Religion and Place

Peter Hopkins • Lily Kong • Elizabeth Olson
Editors

Religion and Place

Landscape, Politics and Piety

 Springer

Editors
Peter Hopkins
School of Geography, Politics and Sociology
Newcastle University
Newcastle Upon Tyne, UK

Lily Kong
Department of Geography
National University of Singapore
Singapore

Elizabeth Olson
Department of Geography
University of North Carolina
  at Chapel Hill, USA

ISBN 978-94-007-4684-8   ISBN 978-94-007-4685-5 (eBook)
DOI 10.1007/978-94-007-4685-5
Springer Dordrecht Heidelberg New York London

Library of Congress Control Number: 2012947588

Printed on acid-free paper

Springer is part of Springer Science+Business Media (www.springer.com)

Acknowlegdements

The editors are very grateful to all chapter authors for their excellent contributions to this collection and for their patience as we have compiled this book. The idea for the book emerged from discussions between Peter Hopkins and Lily Kong in Singapore. Peter is very thankful for funding from the Religion Research Cluster of the Faculty of Arts and Social Sciences at the National University of Singapore that supported his Visiting Scholarship at NUS and enabled these discussions to take place.

Contents

Contributors

Barbara Bompani African Development, School of Social and Political Science, University of Edinburgh, Edinburgh, Scotland, UK

David Conradson Human Geography, Department of Geography, University of Canterbury, Christchurch, New Zealand

Banu Gökarıksel Department of Geography, University of North Carolina at Chapel Hill, Chapel Hill, NC, USA

Julian Holloway Division of Geography and Environmental Management, Manchester Metropolitan University, Manchester, England, UK

Peter Hopkins School of Geography, Politics and Sociology, Newcastle University, Newcastle Upon Tyne, England, UK

Lily Kong Department of Geography, National University of Singapore, Singapore

David Ley Department of Geography, University of British Columbia, Vancouver, BC, Canada

Nimrod Luz Department of Sociology and Anthropology, Western Galilee College, Akko, Israel

Sarah Moser Asian Studies and Culture, Department of Cultural Studies, University of Massachusetts Lowell, Lowell, MA, USA

Caroline Nagel Department of Geography, University of South Carolina, Columbia, SC, USA

Elizabeth Olson Department of Geography, University of North Carolina at Chapel Hill, Chapel Hill, NC, USA

Anna Secor Department of Geography, University of Kentucky, Lexington, KY, USA

Lynn Staeheli Department of Geography, Durham University, Durham, England, UK

Justin Tse Department of Geography, University of British Columbia, Vancouver, BC, Canada

Giselle Vincett School of Geography, Politics and Sociology, Newcastle University, Newcastle Upon Tyne, England, UK

University of Birmingham, Woodbrooke

List of Figures

List of Tables

Chapter 1
Introduction – Religion and Place: Landscape, Politics, and Piety

Elizabeth Olson, Peter Hopkins, and Lily Kong

1.1 Introduction

In 2010, a 14-year-old boy was brutally murdered in a suburb outside of Rio de Janeiro when a group of skinheads observed him at a party and suspected that he might be gay (McLoughlin 2011). This scale of horrific homophobia is not uncommon in Brazil, where rates of violence against gays, lesbians, and transgendered people are reported to be amongst the highest in the world. A study conducted with the support of *Grupo Gay da Bahia* offers the conservative estimate of 260 gays killed in the country in 2010, indicating that rates doubled in only 5 years. The statistic sits uncomfortably with the image of Brazil as a sexually tolerant society, where the legalization of homosexuality was established shortly after the nation's independence from Portugal. It was therefore with a great sense of achievement for proponents of gay rights that, in May 2011, the Brazil Supreme Court agreed to award same-sex couples the same legal rights as married heterosexuals (BBC 2011). Though the decision stops short of approving marriage for same-sex couples, it has been heralded as an important step against discrimination and toward acknowledging the rights of gays, lesbians, and transgenders to love and live without the condemnation of the state.

E. Olson (✉)
Department of Geography, University of North Carolina at Chapel Hill, Saunders Hall, Campus Box 3220, Chapel Hill, North Carolina 27599–3220, USA
e-mail: eaolson@email.unc.edu

P. Hopkins
School of Geography, Politics and Sociology, Newcastle University, Newcastle upon Tyne, England, UK
e-mail: peter.hopkins@ncl.ac.uk

L. Kong
Department of Geography, National University of Singapore, Singapore
e-mail: lilykong@nus.edu.sg

P. Hopkins et al. (eds.), *Religion and Place: Landscape, Politics and Piety*,
DOI 10.1007/978-94-007-4685-5_1, © Springer Science+Business Media Dordrecht 2013

The most vocal opponents to the recognition of same-sex rights were Christian organizations, including the Brazilian Catholic Conference of Bishops, whose lawyer responded to the ruling by stating that that 'plurality has its limits' (Marull 2011). The Catholic Church of Brazil remains influential in a country that is still considered to be the world's most Catholic country despite recent evidence of generational decline.[1] The condemnation of homosexuality is echoed by a conservative Evangelical Christian community in Brazil, which also constitutes one of the most vibrant conservative Evangelical movements in Latin America. Several days after the Supreme Court response, the Evangelical Church announced that it would seek the legal right to prohibit same-sex marriage ceremonies (Maresch 2011). The Sao Paulo local government also responded to a campaign led primarily by Evangelical Christian politicians to approve a bill establishing a 'heterosexual pride day', a clear reference to Sao Paulo's Gay Pride Parade, which is amongst the largest in the world. The author of the legislation, who is himself an Evangelical Christian, argues that the day is intended to resist the 'privileges' enjoyed by the homosexual community and to 'encourage the public to safeguard the (sic) morals and good customs' of Brazilian society (Ko 2011).

However, the relationship between Christianity and homosexuality in Brazil is more complex than might be suggested in the very public battles over the rights of same-sex couples. In 2009, the Catholic Archbishop of Paraiba suspended a priest, Father Luiz Couto, for endorsing contraception and taking a strong stance against homosexual discrimination. Father Couto responded by further condemning homophobia as 'prejudice and intolerance' (Catholic Online 2009). Rio is also home to the gay Evangelical church *Igreja Contemporânea*. Even conservative Christian churches can be important in the lives of queer men. Indeed, research amongst gay and transgendered men/women in Rio suggests that Christian belief and community remains important regardless of sexuality and gender orientation. In his study of queer spaces in Rio de Janeiro, Furlong (2011: 197) found that Christian faith is often at the centre of gay men's well-being, with one young Evangelical Christian explaining that his church's anti-gay stance was irrelevant to his spirituality, insisting that 'my sexuality isn't going to interfere with my love for God'. For some, the gay Evangelical church offers an alternative space in which their Christianity and their sexuality can be simultaneously embraced. For others attending Catholic or conservative Evangelical churches, spaces were still found for personal worship, for meeting other gay men, and for finding personal and spiritual security.

The awkwardly knitted and sometimes unexpected relationships between queer love, Christianity, and public and private life in Brazil are just one illustration of the complexity of studying religion in contemporary lives and societies. Indeed, there are a wide range of illustrations of the new social prominence given to religion: the 2011 decision to ban Muslim women from wearing facial veils in France, the global crisis

---

[1] A recent study conducted by the Getúlio Vargas Foundation suggests that Brazilian middle class and young people consider themselves to be of 'no religion' at higher rates than ever in history, with Catholicism loosing the most ground.

precipitated by the threat of a US Evangelical preacher to burn a copy of the Quran, the fractioning of the Anglican Church over the ordination of female and gay bishops, the cautious and sparse referencing of religion in the context of the Arab Spring, and the resurgence of interest in religion amongst young people and the continuing influence of Falun Gong in China. All excite the global public imagination, and all could be used to assert that religion continues to matter in ways that fundamentally shape not only our private lives but also the organization of our publics. Furthermore, this increased importance does not appear to be contingent on religious growth. Indeed, returning to the context introduced above, though Brazil has the highest numbers of professed Christians in the world, census data suggests that Brazil also has one of the largest populations in Latin America that identifies as having 'no religion'.[2] In a country where Christianity permeates society in such profound and pedantic ways, dismissing affiliation with the default identity of (at least) nominal Christianity signals that non-religious affiliation has also become something of importance in people's lives.

The aim of this collection is to introduce new empirical and theoretical engagements in the geographical study of religion and to contribute to an increasingly diverse and often compelling field of research which as recently as 20 years ago was considered to be in a state of disarray and incoherence (Kong 2001). Our central motivation for compiling the collection is to help reveal a diversity of ways that scholars study 'the religious' from a geographical perspective. This volume thus complements other edited collections and journal special issues that have been produced on various geographies of religion in the past 10 years (Aitchison et al. 2007; Beaumont and Baker 2011; Brace et al. 2011; Holloway and Valins 2002; Hopkins and Gale 2009; Olson and Silvey 2006), but with a particular concern with the co-production of religion and place across a range of contexts, scales, and networks. The contributions herein thus serve as both introduction and provocation, a challenge to our assumptions about religious categories and the ways that geographies of religion might be done. It does this work while introducing religion in a wide range of scales and contexts, from Christian retreats in England to Christian landscapes in Peru, Islamic city visions in the Middle East, and Muslim women's piety in Turkey. The collection is also timely, for it arrives at a moment when religion and its study are considered by many to be on a precipice of revival and renewal. Some scholars have signalled that religion itself is taking on greater importance in the public realm (Beaumont and Baker 2011), while others caution that the greater visibility of religion might be more directly linked to its previous neglect by the academy more broadly, which Habermas (2008) relegates as decidedly secular in standpoint. It is thus not surprising that, once a somewhat moribund sub-discipline, there has been a revival of interest in the geographies of religion in recent years. The chapters in this collection engage different topics in diverse contexts, but together they reveal the importance of place for understanding and analysing religion.

---

[2] Religion-In-Latin-America database: http://www.prolades.com/amertbl06.htm

1.2 Bringing Together Theories of Religion, Space, and Place

The spatial study of religion has a diversity of anchors and interests. Lily Kong (1990, 2001, 2010) has provided comprehensive consideration of the ways which geographers and other scholars in proximate disciplines have studied religion, place, and space. Whereas the geography of religion was often considered to be an incoherent and uncritical subfield at the end of the twentieth century (Kong 2001), the first 10 years of the twenty-first century supplied a great diversity and volume of studies. Religion has emerged as a global concern, not only due to the dramatic events associated with violent religious militancy and the responsive global 'war on terror', but also the less dramatic but perhaps even more influential changes in religious landscapes that have been brought about through migration (Kong 2010). The importance of religion in national and transnational politics and the consequences of the shifting geographies of religious affiliation have become, if anything, even more pronounced as states and citizens respond to new 'problems' in the public presence of religion. Simultaneously, many of the certainties previously associated with private religion are also changing, either through the growth and spread of new religious formations and spiritualities or through the creation of new boundaries and new opportunities within existing traditions.

In response to these empirical changes, geographers have expanded their interests and analyses to new sites of religious practice, new formations and experiences of the sacred, new histories and contexts, new groups of people, and new scales and scalar relationships. Yet the field has also tended to restrict its engagement with theoretical debates about religion in the broader social sciences, until relatively recently, and even now in arguably abbreviated form. It has also arguably struggled to communicate its contributions to a wider academic audience, despite calls to do so at least a decade ago (Kong 2001). Indeed, in an address to a conference on emerging geographies of religion at Newcastle University in 2010, sociologist Kim Knott asked why geographers were not doing more to develop the links between spatial theories and religion.[3] Here, we briefly discuss three broad theoretical considerations – the critical categorization of religion, the emergence of feminist critique, and the emergence of a postsecular critique – which help to situate contemporary geographical contributions. Though we present these three considerations as distinct for the ease of description, they are deeply intertwined, reflecting both the empirical changes in religion in diverse settings and theoretical innovation that emerges from increasingly diversified fields of practice.

---

[3] The 'Geographies of Religion: a new dialogue' conference was on 8 and 9 March 2010 in the School of Geography, Politics, and Sociology at Newcastle University. Keynote presentations were given by Jason Dittmer, Julian Holloway, Kim Knott, Lily Kong, Elizabeth Olson, Jane Pollard, and Andrew Yip. A 'Geographies of Religion Working Papers Series' which is based at Newcastle University presents some of the papers emerging from this conference. Many will recall this event because of the lengthy discussion that it created on the critical geography mailing list when a member of the list posted a statement in opposition to the conference and questioned how it contributed to critical and radical geography.

The first consideration, which has its origins in sociology and anthropology, addresses the question of what religion is and – in postcolonial and post-structural reflection – the composition and consequences of the construction of religious categories. Though it is rarely addressed as such, much of the early theories of religion offered by the likes of Weber (1963), Marx and Engles (1975), and Durkheim (1976) were also inherently spatial in that they asserted a location in which religion resides – the individual, the structures of society, or the institutions. While the study of religion is no longer only the purview of theologians and religious scholars, much of this work was preoccupied with providing systematic means of study, as in Weber's comparative approaches, or for understanding better the functional aspects of religion in society, as encouraged by Durkheim. Grace Davie clarifies that even Marx's best-known assertion that religion is 'the opiate of the people' was not a dismissal of religion as an essential social force but rather a theorization of the character and origin of religion as something that 'cannot be understood apart from the world of which it is part…' (Davie 2007: 27). Yet postcolonial and post-structural theory have further pushed the possibilities for religion, challenging, for instance, the histories underpinning religious categorization (McCutcheon 2004), or Fitzgerald's (2007) offerings on scholarly deployment of rhetorical categories for the maintenance of religion and its counterparts. Taves' (2009) argument in favour of recasting religion as 'special things', and the vigorous debate that it has generated, is an example of just how contested the act of categorization has become.[4]

Geographers have not been central to these debates, but they have contributed uniquely spatial reflections on questions of religious content and category. More specifically, geographical research reveals that scale, space, and place can help us understand and describe how religious categories emerge and fall apart. Some of these approaches are covered in greater detail within the individual chapters in this collection, but concern for the relationships between religion and society is evident in earlier theoretical framings which predate the current interest in religion, including early articulations of cultural ecology (Sauer 1925), humanistic geography (Tuan 1976), and landscape studies (Duncan 1990), to name but a few. In the 1990s, geographical research signalled that presuming coherence in religious categories could be problematic when considered across scales and locations. Studies of the 'unofficially sacred' (Kong 2001), for instance, have highlighted the interrelationship between the formation of religious spaces and the flexibility of religious categories. Despite these recognitions of the power of space in distinguishing and generating the sacred and the profane, geographers have still predominantly tended to focus on traditional or global religions, particularly Christianity, Judaism, and Islam (Kong 2010). However, recent scholarship has expanded and pushed the category of religion to include what Heelas and Woodhead (2005) refer to as 'alternative spiritualities' such as New Age spiritualities, goddess worship, neopagan, as

---

[4] A 2010 special issue of *Religion* (volume 40, issue 4) provided a forum for debating Tevas' assertion of religion and provides an interesting introduction to the sophistication of contemporary theorizations of religion.

well as the transmogrification of yoga, Buddhism, and other world religions as they are adopted and adapted in new places. Holloway (2010, 2011) further extends this research to consider other elements of spiritual life, including ghosts and hauntings and emerging research on the time-space of yoga and daily life (Cadman et al. 2011), and liminality in places of remembrance (Maddrell 2009) suggests that these underexplored beliefs and practices will also yield new theoretical insights into the social presence of religion.

A second consideration is the gradual and sometimes begrudging mainstreaming of feminist theory into the analysis of the social study of religion. Linda Woodhead (2007: 551), writing in reference to the sociology of religion, argues that 'those who engage with gender issues have failed to convince many of their colleagues that such a move is not an optional extra or an interesting specialization, but an essential corrective to the gender-blindness which has, until now, restricted the discipline's field of vision'. The work of Ursula King (1995) helped to draw early attention to the challenges and creativity adopted by women to insert themselves into and reorder dominantly masculine religious domains (see also Walter and Davie 1998). McGuire (2008) develops these concepts in a recasting of lived religion, departing from earlier continental approaches, such as post-war French analyses of lived religion that relied upon fixed Catholic categories, instead emphasizing the multiplicity and plurality of individual and collective religiosity. The message of this existing knowledge of religion and society did not include the positions, perspectives, and practices of the subaltern. The application of feminist theory to the study of religion thus extends beyond the realm of women's religiosity and more recently, into experiences of queer religiosity (Yip 2010).

That the integration of feminist theory has been slow and somewhat contentious might come as a surprise to geographers, given that feminist understandings and concerns have underpinned an important trajectory of the emerging critical research on religion and place (Kong 2001, 2010; Hopkins 2009; Olson 2008). This increasingly diverse body of research has explored women's religiosity (Dwyer 1999a, b, 2000; Falah and Nagel 2005), complex masculinities that intersect with other aspects of identity such as race and nationality (Dwyer et al. 2008; Ehrkamp 2008; Hopkins 2006, 2007), and religiosity of young people (Vincett et al. 2012). Though frequently beginning with the creative and ongoing act of religious subject formation, many of these works are distinguishable from other studies of lived religiosity in the ways that they become part of broader scales, places, and politics. The Anglican debate over gay clergy, for example, challenges us to consider how individual religiosity is simultaneously an important piece and expression of global politics regarding rights, difference, and race (Vanderbeck et al. 2011; see also Butler 2008). Silvey's (2007) research on women's piety in the context of the global labour market presents us with one way that individual religiosity – in this case, of Indonesian Muslim women who work as migrant labourers in Saudi Arabia – intertwines with state and family visions of the labouring, mobile female Muslim. For Gökariskel and Secor (2010), tracing insertions of religion into and through the veiling fashion industry reveals that religion is multiple and contextual, and we are further reminded that Islam becomes itself an internally plural category when considered from the standpoint of female piety (e.g. Secor 2007). This supports the argument that Dwyer (1999a, b, 2000) made in relation to how young Muslim women in Britain experienced Islam as liberating and constraining. These are exciting trends in the field, but as suggested above, the implications of plurality and diversity of religious subjects are not always recognized within geographical work, which still tends largely toward clearly defined religious categories. Lived religion, public piety, and religious embodiment complicate our analyses, for they request a disassemblage of meta-religious categories and their assumptions. Through this, new spatial understandings of religion as producing places, networks, and spaces are revealed that would otherwise be obscured.

A third shift in our understanding and framing of religion emerges in relation to critiques of theories of secularization. Secularization theory predicts certain outcomes for religion in modern societies, including the decline of religious practice, the regression of belief into the private realm, and the removal of religion from the public sphere, especially the function of the state (Berger 1969; Casanova 1994). Still an influential theory for understanding the place of religion in European societies, secularization has been increasingly critiqued. Some of these critiques relate to the previous two points, for much of the evidence of religious decline relies upon declining membership in religious institutions or upon other measures of belief which prioritize those structures which underpin global religions (see, for instance, Bruce 2002). It has also been critiqued for being insufficiently geographical and extrapolating a distinctly European experience as a representative model of what happens to religion in modernity (Berger et al. 2008; Kong 2010). Knott (2005, 2009) develops this spatial critique further in her extended engagement with location and locality. Seeking the location of religion in bodies, objects, buildings, and institutions and incorporating the spatial theory of Lefebvre, Foucault, and Massey, Knott encourages an understanding in which religious space emerges from contestations within and between fields of relation that she deems the 'religious', 'secular', and 'postsecular'. These categories or 'camps' (Knott 2005: 125) do not reflect an evolutionary development, but rather contextualized, located relationships that result in the emergence of new religious spaces. This reflects a broader trend toward emphasizing the emergence of the secular as an essential operational category for the modern state, and Mahmood (2009: 65) provides for us the clearest implication perhaps for this kind of rethink of secularism:

> Secularism here is understood not simply as the doctrinal separation of church from state but also the rearticulation of religion in a manner that is commensurate with modern sensibilities and modes of governance. To rethink the religious is also to rethink the secular and its truth claims, its promise of internal and external goods.

The result of these theoretical developments is a disruption of the totalizing tendencies of secularization theory and new reasons to re-examine both contemporary and historical contexts in light of new theoretical possibilities. If indeed secularization and 'the secular' are, as Knott (2005) argues, cogenerated with 'the religious' through space and in the production of place, then the ways that we study religion in and through society, politics, and history require an engagement which potentially disturbs the categories of 'religious' and 'secular' and their presumed meanings and affiliations (McLennan 2010; see also Olson et al. 2011). Gelder and Jacobs (1998) anticipate many of these conversations in their book, *Uncanny Australia*, where aboriginal sacredness serves as a pivotal discourse in the formation of the modern nation. Yet 10 years later, Wilford (2009) argues that secularization theory and its outcomes are not well understood within geographic research. We believe that the works discussed above, and the works within this collection, demand a different kind of observation which acknowledges what it is that geographic research on religion has done, that is, a systematic demand for greater sensitivity to our terms of description and engagement and, even more importantly for our purposes here, new possibilities for encountering and theorizing relationships between religion and place in ways that are driven by both new empirical insights and new theoretical reflections. This means reclaiming religion in space and place, not in terms of normative endorsement but rather by re-examining the consequences, character, and co-production of religiosities in and through emergent landscapes and through critical engagements with politics and new roles for public and personal piety.

1.3   New Contributions to Religious Landscape, Politics, and Piety

The contributions to this volume address the theoretical shifts described above in rather varied ways, drawing upon experiences in a range of regional contexts from Europe to Asia to Latin America and exploring processes taking place at a diversity of scales encompassing the body and the global. What they share in common is the deployment of fundamentally geographical understandings of space and place in order to reveal new theoretical insights and new empirical expressions. Themes of mobility, scale, subjectivity, and location interweave these chapters in a way that denies easy categorization and have been used by the authors to open up approaches to the study of religion to new experiences and new spaces. The collection is not comprehensive, a point which we reflect on toward the end of this chapter, but instead focuses around three intersecting themes of landscape, politics, and piety. In each chapter, we see hints of the ways that these various forms of religious categorization are constructed, challenged, or modified in the context of new relationships between the religious, the secular, and the postsecular.

In Chap. 2, Lily Kong begins our navigation of emerging religious landscapes by reflecting on the effects of religious globalization as accomplished through the technologies of contemporary Christian evangelizing. Kong focuses her analysis on the Alpha Course, an Evangelical Christian programme which has travelled from its origins in London, England, to be replicated and reinterpreted across the globe. Focusing on the ways that the Alpha Course travels to and is received and interpreted in Singapore, Kong finds that technologies such as videos, websites, booklets, and training manuals provide a path toward coherent practice, ranging in such diverse ways as how to organize a house meeting to the kinds of foods that might be served during the course. These technologies of globalization therefore enable shared practices that are settled through routines that can be only moderately modified and duplicated in diverse parts of the world. The outcome is what Kong refers to as religious transnationalism or religious community constructed across national boundaries. The resulting landscapes of religious transnationalism are also exclusionary communities, built around technologies and texts which, in this case, resonate with a global elite that finds comfort in the emphasis on a rational approach toward Christian belief and recognizes the cultural references deployed in the allusions and metaphors offered in the speeches of Alpha Course leader Nicky Gumbel. In this case, then, religious transnationalism reproduces a 'transnational religious cosmopolitan elite' that are, like the technologies of the Alpha Course, also embedded in networks of global cities and circulating cultural capital. The engagement with and by elites is contrasted with the lack of interest in the course amongst working-class Singapore Christians, who occupy a very different position in the global circulation of ideas, bodies, and capital. Kong thus leaves us with the prospect of religious globalization that both brings together and divides global religious communities, often in unanticipated and not entirely 'religious' ways.

A different kind of technology is deployed in the construction of globalized religious landscapes illustrated by Sarah Moser and her analysis of the emergence of new 'Islamic' cities in the Muslim world in Chap. 3. Moser describes a burgeoning trend in master-planned cities which deploy Islamic themes and a 'pan-Islamic idiom' and considers the meanings of this idiom through the development of Putrajaya, Grozny, and Masdar. Though the three cities represent very different national, historical and political contexts, each illustrates the ways that Islamic building style and aesthetic becomes reimagined and integrated into city architecture with the aim of asserting a different foundation for claims to the status of a global city. 'New cities', Moser explains, 'are not only expected to spark economic growth but to function as public statements about the aspirations and ideology of the state, whether they are to nurture high-tech ambitions, reinforce an official national narrative or communicate religious alliances'. Generic pan-Islamic idiom can thus serve multiple purposes, sometimes acting as the material bridge between secular states and Muslim citizenry and other times deploying Islamic aesthetics as foundations for new visions of the global city.

For Nimrod Luz, religious landscapes function as important spatial metaphors for nationalism and difference while also serving as material expressions of the potential and the challenge of inclusion. In Chap. 4, Luz considers the Judaization of the Israeli landscape in a post-9/11 world, with a focus on the *maqam* of Abu al-Hija, a sacred site in Galilee that valorizes an officer who fought during the Third Crusades. The site, which served as a pilgrimage destination, went through a period of renovation by a secular mayor, only later to be closed off by subsequent leadership. The interplay between the history of the site, material references to the Palestinian nation, and its eventual inaccessibility becomes part of a coherent narrative of exclusion and, Luz argues, a platform for resistance. Religious identity does not provide a clear path for understanding stances toward access, maintenance, and construction of religious landmarks, for at different times and places they function simultaneously as symbols of the politics of difference and as sites of worship. The result is continued development of historical claims to legitimate nationhood through Islamic sites throughout Israel. Impeding access to the site thus functions both as a denial of the right to worship and a denial of the appropriateness of Palestinians to openly occupy and claim a public site.

Whereas the *maqam* demonstrates the importance of material landmarks and sacred sites for the commemoration of history for the purpose of motivating contemporary resistance, in the rural highlands of Peru, the assertion and containment of religious practices is also linked to visions of development for the Andes. In Chap. 5, Elizabeth Olson explores the links between religion, myth, and landscape in the construction of discourses about economic development. Drawing upon historical and contemporary geographical approaches to religious landscape and the centrality of embodiment, Olson considers how the growth of Evangelical Protestantism in Latin America becomes intertwined with the cultural assumptions underpinning development visions. She describes the different ritualistic landscapes that exist in two largely indigenous Quechua communities, one of which is considered a 'traditional' Catholic town, where Andean-Catholic rituals such as planting crosses on hillsides and public celebrations of fiestas are still very much a part of living religious practice, and another which is dominantly Evangelical. In these contexts, *miramiento* – a kind of critical gaze – works to constrain and shift blended religious practices into more acceptable spaces which constrain them within a category of historical beliefs and practices that have little relevance for the future of the Andes. Olson suggests that myths of Evangelical development circulated throughout Latin America are linked to this evocative, visceral ordering of fleeting but defining landscapes and through its ability to anchor modernity to particular forms of religious bodies and practices.

The centrality of religious embodiment for claims upon modernity is similarly reflected in Chap. 6 by Banu Gokariksel and Anna Secor. The authors examine the veil as an 'ambivalent signifier' that allows some women to negotiate the meanings and practices associated with Islamic piety and modern Turkish citizens. Gokariksel and Secor explore the positions of women who wear *tesettür-fashion*, a controversial but popular style of veiling that contrasts with the presumably more modest garment (*çarsaf*) worn by completely veiled women. The technique and style of veiling worn by a woman is subject to critiques from secular and religious publics, who question both levels of piety and secular centre of Turkish contemporary politics. But Gokariksel and Secor also demonstrate how discourses associated with what is inside and outside the veil become an important way for *tesettürlü* women to make claims to both authentic piety and a participating citizen. Associations of the carsaf with hidden nudity, crassness, concealment, and erotic exoticism allow *tesettürlü* women to position their own dress as an appropriate solution for piety and for national concerns with how Turkey itself is positioned as a secular state. Here, embodiment both reveals and creates a 'gap' for the consideration and perpetuation of colonial and contemporary interpretations of the links between women's dress, piety, and geopolitical constructs of terrorism and democratization.

The relationship between religiosity and citizenship is similarly ambivalent in Staeheli and Nagel's examination in Chap. 7 of the political activism of Arab immigrants in the USA and the UK, though in this case, the ambiguity arises from a different set of relationships and very different expectations for how religion can or should be made compatible with a modern state. Staeheli and Nagel consider the arguments which have historically constructed different religions as being incompatible with Western democracy, either due to the threats that they constitute to national autonomy and democratic values, the power that they hold over idealized autonomous citizens, or the threat of new religious values and practices being asserted in the public realm through migration. The Arab immigrants who constituted the study sample engage as democratic citizens in very 'mainstream' ways and assert that democratic values associated with freedom and responsibility are compatible with a state which simultaneously respects both difference and equality amongst its citizens. Islam, from this perspective, is no more political than any other religion, but the testimonies of activists point to the effectiveness of popular constructions of an *innately* political Islam for those who would prefer migrants to remain on the margins of democratic citizenries.

Religious identities, affiliations, and pieties are thus important for positioning individuals and communities in the politics of the public, but they can also be quite distinct from the activities and experiences of religious organizations as political, public actors. In Chap. 8, Barbara Bompani offers an illustration of the politicization of church humanitarian activity in Johannesburg, South Africa, during a refugee crisis that was exacerbated by xenophobic violence against foreign nationals residing in townships and informal settlements throughout South Africa. Bompani provides a case study of the Central Methodist Mission, an inner-city church that provided shelter and diverse support for as many as 3,000 refugees following the 2008 crisis. The church and Bishop Paul Verryn, who was for a time suspended from his ministry in relation to his handling of some components of the CMM's humanitarian activities, became symbols of the tensions that are apparent between the emergence of a democratic state and the profound economic and social marginalization of populations who lack even the vehicle of citizenship to claims upon the state. Though the church provided crucial services for vulnerable populations, it also profoundly altered the local vicinity, including the occupation of public spaces around the church by refugees, who were seen as threats to local business, health, and – ironically, given the circumstances of their precarious situations – to public security.

Bompani's chapter concludes by reiterating the importance of the religious character of their refuge in the eyes of the refugees, many of whom considered Christianity to be at the centre of their own subjectivities. This theme is taken up in greater detail in Chap. 9 by David Ley and Justin Tse through a theological engagement with the religiosity of Chinese migrants to Canada. Migration often brings with it not only new religions but also new charismatic Christianities. That churches can provide migrants with important networks and support has been widely discussed, but Ley and Tse ask us to reconsider how we interpret and explain religion in social life and in particular, the secularist presumptions which allow for a disaggregation of religious life from other aspects of society and self. What would happen, they ask, if religion were interpreted through the categories and language that religion itself offers? The approach exposes concerns related to poverty and vulnerability that are exacerbated by a loss of status. For some migrants, the multiple hardships provide a route toward intensified spiritual experience emerging from a liminal period in which the immigrant church is detached from worldly concerns associated with the material concerns of migrants. For others, it provided a space for reproducing social orders that reflected those from their country of origin, making it simultaneously a space of inclusion, support, and experience, but also of exclusion and retention of residual social orderings to be enacted in a new home.

Giselle Vincett leads us more deeply into the relationship between spirituality and marginality through her analysis in Chap. 10 of the spatial perceptions and performances of Christian feminists in England. For Christian feminists, the spaces and texts of the church necessarily situate women as marginal, in some traditions excluding them from the physical spaces deemed most sacred and in others restricting spaces for conversations about female embodiment and the symbolic and material significance of women's bodily processes, such as breastfeeding and menstruation. Feminist Christians also worry about the effects of pursuing the feminine sacred within Church space, expressing concerns that it might exclude individuals who find it difficult to accept or are squeamish at the thought of discussing a woman's physicality or that a stripping away of masculine language and space from the church could leave very little behind of their valued community. Vincett nonetheless identifies a range of ways that women are challenging the spaces of performance within the existing sacred spaces of the church through preaching and altering the adornments of the church and also beyond it by creating new ritualized spaces. These new spaces do not undo the displacement that women feel from the church space, but Vincett suggests that they act as additional strategies for coping with the persistence of their marginal position.

The importance of alternative material spaces to the experience, expression, and creative force of the sacred is further elaborated by David Conradson's penultimate chapter, in which he considers two retreat centres in England and how their positioning as neither neatly inside or outside of more traditional religious institutions might contribute to our understanding of a possible spirituality revolution. The two retreat centres demonstrate different religious characteristics, with Worth Abby situated on the grounds of a Benedictine monastery and Othona as an independent facility. The former attracts higher numbers of self-identified Christians and is absorbed by the rituals of Benedictine monasticism, and activities, conversations, and meditations reflected Benedictine teachings as a point of return or grounding. Experiences at Othona, Conradson notes, have less institutional touchstone and guidance with greater scope for experimentation or spiritual creativity. He concludes by suggesting that the experiences of the retreatants and the practices and patterns of retreat highlight these special places as existing somewhere between the formal obligations, texts, and institutions of religion and the subjective quests for meaning that define spirituality. Like the spaces created by feminist Christians, retreats provide a space for experience, practice, and emotion that is seen as difficult to achieve in other religious spaces.

As a whole, the contributors to this volume provide new insights into the ways that religion becomes embodied, enacted, asserted, and imagined in ways that both shape and assume a range of 'non-religious' meanings and significations. Indeed, many of these chapters challenge any easy method for disaggregating religion from other social practices that we might consider to be not religion. In the final chapter of the collection – Chap. 12 – Julian Holloway asks us to consider what the implications might be of taking more seriously the imprecision of boundaries between the religious and non-religious, not just from the standpoint of empirical observation but also from epistemological assumptions. Like Ley and Tse, Holloway proposes an approach toward interpreting and understanding religion not through epistemology of the social sciences but through a theological approach that understands the social realm as also, and indistinguishably, the realm of faith. Focusing on Christian theology and on the spatial ordering that is inherent in the structuring of ritual and related faith, Holloway applies the approach to the force of hope and a counter-ethos of revenge, both of which are conceived through the embodiment of hope through the form of Jesus. Connection with non-religious or secular understandings, Holloway suggests, might therefore be found through shared interests and concerns in 'the possibility of the impossible' and a conviction that the future can be different. So-called secular and faith positions can meet, then, in the suspension of a sense of privilege and an acknowledgement of the contestability of perspectives. In his conclusions, Holloway asks if we as scholars and producers of particular forms of knowledge should not also be the subjects of this project.

1.4   Linking Landscape, Politics, and Piety Through Place and Space

By way of both introduction and reflection, we would like to conclude here by drawing out the significance of these chapters for the geographical study of religion and also the broader significance of emerging geographies of religion for our considerations of place and space. Clearly, the landscapes and politics of religion continue to form an important part of geographic thought on religion, but these works indicate that engagement with public religion increasingly requires an understanding of the intimate realms of faith and belief, be it through the texts and technologies of conversion and worship or interpretations of religious politics and piety. Rather than restricting our understanding of the public face of religion, analyses of the intimate practices of faith are described here as more than personal; they are also deeply social and socializing, even when this is not the intent of the religious individual. There is a tremendous amount of labour and effort that goes into constructing religious meaning, evident in the grand plans of states and transnational networks, as well as an unobserved act of rubbing out graffiti from a wall.

Firstly, the authors of this collection offer a range of empirical data detailing new ways that religious landscapes, politics, and piety hold together, create, and pull apart space and place, and in doing so, they reveal the insufficiency of the deployment of secularization and religion as contradictory binaries. In both Moser's case of new Islamic urban design and Luz's example of the maqam, secular ideology and politics, or the relationship between secularism and religiosity, is not always one of contestation. In both examples, secularism allows for the construction or rebuilding of religious spaces. But as Staeheli and Nagel remind us, secularism can also lead to misrepresentations of the intentions of citizens who come to represent the 'religious' public. The existence of religion in secular states is essential to both those who oppose immigration and multiculturalism and those who seek to maintain the possibilities of multiculturalism. Similarly, secularism itself is transformed from the non-religious, understood by activists-with-religion in order to express an expectation of fair treatment that is made possible under a democratic nation.

The second and related point that we would like to emphasize is the significance of these disruptions to – and through – secularization. In the different contexts discussed in the following pages, the ineffectuality or incompleteness of a religious-secular binary encourages us to contemplate other configurations of how things like the profane and the sacred fit together. These alternative configurations have consequences not only for how we think about religion but for how geographers understand space and place. Even more specifically, studies of 'unofficially sacred' sites, lived religion, or public piety are not just studies of religion but are acts of recovery of unacknowledged or discounted spaces. Take Gökariksel and Secor's identification of the gap between clothing and body as deeply meaningful, constructive, and creative, not only for individual identity but also for the ways that gendered religion becomes scripted into the texts of Turkish nationalism. The pious subject is this gap, this absence, the result of inside-outside. This formulation radically transforms our understanding of religious spaces from the standpoint of inclusion and exclusion, religious or secular; it tugs at our expected spatial categories until they come apart, pieced back together through the stories and experiences of people who live them. In Vincett's chapter, both ritual and practice become focused upon acknowledging and resolving a different kind of gap, one which exists between the female body and Christian practice, sometimes surmounting it and other times using it to establish a different space – creating space through the act of crossing over a previously nonexistent space. These insights might suggest that in addition to thinking of the space of religion, we might think of the work that is done by *spaces in* religion or the gaps and in-betweens that call for and allow reinterpretation and manoeuvre.

The third point brings us to reflect upon the mobility of ideas, of bodies, and of rituals and practices across space. The contributors to this volume not only describe emerging contexts of religious practice and belief, but they also suggest new questions about the scope and scale of the restructuring of place in and through religion. We are particularly drawn to the range of technologies, old and new, which mediate the shifts in global religious landscapes. The technologies of religious mobility range from the digital data that underpins the success of the Alpha Course on a global scale to the less evidently 'religious' technologies that go into the production of fabrics, texts, music, and buildings of solitude, worship, or public display. Kong demonstrates the value of paying attention to these technologies, which can reveal much about religion and the role that it plays in the effective construction of a global community – and in the case of the Alpha Course, of maintaining the globalizing culture of a transnational elite. We might further include in our consideration the technologies that circumscribe or restrict, such as the basic infrastructures related to the running and maintenance of a church building, sounds, scents, and visuals. Moser's technology of architecture and buildings facilitates the interweaving of state intentions and ambitions and religious belief systems and the motifs they produce. Bopani's case study reminds us that the technologies of acceptable urban infrastructure, such as sewage and passable pavements, also become part of the politics of religion in society and that these infrastructure technologies and their limits become important pieces in decisions about where religion belongs.[5]

In reflection, then, the contributions herein both reference and drive forward broader conversations within the study of religion in society by engaging with new conversations and considerations of the co-production of place, space, and religion. The chapters by Ley and Tse and by Holloway both set forth several challenges for how we might understand and study religion from the perspective of religiosity itself. As several of our contributors allude, locating religion is not only, or perhaps *should* not only, be about locating the sacred in the materiality and symbolism of a particular place, or indeed, of a bounded Earth. Though not considered in depth in any one chapter of this volume, as a collection, these pieces point to new horizons in quite a literal sense, raising questions about which place the boundary can be drawn between *this world* and *other world* (Bhaskar 2002), or any other range of similar spatial constructions which seek to describe the location of religion. Understanding the consequences of the space of heaven or other world has long been an interest and a motivation in geography, for as MacDonald (2007: 596) reminds us in his analysis of geographies of outer space, 'heaven is no less a geographical imaginary than the Orient or the Occident' as a source of motivation for understanding the unknown. Indeed, knowing these spaces has historically been a driving force in geographic methodology and theory and continues to encourage reflection. Tuan (2010: 5) locates the sacred in nature and thus establishes the 'antithetical' relationship between geography and religion, asking his readers, 'but doesn't religion necessarily imply supernature – something other than nature?' His response is a resolute 'It does', but the subsequent comparative journey is one that takes the reader/viewer through diverse interpretations of the sacred – that which is held paradoxically at the centre of human experience yet also apart from it. In what ways have these conceptions of supernature, the infinite, or the ultimate shaped the ways that we bound our spaces of analysis or influence the ways that we understand and describe our subjects, either historically or in contemporary societies?

---

[5] Research by Claire Dwyer, David Ley, and Justin Tse on suburban religious landscapes in Canada provides a compelling glimpse into the various ways that religious technologies and the logics of regional planning converge and come into conversation.

1.5 Future Directions

The study of religion constitutes a broad field of intellectual engagement, encompassing a range of debates and concerns that span scales from personal faith and subjectivity to transnational organizational arrangements. The chapters in this volume provide a range of reflections upon the ways that geographical approaches to the study of religion are contributing to new empirical and theoretical understandings of religion and place, and we have attempted to both clarify how this work sits within the broader study of religion in the social sciences and within the broader study of geography. We have identified some of the areas in which they are deepening or broadening existing approaches to religion and place. Together, these chapters illustrate the importance and the promise of rethinking religious landscapes, politics, and piety from new theoretical standpoints and in contributing new spatial understandings and theorizations of religion.

There are several topics and empirical contexts which present themselves across the chapters which point to future directions for research. The relationship between class and religion is being actively reconfigured in a range of locations and across a range of scales, and several of the chapters in this book allude to issues surrounding class. As the global economic 'crisis' deepens economic inequalities, these reconfigurations are likely to be increasingly important. Some of these dynamics of class and inequality are situated in the urban setting, and the city continues to be important for providing insights into the place of religion in contemporary societies (e.g. Beaumont and Baker 2011). Indeed, several emerging works seem poised to push the boundaries of our empirical and theoretical engagement with this topic.[6] However, on this front, we also note that the connections between the urban and non-urban can be obscured in a limited focus on the city, and what we see in many of the chapters contained within are new ways in which the urban and the non-urban, or even spaces within the urban, are drawn together through religious acts. Describing and mapping these new religious constructions of places which surmount or transcend our rural–urban categories will likely reveal some unexpected configurations and will also tell us much about how the changing nature of our environments – including changes within the urban setting itself – are incorporated in new logics of worship, ritual, and politics.

These chapters also suggest that the 'how' of geographical research on religion is likely to matter as much as the 'what' in coming years. As we have argued in this introduction, religion retains usefulness as a tool of categorization, but it is also obscuring, inaccurate, at times hierarchical, and at others, perhaps appearing too intimate. The contributors to this collection refer to religion in a range of ways.

---

[6] The Max Planck-funded 'Urban Aspirations in Seoul: Religion and Megacities in Comparative Studies', and the larger project of which it is part, will likely reveal a range of new empirical data about religion in a new configurations of the global city. See http://www.mmg.mpg.de/research/all-projects/comparative-study-of-urban-aspirations-in-mega-cities/

Rather than editing for uniformity, we have allowed the diversity of uses to remain so that the reader might glimpse the various epistemic communities that are shaping our understanding of religion. As such, they not only point to new ways of conceiving of religion but also begin to frame new spaces, places, and localities in which religion might be analysed.

Finally, there are several noticeable absences in this collection that we feel need addressing, as much to acknowledge them as to point out areas where we might encourage further research. Despite a growing emphasis of research on religion and sexuality in the social sciences and humanities more broadly (Yip 2004, 2010), the sparse studies of sexuality and religion in geography suggest that it is an area which deserves more consideration. This should not be restricted to concerns of homosexuality but the full range of sexualities that are often at the centre of religious and spiritual belief and practice, such as celibacy, second-chance virginity, and spiritual sexualities. Vanderbeck et al. (2011) have demonstrated how considerations of sexuality in and with religion reveal relationships that are, in many respects, *more than* religious.

Also relatively under-represented in this collection are considerations of how political borders are being configured and reconfigured. It is the interactions between the state border and the body that Butler (2008) identifies as a key site of the 'age of secularism'. The growing attention to religion and geopolitics includes a range of considerations, from the establishment of peace (Megoran 2011) to postcolonial mission (Han 2011). Scholars will provide a much-needed reconsideration of these issues.[7] Most importantly, new geographies of religious geopolitics (Dittmer and Sturm 2010) offer one example of the consequences of theologies of the infinite and the end of time through an engagement with Evangelical understandings of the rapture from the standpoint of geopolitics and remind us of the expansive possibilities when theology is grounded into material and symbolic practices.

We end, then, by returning to the case with which we begin this chapter. The range of approaches for understanding the intersections between religion and the queer body in Brazil are multiple and complex. We might choose to analyse different sets of strategic alliances and shifts in state practices that mobilize particular religious institutions and values into the public sphere. Alternatively, we might focus on how religion can be understood as a technology that tethers a queer body to society in a very particular way, creating a subject of distinctive consideration in different places and times and complicating notions of institutionalized versus non-institutionalized actions and perspectives. We could also explore the ways that Christianity shapes the ways that a young gay man understands himself as a subject in the world or how the state embodiment of secularism and religion reconstruct domestic and global terror. We might further consider the role that Brazilian conceptualizations of the infinite and the ultimate – afterlife, other worldliness, places beyond place – have played in the public and private placement of gay and lesbian lives.

---

[7] This includes a special issue on religion and politics for the journal *Area* (T. Sturm, ed.).

Each of these inquiries, and those which are evident in the chapters which follow, are clearly relevant beyond a 'narrow' field of geographies of religion; rather, they represent essential understandings of place and space more broadly, whether through recognition of the ways that religions create preconditions of critique (Butler 2009) or the opportunities they present for the recreation of self and society (McGuire 2008). This collection is just one synthesis midst a field of possibilities, but we hope it serves as a reminder that religion has never stopped being relevant in place and that it provides some provocation for future geographical engagement with the work of religion in the world.

References

Aitchison, C., P. Hopkins, and M.P. Kwan. 2007. *Geographies of Muslim identities: Diaspora, gender and belonging*. Aldershot: Ashgate.

BBC. 2011. *Brazil Supreme Court awards gay couples new rights*. 6 May http://www.bbc.co.uk/news/world-13304442. Accessed 7 Sept 2011.

Beaumont, J., and C. Baker. 2011. *Postsecular cities: Space, theory and practice*. New York/London: Continuum.

Berger, P. 1969. *The social reality of religion*. London: Faber.

Berger, P., G. Davie, and E. Fokas. 2008. *Religious America, secular Europe?* Aldershot: Ashgate.

Bhaskar, R. 2002. *From science to emancipation: Journeys towards meta-reality: A philosophy for the present: Alienation and the actuality of enlightenment*. London: Sage.

Brace, C., A. Bailey, S. Carter, D. Harvey, and N. Thomas (eds.). 2011. *Emerging geographies of belief*. Newcastle: Cambridge Scholars Publishing.

Bruce, S. 2002. *God is dead: The secularization of the west*. Oxford: Blackwell.

Butler, J. 2008. Secular politics, torture, and secular time. *The British Journal of Sociology* 59(1): 1–23.

Butler, J. 2009. The sensibility of critique: Response to Asad and Mahmood. In *Is critique secular? Blasphemy, injury, and free speech*, ed. T. Asad, W. Brown, J. Butler, and S. Mahmood, 101–136. Berkeley: The Townsend Center for the Humanities, University of California.

Cadman, L., C. Philo, and J. Lea. 2011. *The new urban spiritual? 'new spiritualities' and new times and spaces*. Working paper. http://web.me.com/jennifer.simmonds/Everyday_Urban_Spiritual/Welcome.html. Accessed 17 Oct 2011.

Casanova, J. 1994. *Public religions in the modern world*. Chicago: Chicago University Press.

Catholic Online. 2009. *Brazil: Archbishop suspends priest for comments on homosexuality/contraception*. http://www.catholic.org/international/international_story.php?id=32398. Accessed on 7 Sept 2011.

Davie, G. 2007. *The sociology of religion*. London: Sage.

Dittmer, J., and T. Sturm (eds.). 2010. *Mapping the end times: American evangelical geopolitics and apocalyptic visions*. Aldershot: Ashgate.

Duncan, J. 1990. *The city as text: The politics of landscape interpretation in the Kandyan Kingdom*. Cambridge: Cambridge University Press.

Durkheim, E. 1976. *The elementary forms of religious life*. London: Harper Collins.

Dwyer, C. 1999a. Contradictions of community: Questions of identity for British Muslim women. *Environment and Planning A* 31(1): 53–68.

Dwyer, C. 1999b. Veiled meanings: British Muslim women and the negotiation of differences. *Gender, Place and Culture* 6(1): 5–26.

Dwyer, C. 2000. Negotiating diasporic identities: Young British South Asian Muslim women. *Women's Studies International Forum* 23(4): 475–486.

Dwyer, C., S. Bindi, and S. Gurchathen. 2008. 'From cricket lover to terror suspect': Challenging representations of young British Muslim men. *Gender Place and Culture* 15(2): 117–136.

Ehrkamp, P. 2008. Risking publicity: Masculinities and the racialization of neighbourhood public space. *Social and Cultural Geography* 9(2): 117–133.

Falah, G.W., and C. Nagel. 2005. *Geographies of Muslim women: Gender, religion, and space.* New York: The Guildford Press.

Fitzgerald, T. 2007. *Discourse on civility and barbarity: A critical history of religion and related categories.* Oxford/New York: Oxford University Press.

Furlong, T. 2011. *Tolerance of queer male performances in Rio de Janeiro.* Unpublished Ph.D. thesis. University of Edinburgh.

Gelder, K., and J.M. Jacobs. 1998. *Uncanny Australia: Sacredness and identity in a postcolonial nation.* Melbourne: University of Melbourne Press.

Gökariskel, B., and A. Secor. 2010. Islamic-ness in the life of the commodity: Veiling-fashion in Turkey. *Transactions of the Institute of British Geographers* 35(3): 313–333.

Habermas, J. 2008. Notes on a post-secular society. Translated to English from *Blatter fur deutsche und internationale Politik*. http://www.signandsight.com/features/1714.html. Accessed 16 Jan 2011.

Han, J. 2011. 'If you don't work, you don't eat': Evangelizing development in Africa. In *New Millennium South Korea: Neoliberal Capital and Transnational Movements*, ed. J. Song, 142–258. London: Routledge.

Heelas, P., and L. Woodhead. 2005. *The spiritual revolution: Why religion is giving way to spirituality.* Oxford: Blackwell Publishing.

Holloway, J. 2010. Legend-tripping in spooky spaces: Ghost tourism and infrastructures of enchantment. *Environment and Planning D: Society and Space* 28(4): 618–637.

Holloway, J. 2011. Spiritual life. In *A companion to social geography*, ed. V. Del Casino, M.E. Thomas, P. Cloke, and R. Panelli, 385–401. Chincester: Wiley-Blackwell.

Holloway, J., and O. Valins. 2002. Editorial: Placing religion and spirituality in geography. *Social and Cultural Geography* 3(1): 5–10.

Hopkins, P. 2006. Youthful Muslim masculinities: Gender and generational relations. *Transactions of the Institute of British Geographers* 31(3): 337–352.

Hopkins, P. 2007. Young people, masculinities, religion and race: New social geographies. *Progress in Human Geography* 31(2): 163–177.

Hopkins, P. 2009. Women, men, positionalities and emotion: doing feminist geographies of religion. *ACME: an International Journal for Critical Geographers* 8(1): 1–17.

Hopkins, P., and R. Gale. 2009. *Muslims in Britain: Race, place and identities.* Edinburgh: Edinburgh University Press.

King, U. (ed.). 1995. *Religion and gender.* Oxford: Blackwell.

Knott, K. 2005. *The location of religion.* London: Equinox Publishing.

Knott, K. 2009. From locality to location and back again: A spatial journey in the study of religion. *Religion* 39: 154–160.

Ko, V. 2011. *Sao Paulo City Council approves 'Heterosexual Pride Day'.* http://newsfeed.time.com/2011/08/05/sao-paulo-city-council-approves-heterosexual-pride-day/. Accessed on 6 Sept 2011.

Kong, L. 1990. Geography and religion: Trends and prospects. *Progress in Human Geography* 14(3): 355–371.

Kong, L. 2001. Mapping 'new' geographies of religion: Politics and poetics in modernity. *Progress in Human Geography* 25(2): 211–233.

Kong, L. 2010. Global shifts, theoretical shifts: Changing geographies of religion. *Progress in Human Geography* 34(6): 755–776.

Maddrell, A. 2009. A place for grief and belief: The Witness Cairn, Isle of Whithorn, Galloway, Scotland. *Social & Cultural Geography* 10(6): 675–693.

Mahmood, S. 2009. Religious reason and secular affect: An incommensurable divide? In *Is critique secular? Blasphemy, injury, and free speech*, ed. T. Asad, W. Brown, J. Butler, and S. Mahmood, 64–100. Berkeley: The Townsend Center for the Humanities. University of California.

Maresch, P. 2011. *Brazil approves same-sex unions*. http://riotimesonline.com/brazil-news/front-page/brazil-approves-same-sex-unions/#. Accessed 10 Oct 2011.

Marull, Y. 2011. *Brazil Top Court recognizes same-sex civil unions' AFP*. http://www.google.com/hostednews/afp/article/ALeqM5gG8v1msdEA7Vz2CE99tzld3Ks5_g?docId=CNG.c45499ec0d03c8e22445e40824338bea.301. Accessed 10 Oct 2011.

Marx, K., and F. Engles. 1975. *Collected worlds*. London: Lawrence and Wishart.

MacDonald, F. 2007. Anti-*Astropolitik* – Outer space and the orbit of geography. *Progress in Human Geography* 31(5): 592–615.

McCutcheon, R.T. 2004. Religion, ire, and dangerous things. *Journal of the American Academy of Religion* 72(1): 173–193.

McGuire, M.B. 2008. *Lived religion: Faith and practice in everyday life*. Oxford: Oxford University Press.

McLennan, G. 2010. The Postsecular turn. *Theory, Culture & Society* 27(3): 3–20.

McLoughlin, B. 2011. *Brazil gay rights progress highlights deep divisions*. http://www.bbc.co.uk/news/world-latin-america-13890258. Accessed on 7 Sept 2011.

Megoran, N. 2011. War and peace? An agenda for peace research and practice in geography. *Political Geography* 30(4): 178–189.

Olson, E. 2008. 'What kind of Catholic are you'? Reflexivity, religion and feminist activism in the Peruvian Andes. *Fieldwork in Religion* 3(2): 103–121.

Olson, E., and R. Silvey. 2006. Transnational geographies: Rescaling development, migration, and religion. *Environment and Planning A* 38(5): 805–808.

Olson, E., P. Hopkins, R. Pain, and G. Vincett. 2011. *Re-theorizing the postsecular present: Embodiment, spatial transcendence, and challenges to authenticity amongst young Christians in Glasgow, Scotland*. Manuscript available from author.

Sauer, C.O. 1925. The morphology of landscape. *University of California Publications in Geography* 2(2): 19–53.

Secor, A.J. 2007. Afterward. In *Women, religion and space: Global perspectives on gender and faith*, ed. K.M. Morin and J.K. Guelke, 148–158. Syracuse: Syracuse University Press.

Silvey, R. 2007. Mobilizing piety: Gendered morality and Indonesian-Saudi transnational migration. *Mobilities* 2(2): 219–229.

Taves, A. 2009. *Religious experience reconsidered: A building-block approach to the study of religion and other special things*. Princeton: Princeton University Press.

Tuan, Y.F. 1976. Humanistic geography. *Annals of the Association of American Geographers* 66(2): 266–276.

Tuan, Y.F. 2010. *Religion: From place to placelessness*. Chicago: University of Chicago Press.

Vanderbeck, R.M., J. Andersson, G. Valentine, J. Sadgrove, and K. Ward. 2011. Sexuality, activism, and witness in the Anglican Communion: The 2008 Lambeth Conference of Anglican bishops. *Annals of the Association of American Geographers* 101(3): 670–689.

Vincett, G., E. Olson, P. Hopkins, and R. Pain. 2012. Young people and performance Christianity in Scotland. *Journal of Contemporary Religion* 27(2): 275–290.

Walter, A., and G. Davie. 1998. The religiosity of women in the modern West. *The British Journal of Sociology* 49: 640–660.

Weber, M. 1963. *The sociology of religion*. London: Methuen.

Wilford, J. 2009. Sacred archipelagos: Geographies of secularization. *Progress in Human Geography* 34(3): 328–348.

Woodhead, L. 2007. Gender differences in religious practice and significance. In *The Sage handbook of the sociology of religion*, ed. J. Beckford and J. Demerath, 550–570. London: Sage.

Yip, A.K.T. 2004. Negotiating space with family and kin in identity construction: The narratives of British non-heterosexual Muslims. *The Sociological Review* 52(3): 336–350.

Yip, A.K.T. 2010. Special feature: Sexuality and religion/spirituality. *Sexualities* 13(6): 667–670.

Chapter 2
Christian Evangelizing Across National Boundaries: Technology, Cultural Capital and the Intellectualization of Religion

Lily Kong

2.1 "New" Landscapes of Religion

For a long time, geographies of religion have focused on how religion influenced and changed physical landscapes, reflecting Isaac's (1959–1960) definition of the geography of religion as "… the study of the part played by the religious motive in man's (sic) transformation of the landscape". In his early conception of the field, the task of a geography of religion was "… to separate the specifically religious from the social, economic and ethnic matrix in which it is embedded, and to determine its relative weight in relation to other forces in transforming the landscape" (Isaac 1961–1962:12). The focus on religion's role in transforming landscapes reflected closely the approaches to cultural geography associated with Carl Sauer and the Berkeley School (see Kong 1990). However, in the last two decades, the field has evolved. Elsewhere, I have mapped "new" geographies of religion, more aligned with the retheorized agendas of cultural geographers, engaging with the discourses and dynamics of plural cultures, and the consequent cultural politics, including the landscape politics arising from the intersections of the sacred and secular (Kong 2001a). "New" geographies of religion take full cognizance of the politics and poetics of religious place and space, identities and communities. Such geographies engage with the dialectical relationship between religion and landscapes rather than a one-dimensional notion of religion impacting landscape form. Further, Kong (2001b) proposes that such "new" geographies need to go further and interrogate the role of technological innovations in refiguring religious landscapes. Finally, attention should also be paid to religious landscapes influenced by global and transnational forces.

L. Kong (✉)
Department of Geography, National University of Singapore, Singapore
e-mail: lilykong@nus.edu.sg

P. Hopkins et al. (eds.), *Religion and Place: Landscape, Politics and Piety*,
DOI 10.1007/978-94-007-4685-5_2, © Springer Science+Business Media Dordrecht 2013

The last 10 years have seen a significant growth in geographical works on religion (Kong 2010). Many scholars have responded to the agendas proposed at the turn of the century (Kong 2001a), though what remains lacking is research on the relationship between technology and religion. Yet, whether we refer to process or procedure; tool, instrument or artefact; vocation or branch of learning, the pervasiveness of technology in human life is undeniable (Newman 1997:39–71). Indeed, technology has opened up new spaces of religious practice – or "techno-religious spaces" (Kong 2001b).

This chapter focuses particularly on one aspect of the "new" landscapes of religion, taking into account the role of technology and global and transnational forces in shaping religious practice. I argue that two related phenomena are increasingly evident in religious practice: religious globalization and religious transnationalism (see also Kong 2006). I distinguish the former as a process of convergence and conformity of religious practice across the globe, while the latter draws on and contributes to the construction of a religious "community" across national boundaries. My conclusions are drawn from analysis of a particular religious occurrence, an evangelical Christian programme (the Alpha course) which originated in London, UK, and its specific (re)production and "consumption" in another culture and setting, 10,800 km away in Singapore.

My key arguments are summed up in two main parts. First, religious landscapes in diverse parts of the world may be integrally connected through a *convergence and conformity of religious practice*, a process in which technology plays an important part. This process, which is conceptualized as *religious globalization* (or the homogenization of religious practice), is possible because there exists a transnational elite community that shares a particular cultural capital. In other words, the commonality of religious practice is facilitated by common values and understandings shared by this transnational elite. In my case study, religious globalization is evidenced in the common course structure, course material and course personnel in the Alpha programme. The original production of the Alpha approach and material in London is recreated in other locations, yielding "new" landscapes of religion, which are mediated in a variety of ways as the "global" meets the local in cross-border intersections. While practices are sometimes mediated and reinterpreted, the basic blueprint remains largely similar and can be effective because of certain pre-existing commonalities in the transnational communities being addressed.

Second, religious globalization, conceptualized as the homogenization of religious practice, is the medium through which a religious community is constructed across national boundaries. In other words, a transnational religious community is the outcome of religious globalization. Through the shared religious practice, an "imagined" community is formed in which the "image of their communion" (Anderson 1983:15) across boundaries is rooted in religious communion, not primordial ethnic ties (e.g. as posited by Anthony Smith (1987)).

These conceptualizations and arguments about the relationship between religion, globalization and transnationalism are situated within broader literatures that have addressed these relationships, which I outline briefly below, before elaborating on my specific empirical research context.

2.2   Religion, Globalization and Transnationalism

While the phenomenon of globalization is not new (Knox 1996), its extent and intensity have increased. Academic engagement with the phenomenon now addresses the different logics of globalization: economic, social, cultural and political (Pieterse 1994:161), and examines, *inter alia*, the medium and outcome of globalization.

In various global flows, the role of communication technology is acknowledged in facilitating movement and exchange of people, ideas, goods, capital and so forth. Technological developments, including travel technology and new media of recent years, have enhanced trade, migration, conquest and colonialism, all of which have in turn facilitated access to information and the flow of ideologies. Within the context of religious practice, technology has facilitated the movement of religious individuals and groups over space and across boundaries, a phenomenon that dates back a long way, with Catholic missionaries, Muslim pilgrims and Buddhist monks travelling across the globe when communication technologies were less advanced than those today. This has prompted Rudolph (1997:1) to argue that "religious communities are among the oldest of the transnationals". In the present technologically more sophisticated times, a further range of cross-border religious phenomena have emerged, from televangelism to radio broadcasts to religious newsgroups and bulletin boards, creating new global "techno-religious spaces" (Kong 2001b, 2006).

Aside from technology as facilitator, the literature has also focused on the outcomes of globalization. One effect has been cultural homogenization (albeit mediated by local forces), wherein a cultural existence characterized by homogenized commodity consumption results in a "McWorld" in which we eat the same food, listen to the same music, watch the same movies and so on (Winchester et al. 2003). In the context of religion, cultural homogenization is translated as a *homogenization of religious practice, or religious globalization*. Nagata (1999) discusses this in terms of a growing convergence and conformity between different religious traditions in which particular religious ideals are sought: regular congregational rituals, adoption of a sacred day a week, a centrality of scriptures and texts, an engagement with secular issues such as human rights, refugees, the environment and so forth. These trends lend themselves to the development of a "global" religious civil society.

A second effect of globalization is the emergence of transnational cultural communities. Proponents of the idea of "transnations" suggest that, with globalization, nation-states have been "reconstituted" in such a way that transnational people assert local loyalties but share in global values and lifestyles (Marden 1997:37). In religious terms, globalization has urged the emergence of *religious transnationalism*, rooted in the *transnational religious community*, best imagined as a religious community constructed across national boundaries. This finds form in the Islamic "*ummah*", for example (Al-Ahsan 1992).

Research on religious transnationalism has spawned varied perspectives. The reach of transnational religious groups set against the mediations of local forces has drawn research attention, as has the question of how pan-religious identities and communities conflict with local and national affiliations. Haynes (2001), for example, argues that globalization facilitates the growth of transnational networks of religious actors which feed off each other's ideas, aid each other with funds and form bodies whose main priority is to improve the well-being of their transnational religious community. The focus here is very much on organized transnational religious activism. Haynes examines whether the activities of transnational religious actors undermine state sovereignty and concludes from his case studies that while they help to undermine the hegemony of authoritarian governments, this is not equivalent to a more general threat to state sovereignty. Rudolph and Piscatori's (1997) oft-cited *Transnational Religion and Fading States* similarly focuses on the question of state sovereignty and whether it is diminished by religious movements that operate across state boundaries. They argue that future conflicts were less likely to result from a "clash of civilizations" but to originate at micro-levels. Conflicts were as likely to arise between states sharing a religion as between those divided by it and more likely to arise within rather than across state boundaries. Rather than seeing transnational religion purely as acting against states, the essays in Rudolph and Piscatori (1997) discuss the dual potential of religious movements as sources of peace and security as well as of violent conflict.

Other aspects of religious transnationalism have also attracted research attention: for example, with globalization and increasing migration of both highly skilled visible minorities and equally visible illegal or low skilled ones, different transnational religious communities have formed. Their experiences and the role of religion in their adaptation deserve research attention. This would parallel research that explores the role of immigrant "voluntary associations" as institutions that assist in the adaptation of newcomers to a new location and as organizations which help to preserve practices and values, even as they assist in adaptation (Schiller et al. 1995; Owusu 2000). Scholars have examined, for example, immigrant religious life and the role of ethnic churches in immigrant assimilation (e.g. Orsi 1985; Brown 1991; Warner 1993; Warner and Wittner 1998), but fewer have explored the transnational nature of their religious lives, the continued relations between home and host-country institutions which modify religious ideologies, practices and expectations in both societies as a consequence (see Levitt 1998, who refers to this as a form of "local-level religious transnationalism").

The limited literature on religious globalization and religious transnationalism, particularly by geographers (see, however, Olson and Silvey 2006; Olson 2006; Mohan 2006), suggests that further scrutiny is in order to refine conceptualizations and expand theoretical ideas about these religious phenomena. There is, however, no "ascent" to theory without "descent" to case study, so I offer in this chapter one case study that focuses attention on the relationships between religion, technology and transnational forces and communities.

2.3   Research Context and Methodology

In this chapter, I explore the case of an evangelical programme (the Alpha course), originating in London, UK, and recreated and reinterpreted in Singapore and other parts of the world. Methodologically, this chapter draws evidence from both textual analysis and field research. The texts and intertexts of the Alpha course are examined, including the talks that form the cornerstone of the course, the course material and the publicity matter. This material was available via VCDs, websites, booklets and training manuals on sale at a local Alpha office. Interviews were also conducted with local organizers and participants to gain insights into the ways in which the course is imported and replicated and the local reinterpretations.

The Alpha course is a 15-weekly session designed to help individuals explore the Christian faith in a "relaxed, non-threatening manner" (http://www.alpha.org.uk). It started almost 30 years ago when Charles Marnham, a clergyman at Holy Trinity Brompton, an Anglican Church in London, UK, devised the course as a way of presenting the basic principles of Christianity to new Christians. The course evolved as other leaders succeeded him. When Nicky Gumbel took over in 1990, he realized the power of the medium for evangelism and turned the course into one that would be attractive to non-churchgoers, with the method of welcome, the atmosphere of small groups, the food, the seating and the substance of the talks themselves tailored to be attractive to the person who walked in "off the street". It was evangelism based on friendship, where friends brought friends, rather than through knocking on doors. It is advertised as "low key, friendly and fun" and is free. Today, central to the Alpha course is Nicky Gumbel, ordained and on the staff of Holy Trinity Brompton in London. Gumbel read law at Cambridge and theology at Oxford and had previously practised as a barrister. His talks form the cornerstone of the Alpha course throughout the world.

The Alpha course is supported by all the main Christian denominations and is targeted especially at those who want to investigate Christianity, new Christians, and those who want to brush up on the basics. In Britain alone, there are more than 8,000 Alpha courses running in churches of all denominations. Throughout the world in 2010, there were at least 163 other countries where the Alpha course was adopted and its reach included over 16 million people.

2.4   Landscapes of Evangelization: Religious Globalization

Religious globalization is evident in the ways in which landscapes in different parts of the world are connected through a convergence of religious practice. Using the current case study, such religious globalization is evident in the close reproduction in Singapore of three dimensions of the Alpha course: the course structure, course material originally produced and course personnel originally trained for the programme in London.

First, the Alpha *course structure* is marketed in a highly detailed convergent manner, from the shape of the entire course to a typical Alpha evening. Throughout the 15 weeks, anywhere in the world, specific topics are covered in the same order, from "Who is Jesus?", "Why and how do I pray?" to "How can I be sure of my faith?" Each week, a typical session begins with a meal when people get to know one another, followed by Nicky Gumbel's talk for the week, delivered via VCD or other technology-mediated means, and then discussions in small groups. Usually, after the fifth week of the course, a "Holy Spirit" weekend is organized, during which there are talks, prayers, worship and counselling, designated for individuals to be touched by the Holy Spirit. This broad structure is entirely adhered to in the Singapore course structures.

The global reach of the course and the dissemination of the "prototype" are facilitated by various technological advances of the modern age. The Alpha website (http://www.uk.alpha.org/) is an easy-to-use information source and includes a detailed step-by-step guide designed to homogenize "preparation", "start", "logistics", "typical evening", "content", "weekend", "invites" and "celebration supper". The close reproduction of the Alpha course from one specific site in Britain to multiple sites in the world is made possible through a variety of detailed instructions: for example, urging the use of the home as the ideal venue, prompting a three-session training course for those leading or helping in a group, exhortations and strategies to help people overcome their nervousness and awkwardness and feel welcome, including the recommendation to provide individualized attention and the use of meals as an icebreaker, the sale of books, the introduction of worship songs, the assignment of people to appropriate groups and so on. Even what happens on a typical evening is outlined as a recommended schedule, beginning at 6.15 p.m., leading to a welcome from the leader with "perhaps even a joke!" and rounding off with the advice that the ending time should be kept consistent at 9.45 p.m. Similarly, a detailed schedule is suggested for the weekend away and made available on the web for groups across the world to follow. Suggestions are likewise made to hold a celebration supper at the end of the course, with the aim that participants will bring friends and family to find out about Alpha.

Even at this level of detailed course implementation, a typical evening of the course in Singapore reveals close consonance with a typical session in the original Holy Brompton version, reflecting a degree of religious globalization at work. Most differences are marginal, such as the start and ending time, and a few reflect specific cultural contexts. For example, not all Alpha courses are held in homes, given the relatively small apartments in land-scarce Singapore. At the same time, as one convenor put it, "it may be less intimidating to go to a church which is kind of public space, rather than to the home of someone you don't know". Apart from these localization factors, the rest of the sessions reflect a remarkable convergence of form across the distance.

Second, religious globalization and the reproduction of practices initiated in London is evidenced in and facilitated by the mass replication of Alpha *course material*. Video tapes, audio tapes and video CDs are sold of Nicky Gumbel presenting his talks in London, and these form the basis of Alpha evenings in many cities across the world, with Alpha evenings centred on a screening of Nicky Gumbel's talk. Additionally, a range of training material is available to assist those running Alpha courses. An Alpha Team Training Video and Audio as well as an Alpha Administrator's Handbook are marketed and include advice on how to select an Alpha team, checklists for each week of the course, forms for recording and organizing information and advice on organizing guest services and celebration services. Many core Alpha resources are available in different languages. For those who prefer to use a live speaker rather than the video/VCD of Nicky Gumbel presenting his talks, the book *Questions of Life* offers the talks in written form.

The globalizing of resources that comes with the (re)production of the Alpha course in myriad parts of the world is further evident in the range of "intertexts" that are made available. Prototype Alpha invitations, car stickers, poster packs, poster boards, balloons and supper invitation postcards of various designs may all be purchased. The Alpha logo can also be obtained in a range of file formats online, as can various Alpha graphics. A most unusual resource is the Alpha Cookbook. Given that leaders are urged to include the meal as an integral part of the Alpha course, the cookbook offers easy-to-prepare recipes that can cater to large numbers. There is also an Alpha Worship pack which includes a CD/tape, songbook, manual and teaching tape. An industry has therefore emerged to support and enhance the globalizing efforts of religion. Capitalism, while promoting acquisitiveness and which is thought to threaten or eclipse religion, is in fact an important contributory factor in the sustenance of religious globalization.

A third set of evidence of the reproduction of practices is the training of *course personnel.* Alpha conferences are held in many major cities across the globe for those leaders who would like to start courses and cover the following areas: how to start an Alpha course; how to develop an existing course and draw in new people; how to train, inspire and deploy a leadership team; how to run a small group; how to lead worship on an Alpha course; how to minister; how to care for the people during and after the course; and how to conduct the Alpha weekend away. The Alpha conferences are held in cities as dispersed as Los Angeles and Chicago in the USA, Cairns and Alice Springs in Australia, Ockelbo in Sweden, Seeland in Denmark and Singapore in Southeast Asia.

Some general observations and conclusions about religious globalization may be made on the basis of this particular case. First, through specific micro-level convergences, a process of religious globalization is effected. Religious globalization, in this instance, occurs as a result of multiple micro-level conformities. Globalization is an everyday, local, "in-here" phenomenon, not a grand-scale "out-there" occurrence.

Second, while the globalization of religious practice within the same faith is perhaps a common enough phenomenon, the source of authority of globalized religious practice may differ. The globalization of same-faith religious practice is verifiable since religions began to spread across the globe, for example, the globalization and replication of worship format, as in the form and structure of Catholic masses across the globe. The difference is in the authority of innovation. Whereas the form and structure of worship emanates from the Church, an evangelical course does not have the same authority and need not have the same influence. The former is a form of religious globalization stemming from the authority and rule of the Church; the latter is a form of religious globalization stemming from hegemonic influence. Alpha succeeds not because it is ordained as a sanctioned evangelical course. Instead, it succeeds because of the hegemonic success of this evangelistic course in appealing to a transnational elite audience (see later discussion on "religious transnationalism").

Third, the evidences of religious globalization outlined above have been facilitated by those very forces that are oftentimes thought to threaten religion – the forces of modernity. In the present instance, the role of capitalist enterprise and technological developments are central to the globalization of religion (its products and information), in this case, through making possible the reproduction of a large range of Alpha material. The large range of Alpha texts and intertexts help to sustain a commercial enterprise, and the commercialization of this material in turn helps to sustain evangelistic endeavours.

2.5 Landscapes of Evangelization: Religious Transnationalism

A second plank of my argument about globalization in religious practice centres on religious transnationalism. Specifically, religious globalization is both medium and outcome of transnational communities. In my empirical study, this particular transnational community shares a specific cultural capital that characterizes a transnational elite. In other words, the convergence of religious practice, in this case, the frequent adoption of the Alpha course in many churches in Singapore, is due to the presence of a transnational elite in this island state that has a shared cultural capital to begin with. At the same time, the shared religious (Alpha) practices across the globe result in the construction of a religious community across national boundaries or a transnational religious community.

To illustrate how religious globalization is medium and outcome of a transnational community, I analyse, first, the ways in which the "texts" of Nicky Gumbel's talks draw on "global landscapes" and speak to a "transnational audience" in making his arguments, thus appealing especially to particular audiences in different parts of the world.

2.5.1 Appealing to the Transnational Elite: "Intellectualizing" and "Capitalizing" Religion

Nicky Gumbel's talks are available on video and audio cassettes, video CDs as well as in the book *Questions of Life* (1993). Textual analysis yields three sets of evidence illustrating how his evangelical work draws on "global landscapes" and speaks to a "transnational audience". This appeals especially to particular audiences in Singapore. First, he is most effective when he can draw on cultural capital that characterizes a cultured and learned audience of the global city. Second, his arguments appeal to the intellect, using evidence-based approaches that characterize the legal mind and drawing on historical knowledge and veracity, and scientific rationality and evidence. Third, the landscapes he refers to are global and transnational landscapes; the lives and lifestyles he characterizes are transnational (post)modern everyday lives.

First, Gumbel frequently makes incursions into the literary and artistic worlds in his talks, drawing on the lives and works of literary and artistic beacons to do his evangelistic work. He relies on the cultural capital that a transnational global elite possesses to be effective. For example, reference is made to David Suchet, a leading Shakespearean actor, who discovered the way that life should be lived through the Bible. Similarly, he details the decadent and promiscuous life of the literary giant, Leo Tolstoy, whose search for meaning led him to find his answer in the faith of the very simple peasant people of Russia and came to understand that only in Jesus Christ were answers found. Apart from elaborating on the lives of such literary greats, Gumbel also drew on their words and works. Musicians, authors, playwrights, artists – all became cultural material for Gumbel to do his religious work with. Referring to the pre-Raphaelite artist Holman Hunt's famous work that hangs in St Paul's Cathedral, "Jesus, the Light of the World", Gumbel points to the ever-closed and overgrown door which shows no handle on the outside where Jesus stood. The evangelical message was a call to non-Christians to open the door from the inside to Jesus Christ. Likewise, Gumbel used the story of Alexander Borodin, the famed composer of the opera *Prince Igor*, who played alongside his daughter on the piano and turned her noise into music. He uses this to make a point about how the Christian God fills the gaps in our lives, turning that which is ugly to that which is beautiful. In accepting Christ, Gumbel argues, there is no fear of boredom, for, like R. L. Stevenson, one might well be able to say: "I've been to church today and I'm not depressed".

Second, Gumbel appeals to the intellect, using evidence-based approaches, drawing on the world of historical research, the realm of scientific rationality and the persuasiveness of legal argumentation. This appeal to intellectual capital is evident very early in his talks when he takes listeners back to the time he was a student and wrote an essay about how god did not exist, priding himself as a "logical determinist". When he started to find out about Christianity at the point his closest friend converted, he decided to seek the truth and started to read the Koran, Karl Marx, existentialism and the Bible. Gumbel's personal journey is anchored in an intellectual discovery, in which he comes to understand an "intellectual truth". In sharing this "intellectual truth", his talks are peppered with the research of professors, historians and scientists and are often evidence-based, building from argument to argument.

For example, drawing attention to Professor Thomas Arnold, Gumbel highlights his role in revolutionizing the concept of English education, his appointment to the chair of modern history at Oxford University and his work with "evidence in determining historical fact". With this intellectual cache, Gumbel quotes Arnold:

> I have been used for many years to studying the histories of other times, and to examining and weighing the evidence of those who have written about them, and I know of no one fact in the history of mankind which is proved by better and fuller evidence of every sort, to the understanding of a fair inquirer, than the great sign which God has given us that Christ died and rose again from the dead.

At points in his various talks, Gumbel cites historical and scientific evidence to support the view that Jesus Christ lived on earth, died and rose from the dead and that the New Testament has not been changed over the years. For example, he points to the Roman historians Tacitus and Suetonius as well as the Jewish historian Josephus (born in AD37), all of whom wrote about Jesus' existence. Gumbel argues that this non-gospel historical writing is independent evidence of Jesus' time on earth. He also takes Alpha course participants through C. S. Lewis' rational arguments about why Christ's assertion that he was the Son of God simply had to hold, looking at his teachings, his actions, his character, the prophecies about him and his conquest of death. He also examines evidence that the resurrection really happened, working through the phenomenon of absence from the tomb, his presence with the disciples and the immediate effect on those who saw him. Ultimately, Gumbel underlines that it is not viable to escape evidence and fact, for, "when the impossible is eliminated, even the remaining improbable is the truth".

Gumbel also shows evidence why the New Testament documents are reliable. Citing the late Professor F.F. Bruce, Rylands Professor of Biblical Criticism and Exegesis at the University of Manchester, and his science of textual criticism, Gumbel points out that the veracity of some very important and very old writings is not doubted despite the very small number of existing manuscripts. The New Testament had many more existing and excellent full manuscripts and therefore did not deserve doubt. Quoting F.J.A. Hort, a key textual critic, Gumbel highlights how the variety and fullness of the evidence suggests that the text of the New Testament "stands absolutely and unapproachably alone among ancient prose writings". The following is an example of his evidence-based approach:

> For Caesar's *Gallic War* we have nine or ten copies and the oldest was written some 900 years later than Caesar's day. For Livy's *Roman History* we have not more than twenty copies, the earliest of which comes from around AD900. Of the fourteen books of the histories of Tacitus only twenty copies survive; of the sixteen books of his *Annals*, ten portions of his two great historical works depend entirely on two manuscripts, one of the ninth century and one of the eleventh century. The history of Thucydides is known almost entirely from eight manuscripts belonging to c. AD 900. The same is true of the history of Herodotus. Yet no classifical scholar doubts the authenticity of these works, in spite of the large time gap and the relatively small number of manuscripts. As regards the New Testament we have a great wealth of material. The New Testament was probably written between AD40 and AD100. We have excellent full manuscripts of the whole New Testament dating from as early as AD350 (a time span of only 300 years), papyri containing most of the New Testament writings dating from the third century and even a fragment of John's Gospel dating from about AD130. There are over 5,000 Greek manuscripts, over 10,000 Latin manuscripts and 9,300 other manuscripts, as well as over 36,000 citings in the writings of the early church fathers.

In short, Gumbel uses the weight of historical and scientific evidence to build his evangelization on an intellectual case. This intellectualization of religion, Tong (2007) argues, appeals increasingly to a younger, more educated population in Singapore, and he illustrates this particularly by reference to the way in which the Taoist Federation in Singapore has sought to appeal to younger Singaporeans who view it as an illogical and superstitious religion. In particular, he refers to the publication of tracts and the offering of public talks to demonstrate the rationality and logic of Taoist beliefs and the attempt to create a canonical context in order to raise the social status of Taoism.

Third, integral to Gumbel's talks are images of global and cosmopolitan landscapes. They emanate from and will resonate with the well-travelled and the migratory class, the well-informed cosmopolitan. References to travels to Moscow and the difficulty of identifying genuine Christians from KGB infiltrators, Kenyan migrants in London, Ugandan missionaries in Cambridge, Tottenham Hotspur footballer Gascoigne in the Italian club Lazio and British royalty at the Niagara Falls all serve to construct the social reality of a modern world in which boundaries are porous. It is a brave new world of "ethnoscapes", or landscapes of persons who constitute the shifting world in which we live: tourists, immigrants, refugees, exiles, guest workers and other moving groups and persons (Appadurai 1990:297). At the same time, many references and analogies are especially relevant to the lives and experiences of the transnational modern capital class, such as the English family with a Swedish *au pair* and the reference to Harley Street for high-order medical treatment. Further, he uses the "language of capital" to make his point:

> The value of a cheque depends not only on the amount, but also on the name that appears at the bottom. … When we go to the bank of heaven, we have nothing deposited there. If I go in my own name I can achieve nothing; but Jesus Christ has unlimited credit in heaven. He has given us the privilege of using his name.

On another occasion, Gumbel even offers a cheque to the audience, signed by Jesus Christ for freedom, cleansing, eternal life and all the riches of Heaven. It is a cheque that can be cashed with the bank of Heaven. The name is left blank and each person is invited to fill up his/her own name. Rejecting Jesus and his sacrifice on the cross would be tantamount to tearing the cheque up, uncashed. The language of evangelism draws from the language of the cosmopolitan capitalist, and the analogies are spoken to the transnational elite.

In sum, the success and spread of the Alpha course and its continued reproduction in places beyond the original London setting reflects a globalization of religious practice. Such globalization is the outcome of a transnational community that shares a specific cultural capital characterizing a transnational elite. This cultural capital is anchored, first, in an intellectualization of religion and, second, in a borrowing from the world of capital and commerce, in short, a "capitalization" of religion. Intellectualization is apparent in the evidence-based approach to evangelism, where the appeal is crafted through references to historical and scientific evidence, while sharing meaning and value with literary and artistic greats. Such "intellectualization" is not only a reference to theology – the study of religion itself – but the deliberate expansion of what "counts" for evidence – the reference to non-theological logics (e.g. other histories, comparative science, art) to underpin belief and to create an incontrovertible truth. "Capitalization" is apparent in the analogies drawn between the world of God and the world of commerce, a way of making sense of human relationships with God, using the language of contemporary capitalism.

Thus far, textual analysis of Alpha material suggests that Gumbel's process of evangelization and religious globalization is based on the strategies of intellectualization and capitalization of religion, designed to hold a distinct appeal for transnational elites. However, as communications research has often enough suggested, "interpretations vary a great deal because each member of the audience is a complex composite of cultural identities and can call on very diverse repertoires of interpretative codes" (White 1997:49). It is therefore important to understand how texts are negotiated and consumed from the perspective of personal and cultural identities. In this regard, research attention must turn to the convenors, facilitators and participants of Alpha courses in Singapore. Field data corroborates the thesis that transnational elites in Singapore are able to appreciate Gumbel's approach and thus participate in the reproduction of religious lives and landscapes originating in London. On the other hand, for those who do not share the cultural capital to begin with, their participation yields less effective outcomes, and they end up participating in the process but investing their own meanings. Two case studies make the point.

2.5.2 Case 1: Patricia Lee, Late 30s, Alpha Participant

Pat is a cosmopolitan citizen of the world. A Singaporean by birth, her formative years were spent in a premier girls' school in Singapore. She speaks impeccable English and travels widely as part of her work in an international foundation in Singapore. A non-Christian at the time of attending the Alpha course, Pat was in search of answers. She hoped to be convinced through a church that was not "deliriously happy or grimly silent" and was introduced to the Alpha course by someone she met in the course of work.

At her first reluctant attendance at the Alpha course, Pat asked: "I don't understand why, if your God is so just, and so beautiful and so omnipresent, and so forgiving, explain to me the holocaust". And then these people were like… "what is she talking about?" So I said, "Okay, okay, maybe let's not talk about the holocaust. Just talk about World War II, let's talk about the Japanese". This signalled Pat's approach to the Alpha course and Christianity. Summing up her perspective was her expression of discomfort that there were some who "just believed", for, in her view, "how can you believe if you don't even see evidence? It's not a feeling, it must be more than a feeling".

Pat found Nicky Gumbel intellectually attractive. In her words, "when Nicky Gumbel came on, it wasn't so much about love or about salvation or anything; it was strictly cross-referencing. And I thought, "Yes! Let's cut out all these feely, touchy stuff, let's go strictly to the point". So, there's a lot of cross referencing between the Old Testament and the New. And I thought, "Yeah, it makes a lot of sense. Okay, seems like an encyclopedic kind of approach. I can stick with this"". By "encyclopedic", Pat was referring to the intellectual content of Gumbel's talks. Further, Pat revealed that she was looking for answers primarily in the Gumbel videos because "he's a barrister and it's all very evidence-based". By her own admissions, it was not so much the discussion sessions that followed the screening of Gumbel's talks that provided answers. Instead, the sessions were more useful in cultivating a sense of togetherness, a sense that the group was in a quest together and provided a feeling of camaraderie.

Pat's reaction to the idea of a Holy Spirit weekend away further underscored her intellectualization of religion. She expressed the dilemma among those who were attracted by the intellectual content of Gumbel's approach but who worried about the more emotional expression of faith and the spontaneity of worship that might be expected of such a weekend. Her words are illustrative: "Then, those of us who are sort of more… I won't use the word cerebral… those of us who were more guided by the head, we had a great dilemma because when we asked what's the weekend all about, we felt this great sense of dread because it's just spontaneity!" In short, for Pat and others like her, the Alpha course was strong on intellectual capital that appealed to an educated class of transnational elites. As Pat articulates, Gumbel "speaks to me as an intelligent, thinking and educated person. He appeals to my experience of the world".

Just as Pat recognized and appreciated the intellectualization of religion evident in Gumbel's approach, she acknowledged the capitalization of religion as a strategy that Gumbel used, to "speak a language that would make sense in the modern world". This acknowledgement was not without some ambivalence though. On the one hand, the analogy cited above of banks and cheques was "quite clever" and was "effective in making the point". On the other hand, it "ran the risk of demeaning religion and reducing something beautiful to something crass".

Pat's case illustrates how religious practices originating in one particular site (London) are reinterpreted by a particular cosmopolitan member of a transnational elite with global experience. It presents evidence of the role of a shared cultural capital in reproducing religious landscapes in different parts of the world.

2.5.3   Case 2: Peter Woo, Late 40s, Alpha Convenor, and Barbara Zheng, Early 40s, Alpha Facilitator

Peter and Barbara are convenor and facilitator, respectively, of an Alpha group in a Roman Catholic Church in a lower middle class public housing neighbourhood. The socio-economic profile of the churchgoers tends to be lower than the average profile of Christians in Singapore.[1]

Prior to the introduction of Alpha in the church, Peter reflected on its appropriateness for largely blue-collar, lesser educated parishioners:

> I was a bit apprehensive about how the members from our church congregation might respond to the video talk because they are a different profile group from the St Ignatius group. It is common knowledge that the congregation of St Ignatius Church is different from our congregation. The congregation over at St Ignatius Church is made up largely of the middle and upper middle income group due to its location. Many of them are younger and made up largely of white collar group, comprising mainly administrative people and professionals, whereas the congregation over here is made up of middle and lower income

---

[1] Data from the 1990 census (Lau 1994) shows how Christians in Singapore tend to be among the better educated and of a higher income bracket.

group due to its location. At our church, a large percentage of the congregation is older and made up of the blue collar group, comprising mainly technical, clerical staff and a handful of small-scale businessmen. There is probably also a difference in the education levels between the two congregations. There is definitely a larger proportion of housewives at our Church.

Peter revealed his concern "that many members of our church may not be accustomed to listen to an Englishman speaking with just the very slightest bit of accent and the British type of humour". Nevertheless, he decided to give it a try as his counterparts at St Ignatius Church had suggested that it was not so important to understand every part of the talk. As Peter put it: "I thought that if the audience could grasp some percentage of the talk (less the humour and literary references), they should know enough to have a stimulating discussion after".

Unfortunately, in the midst of the course, the dropout rate became noticeable. Almost half the participants dropped out by the fourth or fifth session. By the Holy Spirit weekend in the 8th week, almost two-thirds had dropped out and only 15 remained out of the original 44. Even a number of facilitators withdrew, and only about half of the original 15 facilitators remained till the end. The reasons offered for withdrawing were revealing. One participant was pointed, describing Gumbel's talk as "quite long and dry, very difficult to focus and pay attention". Another could not say what it was about the talk but felt that she, like many other participants, was not accustomed to listening to "this kind of talk". A third observed that some "may have a bit of trouble understanding it and appreciating the humour". When prodded, he revealed: "There were certain jokes that I didn't understand so when they were laughing away, I felt stupid. And I thought that most people in the course did not understand his jokes most of the time because hardly anyone laughed or showed any emotions". Barbara herself admitted: "To be honest, I am not always able to follow what he's saying though I get the rough gist of his message. I don't understand all of his jokes and his literature and other references". As a consequence, Peter expressed the likelihood that they would abandon the original thought of running the course on a regular basis twice a year.

On the other hand, Barbara observed that those who understood "British English and its literature" found the talk enjoyable. Those with "less literacy in English humour and literature" found the talk too long. A Britisher living in Singapore, David, who attended the course, echoed this view:

Gumbel's addressing a UK audience and the references are specific to the UK. But I find myself in the context of Singapore and watching him with all the Singaporeans, and I'm laughing at all the things that people don't understand and nodding to things like British football clubs and Oxford paintings. So on the one hand, he's very clear and understandable but at the same time, he can't help drawing on cultural elements that do not mean much to others.

David's observation is partially correct. While Gumbel does literally address a UK audience in the video, his references are not only specific to the UK but are more transnational and global, and his appeal is to the transnational elite, as I illustrated earlier. What the experience in this church reveals is that the absence of a shared cultural capital inhibits the successful reproduction of religious practice in different parts of the world.

2.6   (Re)producing a Transnational Elite: Constructing Transnational Religious Communities

As indicated earlier, the Christian community in Singapore on the whole has a high representation of the better-educated, middle and upper middle classes. These contours of the religious landscape are likely to be reshaped only if evangelistic efforts succeed in reaching out to those of different socio-economic profiles. The Alpha course has gained popularity in recent years in Singapore as an evangelistic programme. The introduction of the course stems often from church leaders who have learnt of its effectiveness in Britain, for example, through Christian magazines, or because convenors and facilitators had attended a course in Britain and found it useful. As one of a range of courses on offer by churches in Singapore, the Alpha course will only have a partial contributory role in (re)shaping the socio-economic profile of churchgoers in Singapore. Nevertheless, it is instructive to examine its likely impacts.

First, the appeal to the intellect through anchoring the understanding of Christianity in historical, literary and scientific evidence predisposes the programme towards the better-educated, transnational elites. In this sense, the socio-economic profile of Christians in Singapore is reproduced and reinforced. Second, as the Alpha course is introduced across the globe, a transnational religious community is produced which shares a common cultural capital and a collective religious induction. In both these senses, a transnational religious community is produced and reproduced.

2.7   Conclusions

Using the specific examination of an evangelical programme with transnational reach, I have clarified two related phenomena in religious practice. The first is religious globalization, the convergence and conformity of particular religious practices across national boundaries. The second is religious transnationalism, reflected in both the elite transnational nature of religious globalization and the (re)production of transnational religious "communities" across national boundaries.

Religious globalization is not a new phenomenon. The great universalizing religions of the world have globalizing missions, "offer[ing] adherents an exclusivist and generalizing set of values and allegiances that [stand] above both state and economy. … [Christianity and Islam] in particular have … sought to convert those defined as heathen or infidel" (Waters 1995:125). On the other hand, the secularization thesis has emphasized that the universalizing religions have been "threatened or eclipsed by modernization and the rise of capitalism" (Waters 1995:125) with the accompanying universalizing values of instrumental rationality, acquisitiveness, individualism, democracy, citizenship and so forth. Yet, modernization, urbanization, capitalism and technological development have not simply caused the demise of religion, as many have illustrated. Just as modernization has on occasion led to atomistic societies in which alienation has prompted a recovery of religion, technological development and capitalistic enterprise have the ability to support rather than suppress religious growth and globalization under specific circumstances.

In my case study, religious globalization is evident in the ways in which religious practices in London, Singapore and elsewhere are connected through the close reproduction of a Christian evangelistic course originally produced in London. Alpha courses are conducted in highly similar ways and in largely similar settings; the same print, audio and visual course material are used; websites are linked; the same symbols, invitation material, banners and other paraphernalia are evident; and facilitators and course leaders go to the same conferences and use the same training manuals. While local influences are apparent, such as the more frequent use of church premises rather than private homes to conduct the courses, in large part, a "prototype" is replicated. Unlike formal church requirements such as the structure of worship services, Alpha succeeds not on the basis of church authority but on the basis of hegemonic appeal and, in particular, to a transnational elite audience. This religious globalization has been facilitated by those very forces that are oftentimes thought to threaten religion – the forces of modernity. I have shown how the role of capitalist enterprise and technological developments (in the mass production and dissemination of Alpha paraphernalia) are central to the globalization of religion (its products and information). As I argued above, the large range of Alpha texts and intertexts help to sustain a commercial enterprise, and the commercialization of this material in turn helps to sustain evangelistic endeavours.

Apart from insights into modern-day processes of religious globalization, I have also illustrated the nature of contemporary religious transnationalism. In my case study, evangelistic effort relies heavily on "texts" which draw on "global landscapes" and speak to a "transnational audience", appealing especially to particular audiences of higher socio-economic and educational status in Singapore with a global outlook, transnational orientation and cultural and intellectual capital. Evangelistic endeavour then relies on "intellectualizing" and "capitalizing" religion. Further, the experiential landscapes created at and by Holy Trinity Brompton for the Alpha course are replicated in Singapore and elsewhere, creating "transnational religious landscapes". The close replication of these experiential landscapes is made possible by a variety of intertexts (manuals, banners, cookbooks, etc.) which are produced and made available in different parts of the world, thereby further replicating the Alpha landscapes that first took shape in London. In all these ways, I argue that transnational religious experiences are (re)produced, creating solidarities and meeting people's needs for a meaningful universe. In these ways, too, it may be argued that as the Alpha course is introduced across the globe, a transnational religious community is produced which shares a common cultural capital and a collective religious induction. Again, a transnational religious community is produced and reproduced, and insofar as these evangelizing efforts and transnational communities are located in cities, the religious meanings of cities are sustained and reproduced. This offers a useful insight to those who study transnational cities, where the cultural character of such cities is (re)produced not just by immediately observable transnational actors such as tourists, migrants and managerial elites (e.g. Hannerz 1993) but by others bound together through religious commonality – a transnational religious cosmopolitan elite. These transnational religious cosmopolitan elites are highly engaged in cosmopolitan social and cultural practices that are embedded in the network of global cities, and these practices constitute part of a cultural capital that contributes to the shared induction to religion.

Finally, the role of "elites" must be re-emphasized from a different perspective. Many analyses of transnational religion have emphasized how transnational religion reaches to the poor and disempowered (see, e.g. Levine and Stoll 1997). These studies offer a theorization of transnational religious phenomena, framed by notions of emancipation and deliverance, power and empowerment. Much as there might be a struggle against analytical notions and practical evidences of neocolonialism, the focus on how transnational religion (often propagated by those richer and more powerful) empowers and emancipates the poor makes it difficult to break away from these theoretical frames. The transnational nature of Christian outreach facilitated by technology, anchored in an "intellectualization" and "capitalization" of religion and appealing to a global transnational elite presents opportunities for alternative theorizations of transnational religious phenomena that emphasize commonality of social formation and cultural capital rather than reliance on differential power structures.

References

Al-Ahsan, A. 1992. *Ummah or nation? Identity crisis in contemporary Muslim society*. Leicester: The Islamic Foundation.

Anderson, B. 1983. *Imagined communities: Reflections on the origin and spread of nationalism*. London: Verso.

Appadurai, A. 1990. Disjuncture and difference in the global cultural economy. In *Global culture*, ed. M. Featherstone, 295–310. London: Sage.

Brown, K.M. 1991. *Mama Lola: A vodou priestess in Brooklyn*. Berkeley: University of California Press.

Hannerz, U. 1993. The cultural roles of world cities. In *Humanizing the city?* ed. A.P. Cohen and K. Fukuo, 67–84. Edinburgh: Edinburgh University Press.

Haynes, J. 2001. Transnational religious actors and international politics. *Third World Quarterly* 22(2): 143–158.

Isaac, E. 1959–1960. Religion, landscape and space. *Landscape* 9: 14–18.

Isaac, E. 1961–1962. The act and the covenant: The impact of religion on the landscape. *Landscape* 11: 12–17.

Knox, P.L. 1996. Globalisation and the world city hypothesis. *Scottish Geographical Magazine* 112(2): 124–126.

Kong, L. 1990. Geography and religion: Trends and prospects. *Progress in Human Geography* 14(3): 355–371.

Kong, L. 2001a. Mapping 'new' geographies of religion: Politics and poetics in modernity. *Progress in Human Geography* 25(2): 211–233.

Kong, L. 2001b. Religion and technology: Refiguring place, space, identity and community. *Area* 33(4): 404–413.

Kong, L. 2006. Religion and spaces of technology: Constructing and contesting nation, transnation and place. *Environment and Planning A* 38(5): 903–918.

Kong, L. 2010. Global shifts, theoretical shifts: Changing geographies of religion. *Progress in Human Geography* 34(6): 755–776.

Lau, K.E. 1994. *Singapore census of population 1990, statistical release 6: Religion, childcare and leisure activities*. Singapore: Department of Statistics.

Levine, D.H., and D. Stoll. 1997. Bridging the gap between empowerment and power in Latin America. In *Transnational religion and fading states*, ed. S.H. Rudolph and J. Piscatori, 63–103. Boulder: Westview Press.

Levitt, P. 1998. Local-level global religion: The case of U.S.-Dominican migration. *Journal for the Scientific Study of Religion* 37(1): 74–89.

Marden, P. 1997. Geographies of dissent: Globalization, identity and the nation. *Political Geography* 16(1): 37–64.

Mohan, G. 2006. Embedded cosmopolitanism and the politics of obligation: The Ghanaian diaspora and development. *Environment and Planning A* 38(5): 867–884.

Nagata, J. 1999. The globalisation of Buddhism and the emergence of religious civil society: The case of the Taiwanese Fo Kuang Shan movement in Asia and the west. *Communal/Plural* 7(2): 231–248.

Newman, J. 1997. Religion and technology: A study in the philosophy of culture. Westport, Conn: Praeger.

Olson, E. 2006. Development, transnational religion, and the power of ideas in the High Provinces of Cusco, Peru. *Environment and Planning A* 38(5): 885–902.

Olson, E., and R. Silvey. 2006. Transnational geographies: Rescaling development, migration, and religion. *Environment and Planning A* 38(5): 805–808.

Orsi, R.A. 1985. *The Madonna of 115th street*. New Haven: Yale University Press.

Owusu, T.Y. 2000. The role of Ghanaian immigrant associations in Toronto, Canada. *International Migration Review* 34(4): 1155–1181.

Pieterse, J.N. 1994. Globalisation as hybridisation. *International Sociology* 9(2): 161–184.

Rudolph, S.H. 1997. Religion, states, and transnational civil society. In *Transnational religion and fading states*, ed. S.H. Rudolph and J. Piscatori, 1–26. Boulder: Westview Press.

Rudolph, S.H., and J. Piscatori (eds.). 1997. *Transnational religion and fading states*. Boulder: Westview Press.

Schiller, N., L. Basch, and C. Szanton-Blanc. 1995. From immigrant to transmigrant: Theorising transnational migration. *Anthropological Quarterly* 68(1): 48–63.

Smith, A.D. 1987. *The ethnic origins of nations*. Oxford/New York: Blackwell.

Tong, C.K. 2007. *Rationalizing religion: Religious conversion, revivalism and competition in Singapore society*. Leiden: Brill.

Warner, S. 1993. Work in progress toward a new paradigm for the sociological study of religion in the United States. *The American Journal of Sociology* 98: 1044–1093.

Warner, S., and J. Wittner. 1998. *Gatherings in Diaspora: Religious communities and the new immigration*. Philadelphia: Temple University Press.

Waters, M. 1995. *Globalization*. London/New York: Routledge.

White, R.A. 1997. Religion and media in the construction of cultures. In *Rethinking media, religion, and culture*, ed. S.M. Hoover and K. Lundby, 37–64. Thousand Oaks/London/New Delhi: Sage.

Winchester, H., L. Kong, and K. Dunn. 2003. *Landscapes: Ways of imagining the world*. Essex: Pearson.

Chapter 3
New Cities in the Muslim World: The Cultural Politics of Planning an 'Islamic' City

Sarah Moser

3.1 Introduction

Contemporary urban planning is broadly assumed to be a secular endeavour, beholden primarily to rational, capitalist values. While planning is dominated by many practical decisions about laying roads, zoning, housing density and transportation networks, cities are powerful vehicles for expressing ideology due to their highly visible and symbolic nature. Not only are cities 'the medium by which the powerful express their influence' (King 2008: 26), they can reveal aspirations of the state and how it wishes to be seen by others (Vale 2008 [1992]). A primary objective in many master-planned cities is to construct, communicate and normalize a particular sense of identity to the citizenry.

There is a widespread assumption that master-planned cities are a relic of modernist experimentation in the decades following World War II. Although it has been over 50 years since their completion, Chandigarh and Brasília are still upheld as the most noteworthy examples of master-planned cities in planning literature and continue to receive much scholarly attention. In the current context of increasingly city-centric development strategies, new master-planned cities are springing up at an astounding speed in such diverse places as Palestine, Jordan, Egypt, Central Asia, Africa, the Gulf States, Iran, China, Vietnam, South Korea, Indonesia and Malaysia.

In this chapter, I investigate the recent trend of new state-created cities in a variety of geographical contexts which have been designed for a variety of purposes using

S. Moser (✉)
Asian Studies and Culture, Department of Cultural Studies,
University of Massachusetts Lowell, Lowell, MA, USA
e-mail: mosersaurus@yahoo.com

P. Hopkins et al. (eds.), *Religion and Place: Landscape, Politics and Piety*,
DOI 10.1007/978-94-007-4685-5_3, © Springer Science+Business Media Dordrecht 2013

a pan-Islamic idiom. While Islamic identity has traditionally been most visible in urban settings through religious architecture, many new cities in Muslim-dominated regions of the world have adopted generic Islamic themes for prominent state buildings and other secular purposes. I suggest that city planning, particularly in the context of new state-funded cities, constitutes a key scale at which pan-Islamic imaginings are made material. In this chapter, I examine how such imaginings at the scale of the city are linked to several related trends. First, I consider how the ruling elite responsible for new cities are influenced by interpretations of the global cities discourse and an emerging sense of competition between cities. Second, I examine how new Islam-themed cities express interpretations of transnational Islam to evoke national identity. Third, I examine how local ethnic and religious tensions and anti-colonial sentiments have produced lavish city-scale displays of Muslim solidarity on several continents.

In this chapter, I examine three very different new cities that have adopted overt Islamic themes in their architecture and urbanism: Putrajaya, the new capital city of Malaysia; Grozny, the reconstructed capital of the Chechen Republic; and Masdar, the new 'eco-city' in Abu Dhabi. The three cities are spectacles of Islamic urbanism built on a *tabula rasa* and are intended to dazzle the visitor with lavish architecture, highly planned urban infrastructure and a controlled, utopian environment. At the same time, the ruling elite and the designers they employ have not employed a placeless modern style but rather have sought to create an environment of 'existential authenticity' (Wang 1999) through Islamic styles. In other words, where no Islam-themed architectural heritage existed (particularly for secular buildings), the state in each case sought to showcase Muslim identity, often for secular reasons.

3.2   The Study of Cities in Islamic Contexts

Scholarship on city design in Muslim contexts can be grouped into two main strands. First, there is an extensive body of scholarship written by Europeans from the colonial era and into the 1970s that attempts to define 'the Islamic city' and catalogue its features in order to draw broad conclusions about how Muslims construct cities (Hourani and Stern 1970; Serjeant 1980). In this literature, there is the tendency to focus on the historical development of 'exotic' Arab cities (Dumper and Stanley 2007), which ultimately serves to orientalize the 'Islamic' city by reducing it to a handful of elements considered typical by westerners (Bennison and Gascoigne 2007).

In the 1980s, there was a turn towards deconstructing previous work on 'the Islamic city' in which earlier scholars were taken to task for their simplistic generalizations about cities built or occupied by Muslims. Janet Abu-Lughod (1984, 1987) argues that scholarship from the first half of the twentieth century sought to catalogue universal elements found in all 'Islamic' cities, a view that she contends was Arab-centric and based on visits to just a handful of cities in specific geographic locations, mainly Morocco and Egypt. While deconstructing the notion that cities can have an 'Islamic essence', Abu-Lughod points out that many urban planners in Saudi Arabia and the Gulf are reproducing features of city building determined by earlier western Orientalists to evoke the essence of the Islamic city. In light of the massive wave of construction in recent years, I suggest there is a need for a continuation of Abu-Lughod's research to further explore connections between religion and urban planning and architecture in the contemporary Muslim world.

A second strand of literature on cities in the Muslim world examines recent mega-projects in oil-producing nations, the focus of which is overwhelmingly on Arab regions. Yasser Elsheshtawy (2004, 2006, 2008a, c, 2010) is the pre-eminent scholar of recent urban developments in the United Arab Emirates and urban change in the Arab world more broadly. His writing and the essays in his edited collections explore urban change and the architectural and urban impacts of globalization in a number of rapidly changing cities located within the Arab world including Abu Dhabi, Cairo, Dubai, Beirut, Kuwait, Doha and Riyadh. Similarly, the June 2010 issue of the journal *Built Environment* examines such recent Arab mega-projects as highways, property development and a harbour redevelopment in existing cities in Syria, Morocco, Sudan, Algiers, Lebanon, Egypt and Iran. The largest volume of scholarly attention has been directed towards massive urban transformation of Dubai, with many scholars critiquing the artificiality and environmental, social and political unsustainability of its recent transformation (Bagaeen 2007; Abdullah 2006; Elsheshtawy 2006, 2010; Schmid 2006; Acuto 2010; Kanna 2011).

This chapter addresses several gaps in the literature on urbanism in regions with substantial Muslim populations. First, the majority of scholarship on urban change in the Muslim world has focused on general urban change in existing older cities, rather than planned cities built on a *tabula rasa*. Lawrence Vale (2008) provides valuable insight into how the nation is intertwined with planning philosophy in a wide variety of new cities examined in his book *Architecture, Power and National Identity*. While several new capital cities in Muslim contexts are examined, Vale does not specifically consider religion as a key dimension of new city planning. Because they are designed and executed during a short period of time under one leadership, master-planned cities can yield fascinating insights into the priorities of the ruling elite and their aspirations. Second, like the colonial-era scholarship that sought to understand the essence of ancient 'Islamic' cities, scholarship to date on mega-projects within the Muslim world has focused overwhelmingly on Arab regions. I suggest that there is value in adopting a comparative approach to examine cities in a variety of contexts across the Muslim world in order to explore trends and the broad set of phenomena that are contributing to the adoption of an Islamic idiom in new master-planned cities. Third, while most scholarship on urban change in Muslim contexts focuses on secular branding, local responses and development challenges, this chapter investigates city design as a key scale at which religion is expressed.

3.3 Orthodox Muslim Culture: A Popular Renaissance?

In regions with large Muslim populations around the world, there is evidence that both popular and state cultures are increasingly embracing outward displays of religiosity. From 'Islamic' soda beverages and nail polish brands in Egypt to Arab-themed 'Paket Ramadan' meals served in McDonald's restaurants in Indonesia, contemporary consumer culture in the Muslim world is increasingly infused with 'Arabized' interpretations of Islam.[1] There has been a parallel increase over the past several decades in more orthodox interpretations of Islam informing various dimensions of daily life with a resurgence of outward expressions of religiosity, including more widespread use of the *hijab* in such moderate countries as Turkey, Egypt, Indonesia and Malaysia.

Shifts towards more orthodox interpretations of Islam and increasing fear of extremists have sparked growing interest in academia, the media and political discourse concerning the spread of a transnational pan-Islamic movement. Scholarship on the Islamic resurgence has primarily focused around several main themes: political Islam (Effendy 2003; Muzaffar 1987; Jomo and Cheek 1992; Kepel 2002; Tibi 2002; Fuller 2002), *sharia* law (Hussin 2007; Henderson 2003; Mir-Hosseini 2006; Lee 2009), *madrasa* schools (Lukens-Bull 2000; Daun and Arjmand 2005; Daun et al. 2004; Bergen and Pandey 2006) and terrorist networks and Islamic militancy (Rashid 2001; Abuza 2002; Ramakrishna and Tan 2003; Smith 2005; Croissant and Barlow 2007; Hussain 2005; Khan 2006; Hiber 2009; Abuza 2003; Speckhard and Akhmedova 2006). The ways in which this transnational Islamic resurgence has been manifested materially in architecture and urbanism have been less examined to date, although a growing body of literature examines representations of Islam in the context of recent change in urban Malaysia (Tajuddin 2005; King 2008; Goh and Liauw 2009; Moser 2010, 2011b).

In this chapter, I do not wish to suggest that a broad Islamic resurgence in various cultural realms is necessarily a step towards a 'global caliphate' or is evidence of a 'clash of civilizations' (Huntington 1996). Rather, I suggest that there are a variety of reasons for the adoption of an Islamic idiom in new cities, many of them secular. As will be discussed in the following sections on Putrajaya, Grozny and Masdar, the adoption of an Islamic idiom in new cities is linked to a variety of factors including global aspirations, the growing interconnectedness of people in distant lands and changing local political and social contexts.

While there is little evidence to suggest that over one billion Muslims are politically or socially united, I suggest that in a globalized world, there are increasing connections to distant places and multiple sources for influences that complicate understandings of a unidirectional spread of culture. For example, while Indonesians may be increasingly influenced by Wahhabi Islam and other more orthodox interpretations of Islam (Ghoshal 2008), one could also note that with increasing globalization,

---

[1] This is the subject of a paper in preparation that examines how and the extent to which popular culture in Muslim Southeast Asia has been 'Arabized' in recent years.

Indonesians are also influenced by 'western' culture and consumerism, manufactured goods from China and Mexican and Korean culture through popular television dramas. With globalization comes a greater awareness of others and different transnational 'imagined communities' (Anderson 1991) that traverse national boundaries. While the concept of transnational Islam appears to be at odds with the modern notion of the nation state, a universal, transcendent religious identity can in fact be a powerful way to make secular claims within the nation state (Jones and Mas 2011).

3.4   Islam as Political Tool: The City as Billboard

In the following sections, I discuss Putrajaya, Grozny and Masdar as empirical examples of new cities within the Muslim world that exemplify the turn towards adopting a transnational Islamic idiom in their architecture and urbanism. I examine the cultural politics behind the design of each city in relation to the local context and to the broader, transnational phenomenon of global Islam and explore the meaning of a transnational Islamic idiom in each context.

3.4.1   Putrajaya

In Malaysia, the state's rapid push to urbanize has been realized, thanks to a lucrative oil industry and its commitment to propelling itself into more powerful regional and global roles. Over the past two decades, the state has developed an ambitious development and modernization agenda evidenced by massive spending on ostentatious and high-profile urban mega-projects. As part of Malaysian Prime Minister Mahathir's (1981–2003) 'Vision 2020', a plan to fully modernize and develop the country by the year 2020, a number of mega-projects have been constructed since the mid-1990s with undisclosed budgets and designed by foreign 'superstar' architects. Mahathir's mega-projects include the Petronas Towers by Cesar Pelli (until recently, the tallest building in the world), the Multimedia Super Corridor, the Kuala Lumpur International Airport by Kisho Kurokawa and the high-tech cities of Cyberjaya and Putrajaya, the new home to all federal government ministries. Officially announced in 1995, Putrajaya replaces the administrative functions of a vibrant and ethnically diverse seat of power established during the colonial era and represents broader development trends in Muslim-dominated Southeast Asia that link religion, national identity and globalization to the scale of the city.

Putrajaya is designed entirely in-house by Malaysian architects employed by the state, rather than by international 'starchitects' commissioned for other recent architectural spectacles in Malaysia. The Islamic architectural idiom selected by Mahathir has produced a fantastical skyline reminiscent of the *Arabian Nights*. The domes, arches and minarets found on government buildings, bridges and shopping malls in Putrajaya are inspired by an imagined Middle East and are taken from such diverse sources as Ottoman, Safavid, Central Asian, Iraqi, Persian, Moorish and Mughal architecture, resulting in an eclectic hodgepodge of recognizably 'Islamic' architecture and urbanism (Moser 2010b). While Malays and other Southeast Asians traditionally use local timber and indigenous building techniques developed over the centuries in response to the tropical climate for their homes, businesses, mosques and palaces, Putrajaya's architecture represents a total rejection of indigenous architectural styles and materials in favour of a broad, unfocused pan-Islamic style.

Similar to other new cities built by a ruling elite with global aspirations, Putrajaya is designed as an urban spectacle and is an attempt to overshadow Kuala Lumpur, the former capital it was designed to replace (King 2008), and to project a new Islamized national identity. The logic for creating a new Islamic capital must be read against Kuala Lumpur and the social dynamic of Malaysia. During the colonial rule, the British imported Chinese and Indians largely to meet the needs of the colonial economy. As a result, Malaysia is a multicultural and multi-religious country consisting of Malays (54%), indigenous peoples (13%), Chinese (25%) and Indians (7%) (Population and Housing Census, Malaysia 2010).

Upon independence from colonial rule in 1957, Chinese residents constituted a majority of urban residents in Malaysia. Due to colonial policies, Chinese Malaysians controlled a majority of the urban economy until the introduction of policies and incentives meant to attract Malays to urban areas in recent years. As has been pointed out by Thompson (2007), such policies have in fact resulted in the perpetuation of ethnic enclaves rather than a blending and sharing of urban space. It is against this backdrop of racial tension and geographical divisions that the new 'Malay' city of Putrajaya was conceived, and its adoption of transnational Islamic architecture announces publicly Muslim supremacy over Chinese Malaysians.

The choice of an international Islamic idiom for Putrajaya also reflects internal Muslim politics, particularly the political agenda of UMNO (United Malays National Organization), a key member of the ruling coalition. In a country divided by the secular-leaning ruling coalition and the Islamic opposition party, urban developments such as mosques, theme parks and new cities have become a key way for the ruling coalition to attempt to showcase UMNO's supposed Islamic core beliefs to PAS (Pan-Malaysian Islamic Party) supporters (Moser 2010, 2011a). As the new capital, Putrajaya is an extravagant attempt 'to be Islamically purer than the strident, fundamentalist-leaning and ever-threatening PAS opposition and thereby to represent a secular state that is still authentically Islamic' (King 2008: 165).

Putrajaya is a fascinating example of the rise of global pan-Islam and its manifestation in urban form. While the 'fantasy Middle Eastern' style has received some criticism from the media and scholars, it is currently the most widely used style for new urban areas in the Malay world, with similar new cities popping up in Indonesia and elsewhere in Malaysia. In this new 'Islamic' development, scrupulous attention is paid to the selection of domes and arches and 'Islamic' details such as orienting new urban developments to face Mecca, a device that had never been employed in the history of Islam until several recent state projects in Malaysia.[2] This Islamic turn

---

[2] Nusajaya, the new capital of Malaysia's Johor state, and *Taman Tamadun Islam* [Islamic Civilizations Park] in Terengganu are both Islam-themed and are oriented towards Mecca (Moser 2011a).

is occurring in the context of growing connections between Malaysia and the Middle East through 'Islamic' banking, development partnerships and growing political ties. By adopting a generic Islamic idiom in Putrajaya, the state is communicating a new national identity to its citizenry while positioning Malaysia to attract the attention and, more importantly, the business of 'global' Muslims (i.e. the wealthy Arab elite) through tourism and investment.

3.4.2   Grozny

Originally established as a Russian military fortress in 1818 as part of the Russian colonization of the North Caucasus, Grozny became a centre for oil and gas industries dominated by a Russian Slavic population. In the 1990s, the two major wars in Grozny occurred in the context of long-standing tensions between Russia and Chechens (Thomas 1997, 1999). In the first war in the mid-1990s, the Russian state sought to restore the sovereignty of Moscow over the self-proclaimed independent Ichkeria Republic. As the seat of the Chechen government, Grozny was the primary target of the federal Russian military, which used tanks and ground troops rather than air strikes in an attempt to overthrow the separatist government. The first Chechen war was so unpopular in Russia that Yeltsin urged troops to finish the operation as soon as possible (German 2003). As a result, Chechen forces were able to regroup and recapture Grozny in 1996, and for 3 years, Chechnya became a *de facto* independent state.

The second major war began in 1999, and Grozny once again became the target of Russian federal troops. This time, the intent was to punish the Chechen nation and terrify the population of the republic. In order to avoid the loss of Russian troops, massive air strikes were carried out. The destruction of Grozny became a symbol of Russian triumph over separatists, and no buildings of historic or economic significance were spared (German 2003).

By the time the violence ceased in 2000, most of the city was damaged beyond repair, and the administration formed between Chechens and President Vladimir Putin's government was unsure what to do with the ruins of Grozny. Akhmad Kadyrov, the new leader of the Chechen Republic, insisted that Grozny be restored as the Chechen capital and, with Russian aid, the post-war reconstruction was carried out on essentially a *tabula rasa*, making Grozny essentially a new city.

Grozny's reconstruction must be read against the long-term hostility between Russia and Chechnya. For centuries, many Chechens have nurtured an intense hatred of Russians and have suffered under various periods of Russian rule. Under the leadership of General Aleksey Yermolov, a Russian Caucasus commander in the early 1800s, Chechens were subjected to extreme disrespect and cruelty. Despite Yermolov's unpopularity among Chechens, the Soviet authorities erected a statue of him in Grozny in 1949 with an inscription that read, 'There is no people under the sun more vile and deceitful than this one' (Gall and De Waal 1999: 39). Significantly, the population of Chechens in Grozny was negligible until the revolution in 1917, when the communist party introduced ethnic quotas that reintroduced Chechens and other indigenous groups back into the North Caucasus. These policies were reversed during WWII when Josef Stalin earned the enmity of Chechens by accusing them of collaborating with the Nazis and deporting the entire population to Kazakhstan and Siberia. Many died during these deportations, which Chechens view as genocide (Park and Brandenberger 2004). They were returned to their homeland 13 years later during the premiership of Nikita Khrushchev. As Grozny grew into an important industrial centre for southern Russia in the decades following WWII, many Chechens moved to the city. However, the Slavic population dominated the industrial sector, and there was a substantial economic and educational gap between the Slavic population and indigenous people. As the capital of the Chechen-Ingush Republic, Grozny attracted a steady influx of Chechens, and by 1991, the year the Soviet Union collapsed, Grozny's Chechens constituted nearly 50% of the population.

Grozny is in the process of being rebuilt after the devastation of the two wars of the 1990s and is a particularly fascinating example of how the city is an important scale through which religiosity is made material. While the old Grozny symbolized Russian dominance, the new rebuilt Grozny has adopted overtly Islamic symbolism that is both a statement against Russian dominance and evidence of Chechnya's recent embrace of more fundamentalist interpretations of Islam.

Grozny's post-war image represents a dramatic shift in the city's demographics and cultural politics. The old Soviet city of Grozny was dominated by Russian bureaucrats and military, Cossack troops and their families, and Slavic (Russian and Ukranian) people employed in Russian industries (German 2003). During the wars of the 1990s, Grozny's heavy industry was destroyed, and the entire Russian population left the city (Wegren and Drury 2001). Before the wars, 326,500 Russian-speaking people lived Chechnya, most of them in Grozny. Between 1989 and 2002, about 308,000 of them moved away from the republic. While no more than 200 Russian-speaking families returned to Chechnya during the post-war period, Chechens from the towns and villages of the Chechen Republic moved to Grozny in large numbers after the second war. While Soviet Grozny was an industrially developed, multi-ethnic city, new Grozny is a predominantly Chechen city that functions as an administrative centre that survives on subsidies from the federal budget (Demchenko 2013).

The significant change of direction in the design for the new city is its overt adoption of an Islamic idiom to symbolize a modern and Islamicized Chechnya. During the wars with Russia, Chechens were provided with funding from Saudi Wahhabi groups and other international fundamentalist Islamist institutions, and Islam played an increasingly significant role in the republic (Wilhelmsen 2005). Predominantly Muslim, Chechens increasingly saw Islam as a source of strength and solidarity against the Russians during the wars. In the second war, the role of Islamic fundamentalist ideology in Chechnya continued to expand as Chechen religious leaders proclaimed a holy war against 'Russian unbelievers' (Wilhelmsen 2005). Sharia law was then introduced in the territories controlled by separatists, and violent incidents allowed Putin's government to present the war not as a separatist movement but rather as an operation against Islamic terrorism and militant fundamentalism.

The reconstruction of Grozny reflects the major social changes resulting from the wars and the complex relationship between Russians and Muslim Chechens. After the wars, the Chechen ruling elite, with Russian funding, looked to Soviet Grozny as a peaceful and stable era in the city's history. In some ways, the new city replicates aspects of Soviet Grozny in the use of post-Soviet architecture and urbanism, particularly in the broad avenues and in the reproduction of several grand Soviet-era buildings in Moscow. Most significantly, the new master plan for Grozny essentially reproduces the Soviet plan, which is designed around major Soviet industrial complexes, which have been destroyed and were only able to exist in the noncompetitive planned Socialist economy (Demchenko 2013). Furthermore, with the dramatic demographic changes in the population, even if the industries were to return, the majority of qualified workers employed in the factories and plants have left the republic.

The reconstruction therefore imitates aspects of the Soviet style but has added a distinct – albeit general – Islamic flavour to the city that was not present in old Grozny. Leaders in Moscow and the Chechen administration learned a lesson in cultural sensitivity from the second phase of the Chechen conflict, when the ideology of many separatists shifted from a nationalist to an Islamist Wahhabi agenda (Wilhelmsen 2005). While mosques, centres of Islamic education and Islamic motifs were completely absent from Soviet Grozny, Russian-funded post-war Grozny prominently features a number of mosques and buildings in an Islamic idiom.

The central focus of Grozny was once the Republican Committee of the Communist Party, which subsequently functioned as the centre of resistance during the wars with Russia. It then became the President's Palace complex. Its most recent iteration as Grozny's symbolic centre is as an extensive Islamic religious and educational complex, officially called 'the Heart of Chechnya' (Markosian 2011; Demchenko 2013). The highly symbolic position of the 'Heart of Chechnya' visually announces a major shift in the state's ideological underpinnings from Russian to Islamic governance. The centre of the city functions solely as a showcase of Chechen nation-building: it has no economic significance or industry, apart from the distribution of federal aid from Russia (Demchenko 2013). Although the sewage system, water and gas supply do not work consistently, the new buildings create the impression of prosperity and Muslim supremacy. Significantly, while the 'Heart of Chechnya' is intended as an iconic monument for the Chechen people, the architecture used is neo-Ottoman rather than vernacular Chechen. Architecturally, a generic Islamic or neo-Ottoman idiom has become a metonym for Chechen independence.

3.4.3   Masdar

Abu Dhabi is the wealthiest of the seven emirates that constitute the United Arab Emirates. With 8% of the world's known oil reserves, Abu Dhabi has over 90 years of oil remaining at present rates of extraction. In contrast to the excesses of neighbouring Dubai, Abu Dhabi's Sheik Zayed, ruler of Abu Dhabi from 1971 to 2004 and first president of the United Arab Emirates, took a more conservative development path. Under his rule, Abu Dhabi transitioned to an oil-based economy and modernized the emirate through the creation of apartment blocks for the masses, universal public education and healthcare and a modern urban environment.

The skylines of Abu Dhabi and Dubai underscore the vastly different approaches to development and modernization. Without a lucrative oil industry like Abu Dhabi, Dubai set out to build its economy through real estate ventures, international banking and urban spectacles intended to attract a global jet-setting elite and provide facilities for executives and tourists, including golf courses, luxury hotels, leisure parks and high-end retail. Furthermore, as Yasser Elsheshtawy (2008b) points out, Dubai was developed by merchant families, whereas Abu Dhabi has a far more conservative and modest background as a temporary shelter for nomadic residents and later a fishing and pearling village. Furthermore, as home to the president of the UAE, Abu Dhabi was developed primarily by the state, giving it a different character than cosmopolitan Dubai. Abu Dhabi's global engagement has also been more tentative than its neighbours. While Dubai has long targeted a global audience, Abu Dhabi, at least until recently, was more inward looking and sought to be a regional centre. The demographics of Abu Dhabi and Dubai emphasize their differences. Dubai's population is 1.2 million with locals constituting between 5 and 12%, while Abu Dhabi's population is 600,000, 12% of whom are locals. Dubai's population is projected to increase to 3 million by 2015 with 15 million visitors per year, while Abu Dhabi's population is expected to rise to 800,000 with 3 million visitors.

Dubai's excesses and recent economic vulnerability, culminating in its recent financial bailout by Abu Dhabi, have been widely publicized. Likewise, Dubai has a global reputation as a 'superlative city' (Kanna 2009), where the world's tallest building is located, massive developments have spread for hundreds of square kilometres into the desert and along the coast towards Abu Dhabi, and massive islands in the shapes of palm fronds, a map of the world and 'the universe' have transformed the coastline. In contrast, Abu Dhabi's development has been pragmatic and designed to cater to the needs of its populace. Unlike Dubai, Abu Dhabi 'never claimed to be another Singapore', and its urban character suggests 'a certain reluctance to become fully global and to engage the region' (Elsheshtawy 2008b: 262). As a result, the city is a rationally planned administrative centre that maintains its traditional and conservative roots, which takes the form of orderly but monotonous grid of indistinguishable tall apartments and office buildings.

In the years following the death of Sheikh Zayed in 2004, Abu Dhabi has dramatically changed course under the leadership of his son, Sheikh Khalifa. While Sheikh Zayed was a conservative developer of the emirate and the future he imagined relied entirely upon the continued extraction of oil (Elsheshtawy 2008a), Sheikh Khalifa has a more global vision for the emirate. After Sheikh Zayed's death, longer-term strategies have been put in place to prepare for Abu Dhabi's future in a post-oil economy. Over the past 5 years, Abu Dhabi has allocated a tremendous amount of resources to becoming a global centre for research and development in 'green' technologies.

The pinnacle of this new 'green' agenda is the city of Masdar, designed to be the world's first carbon-neutral city. Announced in 2007, Masdar, meaning 'the source' in Arabic, is a sophisticated engineered city in the desert outside Abu Dhabi designed by international 'starchitect' Sir Norman Foster's firm, Foster + Partners, with seed capital provided by the government of Abu Dhabi. Still in its early stages, computer-generated models reveal a lavish and innovative city with high-tech buildings and advanced 'green' technologies. A 10-MW solar field within the city is designed to harvest 60% more energy than Masdar requires, with the remaining energy fed into the Abu Dhabi grid. Media attention has focused on the particularly outlandish details of Masdar, including the personal rapid transit system, designed to shuttle people around in pods under the city, and the dynamic energy harvesting technology and cooling technologies that move with the sun to provide maximum shade in the city. Masdar is not intended to be simply an energy-efficient showpiece but to generate leading-edge research innovations in 'green' technologies. The Massachusetts Institute of Technology has collaborated with Abu Dhabi to develop the Masdar Institute of Science and Technology, which Abu Dhabi anticipates will become the world's premier research institute devoted to researching sustainability and renewable forms of energy.

Masdar must be read against the excesses and perceived shortcomings of Dubai, of which Abu Dhabi's ruling elite has long been critical. While the ostentatious scale and the ambitious theme of the project reflect a sense of competition with Dubai, one of the main goals for Masdar is to differentiate itself from its neighbour in critical ways. In developing its 'green' theme, Abu Dhabi has sought to carve a niche for itself in a way that both competes with the scale of Dubai's architectural spectacles while rejecting their highly commercial nature. The scale and ambition of Masdar and its lofty environmental goals have attracted as much international attention as Dubai's Burj Khalifa or man-made luxury archipelagos. However, unlike the placeless mega-projects that have characterized Dubai's development over the past decade, the design for Masdar reveals Abu Dhabi's desire to maintain a sense of Arab Muslim culture. In some ways, Masdar is the anti-Dubai, unlike Dubai's hedonism and generic elite aesthetic.

Despite Masdar's futuristic technology, it has an overtly Islamic aesthetic. Beyond the use of Islamic design motifs, the architects claim to have incorporated lessons from traditional Arabian architecture and urbanism that evolved over centuries (Foster + Partners 2007). Sophisticated, high-tech protective screens cover the city to filter direct sunlight. The screens are perforated with patterns based on traditional Islamic geometric patterns and project a dappled 'Islamic' light and shadow on the city during daylight hours. Masdar's use of leading-edge technology creates a distinct Islamic urban sensibility that goes beyond simply topping buildings with domes. According to the website of Foster + Partners and the official Masdar website, the layout of the city is based on tightly planned, traditional Arab walled cities with the expressed interest of encouraging walking and avoiding low-density sprawl, one of the problems that plagues Dubai. Furthermore, Masdar's distinctive square shape reproduces the 1,700-year-old Yemeni town of Shibam, another nod to regional Arab Muslim urbanism. Masdar carries the connotation of looking to the future while being grounded in traditional Islamic values.

3.5   Interpretations of 'Global Cities' and Cosmopolitanism

Few cities in the Muslim world, particularly new or recently built cities, meet the conventional definition of a 'global city'. However, in recently constructed cities, the ruling elite have clearly aimed for a global, or at least regional, audience while producing unique interpretations of what it means to be 'global'. As numerous scholars have pointed out, the global cities scholarship ranks and classifies cities on economic criteria (e.g. the number of banks, law firms and headquarters for transnational corporations based in a city) (Sassen 2001; Elsheshtawy 2010) in a way that ultimately serves to privilege primarily European and American cities (Robinson 2002). Elsheshtawy (2008a, b, c) argues that the narrow economic focus of the global cities discourse excludes cities such as Jerusalem, Medina and Mecca which are surely global in the sense that they serve as religious centres that attract millions of international pilgrims annually.

Following Carla Jones and Ruth Mas in their essay introducing a special issue of *Nations and Nationalism* dedicated to 'Transnational conceptions of Islamic community' (2011), I suggest there are multiple ways of claiming cosmopolitan or global status, including (and perhaps ironically) through urban expressions of religion. In writing about transnational conceptions of Islamic community, Jones and Mas (2011: 2) cite an Indonesian friend who reminds them that 'the Prophet imagined Islam as global long before anyone was talking about globalization'. Strict economic definitions of the global city need not prevent analysis into other understandings of 'global' and how they shape urban form in new cities (Moser 2011b).

Connections between globalization, transnational Islam and urban form can be seen in Putrajaya, Grozny and Masdar, as well as other new cities designed using an Islamic idiom. Due to globalization, economic development increasingly prioritizes the scale of the city (Castells 1996), and cities are seen as competing with one another for foreign direct investment, tourists and international events. New cities are expected not only to spark economic growth but also to function as public statements about the aspirations and ideology of the state, whether they are to nurture high-tech ambitions, reinforce an official national narrative or communicate religious alliances.

In each case, the use of a generic pan-Islamic idiom in Putrajaya, Grozny and Masdar suggests a conscious awareness of and desire to connect with global currents of Islam. In each context, Islam conveys the power and longevity associated with transnational Islam. While each city desires to appear global, it is through a different mode of expression than gleaming, generic office towers. This rejection of placeless modernism is a widespread phenomenon related to the increase of urban branding. The trend of Islamic urban expression found in new cities is evidence of the sense of competition between cities and the growing importance of cultural identity as a mark of distinction in a globalized world. Expressing religiosity through urban planning and architecture is going a step beyond creating the tallest building, engineering new islands or building extravagant shopping centres that feature ski hills, as it invokes sacred power in secular spaces.

Sharon Zukin (2009) argues that in many ways, globalization is having a homogenizing effect on the appearance of cities: more office space and ostentatious architectural trophies are created in an effort to attract corporate and elite international tenants, cities attract the same luxury shops, and similar leisure landscapes are built.

Putrajaya, Grozny and Masdar demonstrate, however, that global aspirations and the adoption of Islamic idioms can produce dramatically different results. This reflects the theming component of globalization and the divergent local goals of the three cities, as well as the unpredictability of local officials' conceptualizations of Islam and the global.

3.6   Transnational Islam: Secular Goals

While some segments of society in Putrajaya, Grozny and Masdar may aim for a global caliphate, it is apparent that transnational Islamic design has been adopted for primarily secular purposes. First, in each case, the selection of an Islamic idiom can be understood as an exclusionary practice intended to subvert or supercede perceived rivals to power. In the case of Putrajaya, an overtly pan-Islamic identity has been adopted in the national capital to send a strong message of Muslim supremacy to Chinese Malaysians and to convince supporters of the opposition orthodox Muslim political party of the ruling party's commitment to Islam. Similarly, Grozny has tapped into a broad, transnational Islam as a form of resistance against Russian domination. In the case of Masdar, a distinct Islamic sensibility pervades a futuristic city as a response to Dubai's ahistorical and foreign-focused developments. Each example is a lavish city-scale display of Muslim solidarity and demonstrates a strategic symbolic association with a broad and powerful tradition with a cultural legibility and legitimacy more potent than that of their rivals or their own indigenous traditions.

Nation-building is the second way that Islam has been accepted for secular purposes, highlighting the point that transnational Islam and nation-building are not necessarily mutually exclusive concepts. In the case of Putrajaya, Grozny and Masdar, there is a connection between urban-centric development agendas, nation-building efforts and globalization. New state-created 'Islamic' cities can be understood as aspirational, as models to which the rest of the country should aspire.

Through planning and architecture, the cities refashion national identity in a way that privileges particular groups over others and overlooks vernacular Islam in favour of a more transnational and recognizable brand of Islam. In the case of Putrajaya, Malaysia's rich vernacular architectural traditions have been overlooked in favour of an imported generic Middle Eastern style. Likewise, Grozny's 'Heart of Chechnya' is designed by Turkish architects in a neo-Ottoman idiom, a recognizable style that evokes the power and prestige of the Ottoman Empire in the context of a war-torn Russian republic. In these cases, strategically essentializing (Spivak 1996) a group (Malays, Chechens, Abu Dhabians) through borrowing a transnational Islamic identity lends more legitimacy to struggles with local rivals.

A third way in which an Islamic idiom is more related to the secular than the sacred is in the lack of religious function of the city design. None of the Islamic-themed designs for the three cities encourage deeper religious beliefs or practices. The 'Islamic' urban features function as metonyms of a broader Muslim society, intended to reinforce and broadcast one local group's dominance. None of the cities have integrated Quranic concepts into the designs that would encourage residents to live more 'Islamic' lives; they are simply modern cities with shopping centres, jogging trails, government buildings and conventional housing districts that are decorated with Islamic motifs. As Tajuddin, Malaysian architecture scholar and vocal critic of Putrajaya, points out, 'Islamic cultural heritage is not exemplified by big domes, arches and expensive ornaments but [is] rooted in the idea of humility' (Tajuddin 2005: 19).

This chapter draws attention to an emerging transnational sense of identity, specifically a recuperated sense of religiosity, manifested in a generic Islamic architectural idiom. In each context, transnational Islam represents different things: a longing for heritage and a glorious past, a tool in local political manoeuvering and a statement of ascendency over a competing ethnic or religious group. Far from providing evidence of a universal Islam, the empirical examples of Putrajaya, Grozny and Masdar demonstrate that cities are adopting Islamic idioms for a variety of often secular reasons, and that representations of a global Islamic community are subject to the interpretations of the local elite and the designers they employ.

References

Abdullah, A. 2006. Dubai: An Arab city's journey from localism to globalism. *Al-Mustaqbal Al-Arabi (The Arab Future)* 323: 57–84.

Abu-Lughod, J.L. 1984. Culture, 'modes of production,' and the changing nature of cities in the Arab world. In *The city in cultural context*, ed. John A. Agnew, John Mercer, and David E. Sopher, 94–119. London: Allen & Unwin.

Abu-Lughod, J.L. 1987. The Islamic city – Historic myth, Islamic essence, and contemporary relevance. *International Journal of Middle Eastern Studies* 19: 155–176.

Abuza, Z. 2002. Tentacles of terror: Al Qaeda's Southeast Asian network. *Contemporary Southeast Asia* 24: 427–459.

Abuza, Z. 2003. *Militant Islam in Southeast Asia: Crucible of terror*. Boulder: Lynne Rienner Publishers.

Acuto, M. 2010. High-rise Dubai urban entrepreneurialism and the technology of symbolic power. *Cities* 27(4): 272–284.

Anderson, B. 1991. *Imagined communities: Reflections on the origin and spread of nationalism*. London/New York: Verso.

Bagaeen, S. 2007. Brand Dubai: The instant city; or the instantly recognizable city. *International Planning Studies* 12(2): 173–197.

Bennison, A.K., and A.L. Gascoigne. 2007. *Cities in the pre-modern Islamic world: The urban impact of religion, state and society*. London: Routledge.

Bergen, P.L., and S. Pandey. 2006. The madrassa scapegoat. *The Washington Quarterly* 29(2): 117–125.

Castells, M. 1996. *The rise of the network society*. London: Blackwell.

Croissant, A., and D. Barlow. 2007. Following the money trail: Terrorist financing and government responses in Southeast Asia. *Studies in Conflict and Terrorism* 30: 131–156.

Daun, H., and R. Arjmand. 2005. Islamic education. In *International handbook on globalization, education and policy research: Global pedagogies and policies*, ed. J. Zajda, 377–388. Amsterdam: Springer.

Daun, H., R. Arjmand, and W. Geoffrey. 2004. Muslim and education in a global context. In *Educational strategies among Muslims in the context of globalization: Some national case studies*, ed. H. Daun and G. Walford, 5–36. Leiden: Brill.

Demchenko, I. 2013. The illusion of peace: The reconstruction of Grozny and the New Chechen identity. In *New cities in the Muslim world,* ed. S. Moser. London: Reaktion.

Dumper, M., and B. Stanley. (eds.). 2007. *Cities of the Middle East and North Africa: A Historical Encyclopedia*. Santa Barbara, CA / Oxford, England: ABC Clio.

Effendy, B. 2003. *Islam and the state in Indonesia*. Singapore: Institute of Southeast Asian Studies.

Elsheshtawy, Y. 2004. *Planning Middle Eastern cities: An urban kaleidoscope in a globalizing world*. London: Routledge.

Elsheshtawy, Y. 2006. From Dubai to Cairo: Competing against global cities, models and shifting centers of influence. In *Cairo cosmopolitan: Politics, culture and urban space in the new middle east*, ed. D. Singerman and P. Amar, 235–250. Cairo: AUC Press.

Elsheshtawy, Y. 2008a. Cities of sand and fog: Abu Dhabi's global ambitions. In *The evolving Arab city*, ed. Y. Elsheshtawy, 258–304. London/New York: Routledge.

Elsheshtawy, Y. 2008b. *The evolving Arab city: Tradition, modernity & urban development*. New York: Routledge.

Elsheshtawy, Y. 2008c. The great divide: Struggling and emerging cities in the Arab world. In *The evolving Arab city: Tradition, modernity and urban development, planning, history and environment series*, ed. Y. Elsheshtawy, 1–26. New York: Routledge.

Elsheshtawy, Y. 2010. *Dubai: Behind an urban spectacle*. London/New York: Routledge.

Foster + Partners. 2007. Foster + Partners. *Masdar development*. Retrieved February 16, 2011. http://www.fosterandpartners.com/Projects/1515/Default.aspx.

Fuller, G.E. 2002. The future of political Islam. *Foreign Affairs* 81(2): 48–60.

Gall, C., and T. De Waal. 1999. *Chechnya: Calamity in the Caucasus*. New York: NYU Press.

German, T. 2003. *Russia's Chechen war*. London/New York: RoutledgeCurzon.

Ghoshal, B. 2008. Arabization: Changing face of Islam in Asia. *Institute of Peace and Conflict Studies* 81: 1–4.

Goh, B.L., and D. Liauw. 2009. Post-colonial projects of a national culture. *City: Analysis of Urban Trends, Culture, Theory, Policy, Action* 13: 71–79.

Henderson, J.C. 2003. Managing tourism and Islam in Peninsular Malaysia. *Tourism Management* 24: 447–456.

Hiber, A. 2009. *Islamic militancy*. Farmington Hills: Greenhaven Press.

Hourani, A., and S. Stern. 1970. *The Islamic city*. Philadelphia: University of Pennsylvania Press.

Huntington, S. 1996. *Clash of civilizations and the remaking of world order*. New York: Simon & Schuster.

Hussain, R. 2005. *Pakistan and the emergence of Islamic militancy in Afghanistan*. Aldershot: Ashgate.

Hussin, I. 2007. The pursuit of the Perak Regalia: Islam, law, and the politics of authority in the colonial state. *Law & Social Inquiry* 32(3): 759–788.

Jomo, K.S., and A.S. Cheek. 1992. Malaysia's Islamic movements. In *Fragmented vision*, ed. J. Kahn and F.L.K. Wah, 79–106. Honolulu: University of Hawaii Press.

Jones, C., and R. Mas. 2011. Transnational conceptions of Islamic community: National and religious subjectivities. *Nations and Nationalism* 17(1): 2–6.

Kanna, A. (ed.). 2009. *The Superlative City Dubai and the Urban Condition in the Early Twenty-First Century*. Cambridge, MA: Harvard University Graduate School of Design.

Kanna, A. 2011. *Dubai: The city as corporation*. Minneapolis/London: University of Minnesota Press.

Kepel, G. 2002. *Jihad: The trail of political Islam*. London: I.B. Tauris & Co.

Khan, L.A. 2006. *A theory of international terrorism: Understanding Islamic militancy*. Leiden: Brill.

King, R. 2008. *Kuala Lumpur and Putrajaya: Negotiating urban space in Malaysia*. Copenhagen: NIAS Press.

Lee, J.C.H. 2009. Mobilizing for social change in Muslim societies amidst political turmoil and conservatism. *Development* 52: 239–245.

Lukens-Bull, R.A. 2000. Teaching morality: Javanese Islamic education in a globalizing era. *Journal of Arabic and Islamic Studies* 3: 26–48.

Markosian, D. 2011. Amid Chechnya's Islamic revival, some women live in fear. *Voice of America*. Retrieved February 16, 2011. http://www.voanews.com/english/news/europe/Chechnyas-Women-Live-in-Fear-od-Islamic-Revival-116776194.html.

Mir-Hosseini, Z. 2006. Muslim women's quest for equality: Between Islamic law and feminism. *Critical Inquiry* 32: 629–645.

Moser, S. 2010. Putrajaya: Malaysia's new federal administrative capital. *Cities: The International Journal of Urban Policy and Planning* 27: 1–13.

Moser, S. 2011a. Constructing cultural heritage. *International Institute for Asian Studies Newsletter* 57: 30–31.

Moser, S. 2011b. Globalization and the construction of identity in two new Southeast Asian capitals: Putrajaya and Dompak. In *Rethinking global urbanism: Comparative insights from secondary cities*, ed. X. Chen and A. Kanna. London/New York: Routledge.

Moser, S. 2012. 'Circulating visions of 'High Islam': The adoption of fantasy Middle Eastern architecture in constructing Malaysian national identity', *Urban Studies* 49(13): (in press).

Muzaffar, C. 1987. *Islamic resurgence in Malaysia*. Kuala Lumpur: Penerbit Fajar Bakti Sdn. Bhd.

Park, E., and D. Brandenberger. 2004. Imagined community? Rethinking the nationalist origins of the contemporary Chechen crisis. *Kritika: Explorations in Russian and Eurasian History* 5(3): 543–560.

Population and Housing Census, Malaysia. 2010. Population and Housing Census, Malaysia. *Population and Housing Census, Malaysia*. Retrieved February 10, 2011. http://www.statistics.gov.my.

Ramakrishna, K., and S.S. Tan. 2003. *After Bali: The threat of terrorism in Southeast Asia*. Singapore: Institute of Defence and Strategic Studies.

Rashid, A. 2001. *Taliban: Militant Islam, oil and fundamentalism in central Asia*. Princeton: Yale University Press.

Robinson, J. 2002. Global and world cities: A view from off the map, *International Journal for Urban and Regional Research* 26: 531–554.

Sassen, S. 2001. *The global city: London, New York, Tokyo*. Princeton: Princeton University Press.

Schmid, H. 2006. Economy of fascination: Dubai and Las Vegas as examples of themed urban landscapes. *Erdkunde* 60(4): 346–361.

Serjeant, R.B. 1980. The Islamic City, selected papers from the colloquium held at the Middle East Centre, Faculty of Oriental Studies, Cambridge, United Kingdom from 19 to 23 July 1976.

Smith, P.J. 2005. *Terrorism and violence in Southeast Asia: Transnational challenges to states and regional stability*. New York: M.E. Sharpe.

Speckhard, A., and K. Akhmedova. 2006. The new Chechen Jihad: Militant Wahhabism as a radical movement and a source of suicide terrorism in Post-War Chechen Society. *Democracy and Security* 1: 1–53.

Spivak, G. 1996. *Radical democracy: Identity, citizenship, and the state*. New York: Routledge.

Tajuddin, M.H.M.R. 2005. *Malaysian architecture: Crisis within*. Kuala Lumpur: Utusan Publications & Distributors.

Thomas, T. 1997. The Caucasus conflict and Russian security: The Russian armed forces confront Chechnya III. The Battle for Grozny, 1–26 January 1995. *Journal of Slavic Military Studies* 10(1): 50–108.

Thomas, T. 1999. The battle of Grozny: Deadly classroom for urban combat. *Parameters* 29: 87–102.

Thompson, E.C. 2007. *Unsettling Absences: Urbanism in Rural Malaysia*. Singapore: National University of Singapore Press.

Tibi, B. 2002. *The challenge of fundamentalism: Political Islam and the new world disorder*. Los Angeles: University of California Press.

Vale, L.J. 2008. *Architecture, power, and national identity*. New York: Routledge.

Wang, N. 1999. Rethinking authenticity in tourism experience. *Annals of Tourism Research* 26(2): 349–370.

Wegren, S., and A.C. Drury. 2001. Patterns of internal migration during the Russian transition. *Journal of Communist Studies and Transition Politics* 17(4): 15–42.

Wilhelmsen, J. 2005. The Islamisation of the Chechen separatist movement. *Europe-Asia Studies* 57(1): 35–59.

Zukin, S. 2009. Destination culture: How globalization makes all cities look the same. *Center for Urban and Global Studies Working Paper Series* 1: 1–26.

Chapter 4
Metaphors to Live by: Identity Formation and Resistance Among Minority Muslims in Israel

Nimrod Luz

4.1 Experiencing the Sacred on a Cold Winter Morning: Reflections on Religion, Politics, and Landscape

In the winter of 2002, I took students on a field trip that focused on Islamic monuments and landscape in the Galilee region in Israel. Our first stop was a local pilgrimage site called Maqam Abu al-Hijja, namely, the holy place of worship of a certain Abu al-Hijja. It was a fiercely cold morning, and the students relished the time spent inside the relatively warm shrine. As I was talking about the politics reflected in the internal landscape of the shrine – photos of the Dome of the Rock, Palestinian and Islamic symbols, etc. – a student pointed out to me a small graffiti near the entrance door. The handwritten Arabic inscription said: "Please God, help Osama Bin Ladin." Those were the days of post 9/11 and the height of the second Intifada, and the rifts between the Jewish majority and the Palestinian minority in Israel never looked more unbridgeable. I could see that the inscription was deeply disheartening to all the students, Jews and Muslims alike. All of a sudden, cultural-political-ethnical-religious boundaries came alive and were reified in the room. As we were standing there, a group of 25 people, we were no longer just an academic class learning about Islamic civilization and cultural landscape. Rather, we were instantly reduced to clans: Jews, Muslims, Christians, Druze, or so it felt. I did not venture to explore my students' views toward this inscription as I feared it would provoke a heated political debate. I wanted to prevent a situation in which my Muslim students would find themselves between a rock and a hard place. In the Israeli political climate, in a similar fashion to the one prevailing in the USA at that time, one was either with

N. Luz (✉)
Department of Sociology and Anthropology, Western Galilee College, Akko, Israel
e-mail: nimrodluz@hotmail.com

P. Hopkins et al. (eds.), *Religion and Place: Landscape, Politics and Piety*,
DOI 10.1007/978-94-007-4685-5_4, © Springer Science+Business Media Dordrecht 2013

"us" against evil or by default against "us"[1] (Amaney and Naber 2008; Tehranian 2009). Instead, I opted to elaborate on the political nature of the sacred and issues of identity politics and landscape. A few months later, the inscription could no longer be seen; an unknown hand had erased it from the wall; clearly, someone did not like the message.

This short anecdote is just a reminder, if we ever needed one, of the political nature of the sacred. In recent years, religion and sacred sites have gained ample attention in studies ranging from political and cultural geography to sociology, anthropology, and political sciences (Eade and Sallnow 1991; Chidister and Linenthal 1995; Friedland and Hecht 2000; Kong 2001). This chapter is located at the intersection of some of these debates and scholarly attention. It explores the relevancy of the sacred in contemporary life and the importance of religion and religious landscape in sustaining personal and group identity. Specifically, it examines the role of sacred sites among minority groups as a nexus for identity formation, design of collective memory, self-empowerment, and resistance. This chapter focuses on the ways in which minority Islamic sacred sites serve as spatial metaphors. Through an analysis of the transformations of an Islamic sacred site (maqam), this chapter reveals the politics of identity and minority group resistance performed and enacted through the sacred. In this way, the chapter reinforces the theoretical notion that landscape is essentially a political, cultural, and ideological endeavor. In particular, this chapter engages directly with majority-minority relations in contemporary Israel and what seems to be a growing source of conflict in Israeli society – the evolution of a more elaborate, informed, and outspoken Palestinian identity among Arab-Israeli citizens.

4.2   Islamic Sacred Places in Israel as Spatial Metaphors

Landscape is surely one of the more vexing and therefore fascinating human creations. It is anything but self-explanatory, simple, or innocent. In recent years, cultural geographers have promoted time and again an understanding of landscape as a cultural, and therefore highly political, construction, sphere, or process (Cosgrove 1984; Cosgrove and Daniels 1998; Mitchell 2000). At this stage, I would like to build an argument around this understanding regarding the multivalence of landscape as a way to explain the definition of landscape artifacts/icons/landmarks as spatial metaphors. Following which, I will explain the ways landscape and, more specifically, landmarks serve to sustain group identity and transform into spaces of resistance. This will be linked more directly to the main goal of this chapter which is to explore the meaning of sacred sites for minority communities in Israel. I am totally in agreement with Ivakhiv's argument that the phenomena of religion and sacrality ought to be studied as ways of distributing significance across geographic spaces and as

---

[1] "Us" being in this case the Jewish majority.

involving the distinction of different kinds of significance from among those being distributed (2006). It is our task as geographers of religion to explore these landscapes and understand the meanings that are being distributed and fought over.

Landscape, as the argument goes, is not just simply out there to be studied as a natural phenomenon. It is certainly not "nature" (Tuan 1979). Arguably, landscape is "culture" before it is "nature" (Schama 1995). The very word landscape in its cultural meaning entails the existence and work of human agents (Olwig 1993). But if landscape is a product of human labor (work), then Mitchell is right to suggest that it is also about the role played by landscape: to mystify human labor and to make it (i.e., landscape itself) appear natural rather than the product of social-cultural-political forces (Mitchell 2000: 104). It should be seen as a cultural medium that has a dual role:

> It naturalizes a cultural and social construction, representing an artificial world as if it were simply given and inevitable. (Mitchell 2004)

Hence, although landscape is a beguiling phenomenon and is perceived as a seemingly natural outcome of human labor, it is anything but natural or haphazard. The formation of landscape is inexorably linked to politics, power geometries, and struggles over meanings and ownership. The creation, or rather the construction, of landscape is all about power and therefore entails struggles and the use of force. The painting of a mural, the tilling of a field, the production or the demolition of an edifice (Saddam Hussein's monument in Tikrit is just an ostentatious example that comes to mind), and the construction of the Sacrè-Coeur Basilica in Paris[2] are all but parts of negotiations and dialectics among different forces. Thus, the construction of landscape is a continuous dialogue and indeed a struggle among different forces. In this process, power is used, implemented, and contested as there are no power relations without resistance (Foucault 1980).

The use of power in the construction of landscape is unavoidably linked to ideology or, simply put, the way people want to represent themselves (Cosgrove 1984). Landscapes are ideological because they can be used to endorse, legitimize, and/or challenge social and political control (Kong 1993). Thus, landscapes carry signs and symbols which represent social norms, identity, memory, cultural codes, and ways these were, and still are, fought and debated among different forces. It is indeed a text (Meinig 1979; Duncan 1990; Barnes and Duncan 1992) and hence susceptible as any other to many readings. Landscape is one of the most complex and intriguing signifying systems saturated with signs, symbols, and meanings (Barnes and Duncan 1992; Duncan and Duncan 1988). Inevitably, as a signifying system, it needs to be regarded and read as a text and therefore susceptible to all the dialectic and hermeneutic processes that are related to text analysis.

So, who gets to "author" the landscape? Who has the power of authority to write the landscape? (Mitchell 2000). In addition, and more pertinent to this chapter, what are the meanings assigned and the symbolization and cultural codes that may be

---

[2] This is a small tribute to Harvey's powerful cultural-political analysis of an iconic landmark, Harvey (1979).

read through Islamic sacred sites in Israel? The "landscape as text" metaphor is a very useful idea, but at the same time, it leaves us with the following conundrum: what is the metaphor describing? In what ways are those places being used as ideological/political/personal signs and signifiers and which contemporary needs and politics of those communities are being met? Following the understanding that landscapes are texts and may be read as texts, I will offer a "reading" of sacred sites found in local Palestinian communities. However, the evolution of these places in recent years is inescapably connected to general developments within the Israeli landscape, that is, the political geography of Israel at large.

4.3   Minorities and the Judaization of the Israeli Landscape

In order to set the activities related to Islamic sacred sites in Israel in context, it is pertinent at this stage to outline the central developments of the Israeli landscape – in other words, the cultural-political geography. It should be clear from the outset that the following are brief notes on the issues relevant to our discussion on the meaning of Islamic sacred sites (for more elaborate studies on the political geography of Israel for example, see Kimmerling 2001; Don Yihya 2001; Hilal 2006; Rouhana 2004; Yiftachel 2006).

The Israeli (then Palestine) landscape experienced dramatic changes and transformations during the nineteenth century mainly due to the growing interest and activities of European powers and the influx of new ideological groups to the region (Kark 1990). One of the most influential and meaningful changes was the growing presence of Jewish settlers and settlements which later served as the crucial platform for the emergence of the state of Israel. The return of the Jewish people to their historical homeland was a direct outcome of the advancement of the Herzlian concept of practical Zionism (Vital 1975). The years under the British Mandate (1917–1948) were crucial to the changes in the political geography with the massive influx of Jewish immigrants and refugees. However, the land was far from being deserted, and the Arab population located between the Jordan and the Mediterranean Sea did not sit idly by as Zionists established roots. Against the Jewish nationalistic project, the local Arab population promoted its own national Palestinian movement (Muslih 1998). The tension between these two opposing ethnic groups and ideological movements grew as both sides came to the realization that the war for Palestine was imminent following the UN vote for partition of the land (Laqueur and Rubin 2001). Shortly after the final British withdrawal on May 15, 1948, a full-scale war was launched between the Jews (soon to be the state of Israel) and their Arab counterparts. As a result of the war, Israel was established as a Jewish State and imposed ethnic rule within its sovereign territory, now covering 78% of Israel/Palestine (Yiftachel and Ghanem 2004). The majority of the Arab-Palestinian population fled or was forced out of the new emerging Jewish state, thus transforming the native Arab majority into a dispersed and marginalized minority in its previous homeland (Ghanem 2001; Morris 2001). The Israeli-Palestinians have become a "trapped minority" which means that their Arab-Palestinian identity contradicted the hegemonic Jewish character of the state in which they were supposed to be equal rights citizens (Rabinowitz 2001).

As a sovereign state, Israel began a concerted project known as the Judaization policy and built over 500 settlements and cities in areas previously inhabited by Palestinians (Benvenisti 2000; Yiftachel 2006). One of the most important results of this project (which is still underway) was the disappearance of former non-Jewish cultural artifacts, landmarks, houses, villages, and other cultural spatial presentations of the Arab-Palestinian past and heritage. The outcome of this state-hegemonic project meant that the Arab minority was by and large deprived of accessibility to public space that it could identify with outside of its own settlements. Arguably, the public space – the cultural-national landscape – was dominated by Jewish-Zionistic icons and symbols. Meron Benvenisti – an Israeli historian, a public figure, and an avid advocate of reconciliation and mutual recognition of the loss on both sides – encapsulates the gist of the contemporary Israeli landscape vis-à-vis its Arab-Palestinian origins through the following words:

> One need only read Israeli textbooks or see the albums of "before and after" photos – the land of 1948 and today – to realize how close we are to the point when the vanished Arab landscape will be considered just a piece of Arab propaganda, a fabrication aimed at the destruction of Israel. (Benvenisti 2000: 5)

In recent years, there has been growing activity among Palestinian citizens and groups in Israel regarding heritage locations that are mostly religious in nature. Thus, deserted mosques, religious endowments, graveyards, and other landmarks are being contested both publicly and legally. For this reason and as a part of an emancipatory process, several NGOs were established (Jabarin 2007). One of the more prominent ones is an offshoot of the Israeli Islamic movement appropriately named "the Al-Aqsa Association to Deal with the Property of Islamic Waqf." According to its director Sheikh Kamil Rayan, the organization focuses its activities on "the demand to apply Waqf assets to the preservations and development of neglected sites" (Haaretz, 19 April 1991; cited in Ghanem 2001: 128). Following the Oslo Accords (1995), there is a growing involvement of the Israeli-Palestinian minority in the Israeli public sphere. This followed the realization that the negotiations between Israel and Palestinian authority do not contribute to any significant improvement in their civil status or rights. This realization was translated into activities that "localize the national struggle" (Rekhess 2002). Thus, issues that had haunted Palestinian communities for decades, such as the right of return, accessibility to heritage sites, the "opening of the 48 files," refugees, land ownership, and their very definition as a national minority, began to surface more and more in the public media, in the courts, as well as in the Israeli parliament.

The battle for the (sacred) landscape is fought over many fronts from the local to the national scale and is manifested in various forms, for example, the struggle over the right to renovate the ruined minaret at the deserted village of Hittin, the contestation over the ownership of the mosque of Hassan Bey in Tel Aviv-Jaffa or the more photogenic and globalized conflict over the Haram al-Sharif in Jerusalem (Luz 2004, 2005, 2008). These places are highly effective in this cultural war.

Due to their religious connotations and social sensitivities (indeed, deep sense of place), they are less susceptible to the hegemonic machinery. Sacred places are highly evocative and therefore can successfully serve as efficient platforms to rally together people and groups that do not necessarily agree or cooperate on a daily basis. Thus, one may find adherents of the Israeli Islamic movement working shoulder to shoulder with representatives and supporters of the former Arab communist party in the struggle over the right to pray at the al-Aqsa mosque. In a different struggle, Arab Christians from Jaffa were at the forefront of a public struggle over the ownership of a mosque (Luz 2008). These places serve as locations and nexuses where various processes are underway: self-empowerment, memory design, identity politics, and more.

In the northern part of Israel, the Galilee, the state faces problems of control (at least according to the "official" perception) as the Jewish citizens of the region constitute less than 50% of the entire population. Over the years, different ideas and projects were offered in order to strengthen state control over this ethnically mixed region (Yiftachel 1992). One such solution to change the demographic balance (i.e., ratio between Jews and non-Jewish citizens) was the "Judaization of the Galilee" project that was launched in the late 1970s. The most successful part of this project was the construction of a new Jewish regional council named "Misgav," stretching over 200,000 dunums in the center of Lower Galilee (Sofer and Finkel 1988). Set between various existing Arab municipalities and built, partially at least, on appropriations of Israeli-Palestinians' land, this council was designated mostly for Jewish citizens (Luz 2007).[3] The formation of a new council consisting of 35 small villages scattered mainly on hills overlooking Arab-existing settlements contributed not only to changes in local demography but also to changes among respective local Arab communities. Against the background of years of marginalization and state-authored discriminatory laws against the non-Jewish population, this state-supported endeavor contributed directly to growing friction and contestations between Arab and Jewish councils in the Lower Galilee. During the early days of the October 2000 events (local name for the second Intifada within the Green Line), the region was in turmoil and Jewish settlements as well as various state symbols were attacked by Arab citizens of the neighboring villages. One cannot help but see the connection between the state project "Judaization of the Galilee" and local responses to the apparent discrimination against Arab-Israeli citizens of the Galilee. Indeed, as Don Mitchell already suggested, cultural wars were not confined to the field of representation but rather were raged across the landscape itself (Mitchell 2000).

Amidst these affluent new Jewish settlements lies the maqam of Abu al-Hijja, which is a local shrine that serves mostly people from the region. This sacred site is the point of departure and main case study for the current analysis. It will be demonstrated in the following text that this location and the recent changes of the region's landscape contributed significantly to the development and the changing perceptions of this shrine.

_____

[3] Misgav Regional Council entails also six Bedouin villages.

4.4   The Rewriting of a Sacred Landmark: Historical and Recent Development at Maqam Abu al-Hijja

Maqam in Arabic literally means "a place." However, when the term is applied to places of this nature, it should be understood as "a sacred site" (Goldziher 1967). According to local and mostly oral traditions, the shrine of Abu al-Hijja is the tomb of a certain Husam al-Din Abu al-Hijja (Arraf 1993). Who was this person and what were his virtues that led to his burial site being transformed into a local pilgrimage shrine? The data is rather scarce as little is written about him in historical sources. His name Abu al-Hijja carries a rather military tone and means "father of the war" but probably should be translated as the "fearless warrior." His nickname was al-Samin, that is, "the fat which should be read as a sign of good health." He was of Kurdish origin and served as a high-ranking officer (Amir) in the army of Saladin during the famous third crusade led by Richard the Lion Heart from 1191 to 1192 (Holt 1986). He excelled in the battlefield and was awarded accordingly with the revenues from vast tracts of taxable lands (Iqta') mostly in the Lower Galilee. The village in which the maqam is found was also part of this fiefdom.[4] Abu al-Hijja died in 1196 on his way back to his hometown, Irbil, which is in contemporary northern Iraq (Ibn Taghri Birdi 1913). There are no indications that he met his death in this very village or that this tomb indeed holds his remains. What is even more intriguing is the very process of consecration of this persona who had neither religious background nor any known spiritual virtues and whose only real connection to the area was his short army career and revenues he exploited from the locals. Why then would the people of the region promote an understanding of this military figure as a wali – an Islamic term referring to a righteous person who is considered a "friend of God"? To put this in a Weberian perspective, what was his charismatic lure and why would the local population attribute any special virtues to him? It would seem that his main claim to fame was his role in the holy war (Jihad) against the Crusaders.

Abu al-Hijja is not a singular or a unique example. The consecration of this place and person is but a case in point for a much wider phenomenon. Throughout the region, places and figures associated with the struggle against the Crusades have over the years become part of the mythologized and valorized local (and contemporary Palestinian) history and collective memory. Thus, for example, the alleged burial ground of the nephew of Saladin, Shihab al-Din, in Nazareth has become a pilgrimage site. The name Hittin, which is the place where Saladin defeated the Crusader army, was given to numerous Palestinian schools as well as to one of the divisions of the Army for the Liberation of Palestine. The "reconquista" against the Crusades and especially the period of Saladin have become part of a mythologized past for contemporary local Palestinian communities. It functions as a regulatory mechanism in the construction of landmarks and sacred landscape (Frenkel 2001; Luz 2002).

---

[4] For lack of better word, I use the European term fiefdom. However, it should be noted that the Islamic grant system of land was not similar to the European one.

It is rather difficult to reconstruct the historical geography of the maqam. It is not at all certain that the compound was actually constructed in this location prior to the late nineteenth century and certainly not in the format that exists today. Victor Guerin, a renowned and highly reliable French scholar, whose vast knowledge and meticulous surveys of the region are generally acclaimed, visited the small village of Kawkab on August 13, 1875. His description fails to mention a sacred site by that name although he does refer to another sacred site related to a certain local saint (wali) by the name of Ali (Guérin 1870). Surely this omission does not connote that maqam Abu al-Hijja did not exist at the time. But against the general lack of sources, it certainly poses some serious doubts as to the prevailing local historical reconstruction. So, in addition to the uncertain death place of Abu al-Hijja, we are also faced with inconclusive evidence regarding the construction date of the maqam. Indeed, as argued by Nora, there is a striking difference between memory and history. While history, as explored by historians, is about the representation of the past,[5] memory is life, borne by living societies (Nora 1989: 8–9). Put differently, memory is the vehicle through which myths are carried further. Memory and what is fashionably called collective memory rarely need verifications. It is the very essence of myth or as brilliantly formulated by Lincoln: "strategic tinkering with the past introduces the question of myth" (Lincoln 1989: 21). In my numerous visitations to the site, through conducting talks and interviews, or even when upon examining the fragmentary literature, not a single doubt was ever cast on the accepted (hi)story of the maqam. An assumed past (history as the case may be) is agreed upon according to which the place served as a sacred site since its inception subsequent to Abu al-Hijja's demise in the late twelfth century.

Today, the site is an integral part of the local sacred geography. One of the traditions that entailed visitations of the maqam was the annual ritual antecedent to the rainy season. Shortly before the "official" beginning of the winter (usually late October), the people of the village, accompanied by pilgrims from more distant locations, perform a pilgrimage to several sacred locations surrounding the village. The parade would end in a public gathering at maqam Abu al-Hijja during which a special prayer for rain (Istisqa) was performed (Arraf 1993). The upheaval of 1948 and the dramatic geopolitical changes that followed, in particular the formation of the state of Israel as a sovereign Jewish state, have led to the cessation of this pilgrimage. During the 1990s, as part of an initiative to transform the village into a tourist attraction, the ceremony was reenacted a few times but with meager success (Mustafa Abd al-Fatah, Interview with Author, April 28, 2005). In recent years, this initiative is no longer being carried out.

Located amidst an olive orchard, Maqam Abu al-Hijja today is far from being an impressive or extravagant landmark. It consists of two small halls, one serves as the entrance through which pilgrims can sit and pray and another one in which the tombs are located. This is the sacred center of the maqam where the pilgrims visit

---

[5] I think Nora is oversimplifying here as to the power-knowledge complexities of writing history, but his discussion opens up the debate about these distinctions.

with their special requests to ask for the intercession of Abu al-Hijja. The compound also consists of a courtyard in which a cistern can be found. The entrance to the sacred area is through a gate in this courtyard which is never really locked. The roof is adorned with two identical domes. Over the years, the ground surrounding the maqam serves as the village's main graveyard which is another reason for frequent visitations.

In 1989, a new mayor was elected to the village municipality. The new elected mayor was Ahmad Hajj of the left wing secular Arab-Jewish party of Hadash.[6] Shortly after beginning his time in office, he launched a renovation project which included among other historical sites the maqam of Abu al-Hijja:

> I wanted to renovate all historical sites. True, I am not a religious person but I think that some places need to be preserved by the people they belong to because they are part of their history. If you do not have a history you do not have anything, and especially because I am not religious I renovated the place because I wanted that my history in the area will not be erased. (Interview with author, December 28, 2005)

The renovation project included a complete do-over of internal parts of the maqam. In addition to renewal of the plaster and repainting of the walls, the external side of the domes was painted with the traditional green. New pictures were hanged inside the maqam. The themes of the pictures are quite intriguing. Along with traditional depictions of the sacred sites at Mecca and Madina, one could also find a number of pictures of the al-Aqsa mosque and the Dome of the Rock. Beside placards carrying Quranic verses, pictures of a more nationalistic Palestinian nature were hanged. One such picture was that of a young crying boy clad in a Palestinian kefiyyeh. This is one of the most popular "Palestinian" self-presentations of the current occupation and predicament of the Palestinians. The boy in the picture personifies Palestine and the struggle for the lost land as well as the catastrophe (Nakba) suffered by the Palestinian people. Should this rather unsubtle symbolization escape the beholder, the following caption is inscribed: "My beloved Palestine, how can I sleep while my eyes are clouded by the shadows of agony?" Thus, along with acknowledged and well-recognized religious symbols, one could find signs of the political national struggle. Furthermore, these symbols are often fused together to establish an understanding of the place as a religious-national icon. Indeed, maqam Abu al-Hijja is an Islamic sacred site and is promoted as such, but the construction of a layer of national meaning around it promotes it as a religious-national symbol. This fusion can be found across the board all around Israel. Several years ago, the Palestinian community of Jaffa joined hands in a public struggle to reclaim the mosque of Hassan Bey which was going to be transformed into a shopping mall (Luz 2005, 2008). Among the leaders of this public struggle were Christians, seculars, as well as other Jaffa residents who clearly were not members or adherents of the Islamic movement. These people went into conflict over a cultural icon or a

---

[6] This is the only political party in the Israeli parliament which advances the concept of full Arab-Jewish cooperation and promotes the idea of Israel as state of all its citizens as opposed to the current definition of a Jewish and a democratic state.

heritage site rather than a religious compound. Against the prevailing forces in Israeli society and after years of marginalization, the mosque has become an icon that symbolizes their civilian and political status. Another case in point is the promotion of the Haram al-Sharif – the Islamic noble sanctuary in Jerusalem – as the most revered national symbol (Luz 2004, 2009). The sacred sites in Jerusalem became coterminous with the idea of the Palestinian national struggle and national revival. Muslims and Christians, religious and seculars, and otherwise bitter enemies are firmly united regarding the importance and sanctity of this place. Its importance as a religious-national symbol rises high above any political differences and contestations. These new significances that are being distributed to sacred sites are part of the localization of the Palestinian national struggle. Put differently, in recent years, the war for national independence has been waged internally in Israel over numerous internal Israeli civic issues, sacred sites being but one sterling example of that.

To ensure a safe and fulfilling visit to the maqam, a new parking lot was constructed for the pilgrims and visitors. The dirt road leading from the village to the maqam was freshly covered with asphalt. A new gate was opened to the parking lot which enabled the visitors to enter directly from the local regional highway which ran parallel and was close to the maqam. New lawns and olive trees were planted, and the area surrounding the maqam was transformed into a recreation site. In recent years, the number of visitors coming to enjoy the maqam solely as a recreation site has been on the increase. Families, groups, and young people who want to avoid the public gaze and scrutiny[7] come here to enjoy peaceful hours in a place where they can truly identify with as their own. This may be better understood against wide-ranging processes of polarization and exclusion of Israeli society and in particular the growing animosity between Jews and Arabs in recent years. Parts of these processes are the ongoing efforts to exclude Arab citizens from public places. In the nearby town of Karmiel, dominated by the Jewish population, members of the city council were trying time and again to pass a new bylaw that would ensure that only citizens holding city passports would be allowed in the city parks (Zafon December 1, 2003). Plainly, this was an initiative to ban Arabs from surrounding villages from enjoying the city public spaces and using its parks for recreation. Attempts to gentrify the urban landscape are surely not endemic to the Israeli landscape but additions to the general class struggle in Israel where contestations and public debates are also fueled by ethno-national politics (see, e.g., Smith 1992, 1996).

In 1999, a new mayor was elected to the Kawkab municipality. The mayor, Nawaf Hajuj, was considered to be a sympathizer of the Islamic movement. Shortly after his election, he ordered the gate of the car park entrance to be sealed. Apparently, he was concerned about the "illicit" activities taking place in the vicinity of the maqam and took measures to minimize them. Ironically, it was the "secular" mayor who opened up the place and the more religious one who symbolically reduced accessibility to the place. Be that as it may, over the last 20 years, the maqam has

---

[7] I am particularly referring to the consumption of alcoholic beverages and social encounters in a mixed company which are by and large condemned in local traditional Arab communities.

undergone significant changes both in its physical appearance and in its growing importance and visibility among local communities. In the following pages, I will delve into the issue of resistance through the sacred and the symbolical uses of the sacred as part of the national struggle and resistance.

4.5 Resistance, Identity Politics, and the Sacred

On a warm Friday afternoon in April 2003, three women arrived at the gates of the maqam. For Ibtisam, who drove 2 h from the city of Ramle, this was her annual visit in which she asks for her family's health and well-being. Umm Hanni came from the nearby town of Sakhnin to pray for the quick recovery of her mother-in-law from a recent surgery. Hadija, who just recently divorced, walked with her three children from her house in Kawkab to seek solace from her current quandary. Normally, I refrain from making conversation with unescorted single women, but it was Hadija who first approached me asking if I knew if any of my neighbors might be in need of her services as a manual laborer.[8] Although I could not offer her any crumb of comfort, the conversation flowed, and the three of them were very open about their pilgrimage and visitation at the maqam. In fact, despite gender, religious, and ethnic differences, I was invited to attend their prayers at the tombs and later to the repast in the small picnic area. As we sat and enjoyed the meal, I ventured to ask them about the maqam and the man associated with it. Regardless of their total ignorance about his true identity and history, they assured me that he was a saint and a venerated man who helped many people over the years. If anything at all, they were willingly sharing their worldviews and expressing their identity without the tiniest doubt or fear. No words were said about the conflict, the problems of the Arab minority in Israel, and indeed anything that might be understood as relating to contemporary political or public issues. This brings us to the question of resistance and identity politics in sacred sites.

Resistance is typically reactive and cannot be understood apart from domination and power relations. It relates to those behaviors and cultural practices applied by subordinate groups that contest hegemonic social formation and threaten to unravel the strategies of domination (Haynes and Parkash 1991). It is also the ability of people to alter situations and realities through a myriad of tactics and behaviors. Resistance is therefore the weapon of those occupying subordinate positions in power-geography relations, who are therefore less likely to influence or change their spatialities. Naturally, those who have more access to resources (hegemonic groups) will also be those who will be able to codify space in accordance with their ideologies and political aims. Consequently, Islamic sacred sites within the Israeli landscape are inexorably linked, in my mind, with resistance and counter-hegemonic politics.

---

[8] She asked me that after she discovered that I lived in one of the new Jewish villages nearby.

Following Gramsci, I would claim that relations between dominant and subordinate groups are a process in which boundaries and consensual norms are always shifting and being negotiated (1971). Tangled in a web of political and social relations, dominant and subordinate groups are constantly competing and transforming the spaces they are sharing (or competing for) in accordance with their cultural, economical, and political stances. Resistance arrives from a place (and can take place) outside of the hegemonic control or less monitored by dominant agencies, be they state-controlled or socially constructed ones. Resistance therefore can be mapped as it is inevitably spatial (Pile 1997). It does not just simply take place but also seeks to appropriate place, a place that was subjected to hegemonic manipulations or is about to succumb to such dominant maneuvers that alter its character, accessibility, etc. From this perspective, resistance is less about particular acts than about the desire to find a place in a power-geography where space is denied or totally controlled (Scott 1990). The struggle for a particular space and the spatial changes in the socio-spatial boundaries of a place are inexorably linked to politics of identity. The struggle of a subordinate group over a particular place (resistance) is by and large a spatial-ization of identity conflicts and at the same time identity constructions around a particular object.

Resistance, according to Scott, includes any act(s) by member(s) of a subordinate class that is or are intended either to mitigate or deny claims or to advance its own claims vis-à-vis any external or hegemonic power (Scott 1985). In my mind, one of Scott's strongest contributions is his claim that resistance predominantly is informal, hidden, and nonconfrontational. However, Scott demands political awareness on the part of the subordinate and a reactive approach to claims made by the powers that be. Scott therefore demands political consciousness on the part of the subaltern or subordinate. But sometimes, even when the intention is unclear or even when one completely denies the very existence of resistance or intention, the very posing of an alternative politics and cultural traits that are different from those of power may be/ need to be considered as resistance. My argument here is more expansive than Scott's as I regard nonpolitical, unintended, or even unintentional acts as forms of resis-tance if they emanate from identity politics of subordinate or subaltern positions (Vinthagen 2007). The three women that performed their identity at the maqam may be totally oblivious to the nature or possible interpretations of their acts. They might even rule out such a statement on their part. However, I read it as resistance in the context of the Lower Galilee and Israeli society at large, and given the current politi-cal situation, the very portrayal of social behaviors which are inconsistent or at odds with that of the Jewish-hegemonic majority calls for a highly politicized read-ing. Therefore, resistance may be defined as positions, intended or unintended, which have the potential to influence power or hegemonic positions. Put bluntly, I hold the three women's activities in a minority sacred site as resistance even if they fail (or refute) to acknowledge these acts as such.[9] The very projection of alternative

---

[9] It might be argued that it is not against me that they resist but rather internal politics among the minority group and particularly male domination. I as an outsider might not be their frame of reference, and therefore, no such claims or statements were made.

cultural traits needs to be considered as resistance as they carry political implications or at least possibilities. This is certainly true in cases when the subject is fully aware of his acts and defines them against the hegemonic group.

Another pertinent issue is raised by Chivallon in her exploration of religion as an essential feature of the diasporic experience of the Caribbean in the UK (2001). Chivallon takes issue with Pile's formulation of resistance in/through a place, in particular the question of ownership and resistance. Chivallon claims that as soon as the subordinate is in control of a place, his performance therein can no longer be considered as resistance:

> I agree completely with Pile's analysis (1997), in which he remains wary of a working of power relationships which is seen as "a separation of one space (of domination) from another (of resistance) … . Resistance, then, not only takes place in places, but also seeks to appropriate space, to make new spaces" (page 16). I believe, however, that from the moment when forms of resistance have access to the full codification of the physical space, they are no longer in a position of resistance (Chivallon 2001).

The ownership of maqam Abu al-Hijja was never in question. It is owned, operated, and controlled by the people of Kawkab who naturally regard it as their own. Nevertheless, I chose to read their activities therein as resistance because even if they were unintentional, they are contrasted with hegemonic positions and carry the potential to undermine them. The fact that the people of Kawkab have access to the full codification of the physical space does not change either their subordinate position or their relations vis-à-vis the state and the Jewish majority. But even if the issue of resistance could be put to question, at least theoretically, where activities of uncertain political implications are concerned, the following statement leaves little doubt as to the identity politics entailed in adhering to Islamic sacred sites:

> The holy Islamic places are more important to me than the Christian ones…the mosque in Jaffa or in Acre, and the mosque in a ruined village are all signs for the continuation of Palestine… I would pay good money for a mosque to be built atop Mount Carmel because it challenges the political Jewish identity of the State of Israel. (Nadim Rouhana, interview with author, August 2002)

The speaker was Nadim Rouhana, a Palestinian from a Christian family who grew up in Israel and currently resides as Professor of International Negotiation and Conflict Studies at Tufts University (http://fletcher.tufts.edu/faculty/Rouhana/default.shtml).

For him, the identity politics involved with Islamic sacred sites in Israel are apparent and undeniable. The existence of such places, the contestations involved with them, and their symbolic meanings are part and parcel of the ethno-national conflict. The fact that he is not a Muslim and yet can fully identify with such places clearly suggests that these locations have long since surpassed their religious, cultural, or historical framework. Within the Israeli context, these places are becoming highly politicized as they are perceived as part of the Palestinian national identity and heritage. Indeed, as stated by Rouhana, they have the capacity to challenge the Jewish identity of the state. But these places are also highly instrumental on a local scale for individuals and communities while sustaining and performing their identity. Surely, the growing activities in sacred sites cannot be fully explained simply by religious motivations.

Jamil is a young man I met in Kawkab. He was entertaining friends on his front porch as I passed his house. I asked for his permission to take a picture of the emblems above his front door. I was duly invited to join the conversation, and while we were sipping our drinks, he showed interest in my work. I explained that I was trying to understand how Israeli-Palestinians relate to their sacred sites. We discussed maqam Abu al-Hijja, and he shared with me some of the traditions assigned to the place. He told me that his father who suffered from a walking disability stayed by the tombs an entire night and in the morning he walked all the way back home fully cured. Jamil insisted that he did not consider himself a religious person but time and again he visited the maqam:

> I do not go there because I believe in the sanctity of Abu al-Hijja or that I actually pray there. For me this is my place and it is important for me that it will look nice and particularly now because of the new Jewish places that were recently developed around us. I am not ashamed of what I have; far from it. Abu al-Hijja is part of my history even though I am not a religious person. (Interview with author, June 2005)

His answer reminds us of what was previously quoted from Ahmad Hajj, the former mayor, who insisted that his initiative to renovate the maqam should not be perceived solely as a religious issue. For him, the maqam was a part of his heritage and therefore a venerated cultural attribute. Hajj was very upfront about the political implications of this site. He supplied an explanation, at least a partial one, of the importance of the period of Saladin among Palestinians and why sites affiliated with that period have grown in significance in recent years:

> Q: But what is so special about Abu al-Hijja? After all has been said and done, he was but a military figure, a general in the army of Saladin. What do you have in common with this man from the twelfth century who was a Kurd and exploited the peasants of this region?

> A: I feel close to Abu al-Hijja, not because he was a general or a Kurd, but because he was involved and helpful with the battle against the Crusaders. Through fighting the Crusaders he ultimately helped the Palestinian cause and people. (Interview with author, December 28, 2005)

Thus, the mythical "glorious" victory against the Christian-European forces of the 12th Crusade is fused with the contemporary Israeli-Palestinian conflict and the Palestinian national struggle. This fusion of religion, history, and past and contemporary politics is even more intriguing when we are reminded that Hajj, according to his own self-definition, was a highly secular person. This fusion allows for a highly speculative interpretation and understanding of the past to sustain contemporary needs. Thus, a history of the place is being formed and concretized to sustain the dire needs of the present. The maqam, as any other "place," is a complex web of relations, of domination and subordination, and of solidarities and cooperation (Massey 1993). At the same time, it is inexorably linked with controversies, conflicts, struggles over control, and debates (as well as more physical contestations) over meaning and symbolism. Being a "web of signification" (Ley and Olds 1988) inevitably transforms the place into a site where that significance and its "true" nature is up for grabs for those already in power or those in the search for power. Places, as the argument goes, are spatial metaphors through which people (singular and plural) can represent themselves and thus concretize their culture; that is, through places, cultural ideas and abstracts become concrete. The maqam and the person commemorated therein are refashioned and are perceived as parts of the national heritage. Thus, the place is able to accommodate and sustain a highly complex and flexible identity politics as well as serve as an accessible and handy platform where resistance can be performed.

4.6   Concluding Remarks

The analysis of the process of placemaking in the construction of sacredness and a sacred site is the foreground of the politics of spatial relations. Indeed, as the case of Abu al-Hijja reveals, the encounter with the sacred is a mediated and negotiated experience rather than an inherent one. The construction of the place follows other sociopolitical processes within and without the community of Kawkab. The ways in which the construction of a religious-political community and particular identity politics are understood are embedded within wider Palestinian national discourses. All around Israel, Islamic (Palestinian) religious sites are becoming highly politicized and serve as platforms where new identity politics are being formed to meet with contemporary needs.

Maqam Abu al-Hijja is also a case in which the past of the place is used and transformed in order to meet with contemporary needs. The sacred site of the minority is promoted as a religious-national icon and therefore part of an emancipatory process. This hybrid of meaning and rather unreserved construction of historical events emanate from a rather unique process of identity politics which is underway among Palestinian communities in Israel. In this sense, identity has both an individualist and a collective meaning. Going back to the very basic definitions, identity can simply relate to "a person's sense of belonging to a group if (it) influences his political behaviors" (Erickson 1968). The common interest calls for a common identity. In order for different people to join together, a very rich understanding of this identity is being formed. Thus, identity politics serve as rallying and organizing principles of social action among Israeli-Palestinians. They inform and guide cultural political behavior and enable different forces to unite over an all-encompassing understanding of the sacred site. Identity is not only about individuality and self-awareness but also and especially about identification with, and commitment to, shared values and beliefs in a social collectivity to which a person belongs. At any given time, a person may have multiple identities, each of which may always have some bearing on his or her political conduct and social roles in society. In the case of maqam Abu al-Hijja, the construction of a "mythical" past and the nationalization of the sacred allow individuals who might otherwise be at odds with each other to find a common ground: a common interest that involves a shared identity and collective hi(story) through politics of resistance. The maqam of Abu al-Hijja is a relevant case in point through which one can study the phenomena of religion and sacrality as ways of distributing significance across geographic spaces and involving the distinction of different kinds of significance from among those being distributed.

The study of the changing landscape and socio-spatial activities therein reveal the importance of critical geography of religion as a way to explore sacred places and understand what meanings are being distributed and fought over.

References

Amaney, J., and N. Naber (eds.). 2008. *Race and Arab Americans before and after 9/11: From invisible citizens to visible subjects*. Syracuse: Syracuse University Press.
Arraf, S. 1993. *Tabaqat al-Anbiyya w-al-Salihin fi al-Ard al-Muqadssa*. Tarshiha: Matbaat al-Ikhqan Makul.
Barnes, T., and J. Duncan. 1992. Introduction: Writing worlds. In *Writing worlds: Discourse, text and metaphor in the representation of landscape*, ed. T. Barnes and J. Duncan, 1–17. London: Routledge.
Benvenisti, M. 2000. *Sacred landscape: The buried history of the Holy Land since 1948*. Berkeley: University of California University.
Chidister, D., and E. Linenthal. 1995. Introduction. In *American sacred space*, ed. D. Chidister and E. Linenthal, 1–42. Bloomington: Indiana University Press.
Chivallon, C. 2001. Religion as space for the expression of Caribbean identity in the United Kingdom. *Environment and Planning D: Society and Space* 19: 461–483.
Cosgrove, D. 1984. *Social formation and symbolic landscape*. London: Croom Helm.
Cosgrove, D., and S. Daniels (eds.). 1998. *The Iconography of landscape: Essays on the symbolic representation, design, and use of past landscapes*. Cambridge: Cambridge University Press.
Don Yihya, E. 2001. *Studies in religious Zionism and Jewish law*. Ramat Gan: Bar-Ilan University.
Duncan, J. 1990. *The city as text: The politics of landscape interpretation in the Kandyan kingdom*. Cambridge: Cambridge University Press.
Duncan, J., and N. Duncan. 1988. Re(reading) the landscape. *Environment and Planning D: Society and Space* 6: 117–126.
Eade, J., and M. Sallnow. 1991. Introduction: Contesting the sacred. In *Contesting the sacred: The anthropology of Christian pilgrimage*, ed. J. Eade and M. Sallnow, 1–29. London: Routledge.
Erickson, E. 1968. *Identity: Youth and crisis*. New York: Norton.
Foucault, M. 1980. *Power/knowledge: Selected interviews and other writings 1972–1977*, ed. Colin Gordon. London: Harvester.
Frenkel, Y. 2001. Baybars and the sacred geography of Bilad al-Sham: A chapter in the Islamization of Syria's landscape. *Jerusalem Studies in Arabic and Islam* 25: 153–170.
Friedland, R., and R. Hecht. 2000. *To rule Jerusalem*. Cambridge: Cambridge University Press.
Ghanem, A. 2001. *The Palestinian-Arab minority in Israel, 1948–2000*. Albany: SUNY Press.
Goldziher, I. 1967. *Muslim studies*. London: Allen and Unwin.
Gramsci, A. 1971. *Selection from the Prison Notebooks,* eds. and trans. Quentin Hoare and Geoffrey Nowell-Smith. London: Lawrence and Wishart.
Guérin, V. 1870. *Description géographique, historique et archéologique de la Palestine*. Paris: A L'Imprimerie Nationale, Galilee I.
Harvey, D. 1979. Monument and Myth. *Annals of the Association of American Geographers* 69: 362–381.
Haynes, D., and G. Parkash. 1991. Introduction: The entanglement of power and resistance. In *Contesting power: Resistance and everyday social relations in South Asia*, ed. D. Haynes and G. Parkash, 1–22. Delhi: Oxford University Press.
Hilal, J. (ed.). 2006. *Where now for palestine?: The demise of the two-state solution*. London: Zed Books.
Holt, P. 1986. *The age of the Crusades*. London/New York: Longman.
Ibn T.B. 1913. *Al-Nujum al-Zahira fi Muluk Misr w-al-Qahira*, vol. 5. Berkeley: The University of California Press.

Ivakhiv, A. 2006. Toward a geography of "Religion": Mapping the distribution of an unstable signifier. *Annals of the Association of American Geographers* 96(1): 169–175.

Jabarin, Y. 2007. NGOs as a political alternative – A critical analysis. In *The Arab minority in Israel and the 17th Kenesset elections*, ed. E. Rekhess, 93–99. Tel Aviv: Tel Aviv University Press [Hebrew].

Kark, R. (ed.). 1990. *The land that became Israel: Studies in historical geography*. New Haven/Jerusalem: Yale University Press/Magnes Press.

Kimmerling, B. 2001. *The invention and decline of Israeliness*. Berkeley: University of California Press.

Kong, L. 1993. Ideological hegemony and the political symbolism of religious buildings in Singapore. *Environment and Planning D: Society and Space* 11: 23–45.

Kong, L. 2001. Mapping 'New' geographies of religion: Politics and poetics in modernity. *Progress in Human Geography* 25: 211–233.

Laqueur, W., and B. Rubin (eds.). 2001. *The Israel-Arab reader: A documentary history of the Middle East Conflict*. New York/London: Penguin.

Ley, D., and K. Olds. 1988. Landscape as spectacle: World's fairs and the culture of heroic consumption. *Environment and Planning D: Society and Space* 6: 191–212.

Lincoln, B. 1989. *Discourse and the construction of society: Comparative studies of myth, ritual, and classification*. New York: Oxford University Press.

Luz, N. 2002. Islamization of space and society in Mamluk Jerusalem and its Hinterlan. *Mamluk Studies Review* 6: 135–155.

Luz, N. 2004. *Al-Haram Al-Sharif in the Arab-Palestinian public discourse in Israel: Identity, collective memory and social construction*, Floersheimer Institute for Policy Study. Jerusalem: Achva Press.

Luz, N. 2005. *The Arab Community of Jaffa and the Hassan Bey Mosque. Collective identity and empowerment of the Arabs in Israel via Holy Places*, Floersheimer Institute for Policy Study. Jerusalem: Achva Press.

Luz, N. 2007. *On land and planning majority-minority narrative in Israel: The Misgav-Sakhnin Conflict as a Parable*, Floersheimer Institute for Policy Study, Jerusalem: Achva Press [Hebrew].

Luz, N. 2008. The politics of sacred places. Palestinian identity, collective memory, and resistance in the Hassan Bek Mosque Conflict. *Environment and Planning D: Society and Space* 26(6): 1036–1052.

Luz, N. 2009. *The Glocalisation of al-Haram al-Sharif Landscape of Islamic resurgence and national revival: Designing memory, mystification of place*. Paper presented at the International conference on: Islamic Resurgence in the age of globalization: Myth, memory, emotion, NTNU, Trondheim Norway, 4–6 September 2009.

Massey, D. 1993. Power-geometry and a progressive sense of place. In *Mapping the futures: Local cultures, global change*, ed. J. Bird, B. Curtis, T. Putnam, G. Robertson, and L. Tickner, 59–69. London: Routledge.

Meinig, D. (ed.). 1979. *Interpretations of ordinary landscapes: Geographic essays*. New York: Oxford University Press.

Mitchell, D. 2000. *Cultural geography: A critical introduction*. Oxford: Blackwell.

Mitchell, W.J.T. 2004. *Landscape and power*. Chicago: University of Chicago Press.

Morris, B. 2001. *Righteous victims: A history of the Zionist-Arab conflict 1881–2001*. New York: Vintage Press.

Muslih, M. 1998. *The origins of Palestinian nationalism*. New York: Columbia University Press.

Nora, P. 1989. Between memory and history: Les lieux de mémoire. *Representations* 26: 7–24.

Olwig, K. 1993. Sexual cosmology: Nation and landscape at the conceptual interstices of nature and culture, or: What does landscape really mean? In *Landscape: Politics and perspectives*, ed. B. Bender, 307–343. Oxford: Berg.

Pile, S. 1997. Introduction: Oppositional, political identities and spaces of resistance. In *Geographies of resistance*, ed. S. Pile and M. Keith, 1–32. London/New York: Routledge.

Rabinowitz, D. 2001. The Palestinian citizens of Israel, the concept of trapped minority and the discourse of transnationalism in anthropology. *Ethnic and Racial Studies* 24(1): 64–85.

Rekhess, E. 2002. The Arabs in Israel: Localization of the national struggle. *Israel Studies* 7(3): 175–198.

Rouhana, N. (ed.). 2004. *Citizenship without voice: The Palestinians in Israel*. Haifa: Mada al-Karmel Center.

Schama, S. 1995. *Landscape and memory*. New York: Alfred Knopf.

Scott, J. 1985. *Weapons of the weak: Everyday forms of peasant resistance*. New Haven: Yale University Press.

Scott, J. 1990. *Domination and the arts of resistance: Hidden transcripts*. New Haven: Yale University Press.

Smith, N. 1992. New city, new frontier: The lower east side as wild, wild, west. In *Variations on a theme park: The new American city and the end of public space*, ed. S. Michael, 61–93. New York: Hill and Wang.

Smith, N. 1996. *The new urban frontier: Gentrification and the revanchist city*. New York: Routledge.

Sofer, A., and R. Finkel 1988. *The new outposts in the Galilee – Aims, achievements, lessons* (Publications in problems of regional development 43). Rehovot: The Center for the Study of Rural and Urban Settlements (Hebrew).

Tehranian, J. 2009. *Whitewashed: America's invisible middle eastern minority*. New York: New York University Press.

Tuan, Y.F. 1979. Thought and landscape. In *Interpretations of ordinary landscapes: Geographic essays*, ed. M. Donald, 89–102. New York: Oxford University Press.

Vinthagen, S. 2007. *Understanding resistance: Exploring definitions, perspectives, forms and implications*. www.resistancestudies.org (permission by author).

Vital, D. 1975. *The origins of Zionism*. Oxford: Clarendon.

Yiftachel, O. 1992. *Planning a mixed region in Israel: The political geography of Arab-Jewish relations in the Galilee*. Avebury: Gower Publishing Limited.

Yiftachel, O. 2006. *Ethnocracy: Land, politics and identities in Israel/Palestine*. Philadelphia: Pen Press.

Yiftachel, O., and A. Ghanem. 2004. Ethnocratic regimes: The politics of seizing contested territories. *Political Geography* 23: 647–676.

Chapter 5
Myth, *Miramiento*, and the Making of Religious Landscapes

Elizabeth Olson

5.1 Introduction

It looks just like Switzerland…

This comment came from a Peruvian development practitioner with extensive experience of resource development in the rural Andes. We were having lunch and discussing watershed governance, and the conversation drifted to my interest in the links between religious affiliation and social organization in Latin America. He began explaining the development success of several indigenous communities in a region of the Andes where investment in an Evangelical community had resulted in unequaled development. As we continued talking about this place, he soon revealed that he had never been there, but that he had seen pictures shown to him by other development professionals who had been there. My curiosity was less in the mechanical aspects of the success, for his narrative of fat cows and healthy children raised a very different question – why, in the several years that I had been working in Latin America, did this narrative of Evangelical success always adhere so tightly to concepts of landscape? How were these "Evangelical" places being made so convincingly that they were described to me first by a Spanish tutor in Guatemala and, 3 years later, by this development practitioner in Peru?

The purpose of this chapter is to reflect upon the ways that religious difference becomes produced in and through embodied religious landscapes. I begin by outlining some of the central arguments emerging from geographic research on the construction of religious landscapes. The data is drawn from ethnographic research conducted in 2002 and 2003 in two rural districts of the high provinces of Cusco, Peru. I explore the ways that religious boundaries and differences become part of a rural landscape and gain shape through *miramiento*, a gaze which acts as a strong

E. Olson (✉)
Department of Geography, University of North Carolina at Chapel Hill, Saunders Hall,
Campus Box 3220, Chapel Hill, North Carolina 27599–3220, USA
e-mail: eaolson@email.unc.edu

P. Hopkins et al. (eds.), *Religion and Place: Landscape, Politics and Piety*,
DOI 10.1007/978-94-007-4685-5_5, © Springer Science+Business Media Dordrecht 2013

force for social order, and the myths that become attached to particular aspects of lived religion. Beginning with the assumption that the meanings and functions of the material landscape are left incomplete when the narratives and stories that simultaneously describe it and construct it are excluded from analysis (Price 2004), I consider the intersection between the gaze, myth, and landscape in the construction and maintenance of religious landscapes. I conclude by reflecting on the ways that embodied landscapes might help to inform our understanding of the scaling of religious identities and belonging.

5.2 Religious Landscape and Lived Religion

References to landscape and religious landscape are common in the spatial studies of religious phenomena, but the concept of religious landscape is often left rather unconsidered in comparison to other spatial categories. In her compelling and insightful analysis of the location of religion, Knott (2005) envisioned an embodied experience of space, and though other geographic terms are painstakingly explored, landscape is applied far less judiciously. Thus, the subject of Knott's analysis, the left hand, becomes a "place," whereas a street or neighborhood becomes an "urban landscape" (Knott 2009: 157). Similarly, Cladis (2008), in his analysis of religion in the public realm, is careful to define terms such as modernity, but not landscape, which becomes synonymous with public landscape, or the spaces that lie outside of the individual and its contours. In the following, I outline two ways geographers have used the concept of religious landscapes to analyze and describe religious presence in diverse societies: first, as a reflection on religious affiliation and the built environment and, second, as a meditation on the embodied practices that become constructive parts of the social landscapes of religion.

The first and perhaps most prevalent way that geographers have thought about the religious landscape refers to shifting demographics of religious affiliation and new religious places in the built environment, or what we might think of as the built religious environment. Zelinsky (2001: 565) – in writing about the religious landscape of North America – writes of the "visible, tangible man-made landscape" and extends our attention to what might now be considered unofficially sites of the sacred, such as cemeteries and religious bookshops (Kong 2010). But far from a simple accounting of places and boundaries, accounts of religious landscapes have emphasized how changes in the religious landscape pull the private aspects of faith and practice into very public processes of governance. Peach and Gale's (2003: 487) focus on the "social and aesthetic trends" associated with religious change in England is one example, with religious landscapes emerging out of immigration and settlement and new forms of occupation of space. In this instance, the presence of religious people and religious buildings is intimately linked, for when religious communities are present for longer periods of time, they might then have to engage with local planning regulations in order to construct purpose-built facilities rather than occupying existing places of worship or modifying previously profane sites for sacred use.

Thus, current studies of religious landscapes are often distinguishable from earlier geographies of religion by what might be called a critical focus on the reasons for how and why religious communities, their buildings, and their symbols end up where they do. In places where efforts by religious communities to establish formalized religious spaces have been rebuked by their neighbors, the landscape becomes not only the pattern of religious practice and identity but also a source of its politics. As Kong (2010) notes, there is now a substantial body of academic work on "minority" religions, such as mosques being constructed in non-Muslim countries. However, it is not only the erection of buildings that religious spaces become publically claimed. Watson (2005) draws out this dimension of religious landscape in her analysis of the ultimately successful attempts by Orthodox Jews to establish an eruv in Barnet, London, that was opposed by non-Jewish neighbors and other Jews who feared that it would attract anti-Semitism. The boundaries of the eruv required mostly preexisting poles, wires, walls, and buildings, but the symbolic transformation of these objects effectively changed the landscape not just for observant Jews but also for nonobservant neighbors. Though some complaints about the establishment of the eruv referred to the potential interruption to the material landscape, Watson exposes the underpinning intolerance toward making otherwise invisible religious practices visible and occupying. As one objector, whose property was to form part of the eruv, wrote in a letter to the Chairman of the United Synagogue Eruv Committee, "We will constantly be reminded of this religious significance every time we arrive at and leave our homes. We consider this to be an unfair and unreasonable imposition of a religious belief upon us" (Watson 2005: 607).

Claims about symbolism or religious difference might be stringently avoided, as alluded in Trudeau's (2006) account of the rejection of a slaughterhouse used for Hmong ritual animal sacrifice (*Ua Dab*) and the preparation of Halal meat in Hugo, Minnesota. Though located in a rural setting and one that would not be unusual for animal production and rendering of much larger scales, the slaughterhouse attracted a large number of immigrants and ex-refugees to the area. Neighbors objected to increased traffic and the techniques of slaughter, and the city refused to give the owner the planning permission that would allow compliance with state sanitation rules. The rejection was worded in a way to clarify that the cultural and religious concerns were not considered in making the decision but was "nothing more than a question of land use" (Trudeau 2006: 430). In this case, it is through the divorce of the symbolic relevance of this landscape, and the unwillingness to acknowledge formally the changed human landscape, which then allows the city to effectively limit the religious and cultural practices of a minority of its citizens. Thus, in the case of the Hugo slaughterhouse, racism is denied through a language of planning and of citizenship, a turn that is accomplished by denying a discussion of belief, practice, and the symbolic meaning of the slaughterhouse for both proponents and opponents. Dunn (2005) makes a similar point in the context of Australia by illustrating how the symbolism of multiculturalism is ultimately used to situate anti-mosque discourse as racist, and in her spatial analysis of religion, Knott (2005) emphasizes:

> As power struggles of all kinds are played out in space – whether social, mental or physical space – a spatial analysis of religion cannot avoid confronting them, both directly and through their representations. The spaces that religion occupies and participates in are spaces of power – the challenge will be to discover the relationship between religion and power in any given space. This will require a close examination of the complexity of the social relations which constitute that space and the cultural symbols that represent it. (2005: 28)

These studies of religious landscape offer important insights into the ways that the built landscapes of religion, particularly religious buildings, are constructed, contested, and accommodated. But they also remind us that religious landscapes are not only about material buildings and boundaries but also – perhaps even ultimately – about the people, beliefs, and practices that they are presumed to represent and the attempts that they make to materialize those aspects of self that are essential to faith. Cultural symbols, or other forms of materialized culture, are thus important means by which religion takes hold of and shapes place, and this underpins the second category of landscape studies, that which focuses on the ways that lived religion become transformed or expressed through a religious landscape. Lived religion emphasizes the embodied character of religion, focusing on the embodied emotions, experiences, and biographies of being religious (Streib et al. 2008), but it is only through a grounding in space and scale that lived religion transforms into lived landscape. Gökariksel (2009: 658) provides one example, drawing our attention to "different scales and geographies related to the fluid and mobile body" in her analysis of Muslim women's veiling practices, and the urban material landscapes which mark religious practice and religious identity are generated as much through embodiment as they are through the political debates which have hung heavy over multicultural Europe (see also Secor 2002). In the consumptive practices of the secular Turkish state, veiling becomes a symbol of class in the painstakingly secular landscapes of shopping malls. The material practice of religion – in this case, veiling – becomes synonymous with a lower class, and less accepted, vision of the nation. In the case of shopping malls, the symbolic landscape is as powerful as the material one in establishing norms of behavior, and the secularization of the space is secured by making veiled women feel out of place in these environments (Gökariksel and Secor 2010).

How, then, do these embodied religious landscapes work? Price (2004) offers one possibility in her study of the US-Mexico border. Rejecting Mitchell's (2003) critique of cultural landscape studies and his concern with the "facts of place," Price draws upon Edward Casey's phenomenological view of place and space[1] to craft an alternative to the "enduring substrate, a straightforward power of place that

---

[1] Casey (1993, 1996) suggests that there is no "place qua place," where space is in fact derived from place rather than the other way around. The emplaced body, according to Casey, is the means for retrieving place.

undergirds, drives, and is effaced by its representations" (Price 2004: 19). Suggesting that representation can be stripped away to reveal the "truth" about place, Price warns, reinforces a hierarchy of "fact" over "fiction" and, as such, imposes an order of truth and reality that is itself the product of a privileged scientific position. Her solution is to engage the embodied landscape by listening to the stories of the insider. Rather than rejecting landscape as either text or morphology, she suggests that "…the narrative construction of landscape is so tightly bound to material processes that to separate the two, let alone relegate stories to a secondary role, would be to profoundly miss the point" (Price 2004: 22). The meanings of the shrines that migrants from Mexico build under bridges and on borders can be missed if the narrative compositions of landscape, the stories, are considered "only fiction" (see also Duncan 1990). The alternative truths that go into constructing the material landscape, such as a seductive gringo devil that reinforces the "trickster" quality of the borderlands or the importance of the Virgin and other popular saints that dictate routes of migration, can be similarly missed. Thus, whereas in Mitchell's (2003) critique, we are told that the landscape vision falls apart when the real, powerful relations of production are exposed, Price's landscape is layered, and the outsider's vision of production is only one of these layers.

Taken together with the cases of eruv opposition and the Hmong slaughterhouse, Price's study also suggests that the materialization of symbolic or sacred meanings can be powerful for both those who believe they posses sacred or spiritual significance and those who do not, and that those perceived religious landscapes are not limited to "immovable," formal religious landscapes such as buildings. I would like to clarify this latter point, for as the case study from Peru suggests, it is important to establish that a landscape is no less real when it is temporary. Doreen Massey (2006), when reflecting on the "nature" of landscape, reminds us that even the most apparently solid earth beneath our feet is changing and that "the very rocks were/are moving on" (2006: 9). Her point is that all landscapes are ones that are moving, sometimes fleeting, even (and her point is, in fact, *especially*) when perceived from a scientific perspective, or that which seeks truth through the virtue of being able to be incorrect or proven wrong. "The reorientation stimulated by the conceptualization of the rocks as on the move leads even more clearly to an understanding of both place and landscape as *events*, as happenings, as moments that will be again dispersed" (2006: 21). Massey suggests replacing the idea of landscape as something only material and as "something that we travel across" with the alternative of "provisionally intertwined simultaneities of ongoing, unfinished stories" (*ibid*).

In short, embodied religious landscapes are not only about fleeting or temporary landscapes, though these may be important components of them. They signal the centrality of authorship, of storytelling, in that landscape, not by landscape portraitists or by landowners. There is a danger that all embodied scales of analysis could be conflated with embodied religious landscapes, and I think it is important to distinguish the kinds of religious landscapes that I am referring here from those described by Dewsbury and Cloke (2009) as spiritual landscape faith. Whereas spiritual landscapes are primarily concerned with the ways that faith and belief adhere to material landscapes and aspects of sacredness, embodied religious landscapes are concerned with issues of identification and acknowledgement. Thus, spiritual landscapes and embodied religious landscapes are clearly related and arguably inseparable from the standpoint of a faithful individual, but as the studies above demonstrate, it is useful and arguably important to distinguish between the two for the purpose of empirical analysis for they are likely to express different dimensions of contemporary religion.[2]

In the remainder of this chapter, I would like to draw upon the concept of a lived religious landscape to examine what I have called the myth of Evangelical development. Throughout Latin America, religious difference has become linked to economic success and modernity, both by the popular press and in academic analysis.[3] David Martin (1990: 206) argued that though there is little evidence to suggest that religious change can lead to economic success, "Evangelical religion and economic advancement do *often* go together, and when they do so appear mutually to support and *reinforce* one another." In 2002, *Somos*, a magazine supplement to the Peruvian paper *El Comerico*, published an article titled *"La Tierra Prometida,"* The Promised Land (Rocha 2002). The first page of the article shows the image of a man, hands outstretched toward the camera, gleefully displaying a massive trout. Behind him lie hillsides of brilliant green, interspersed with small patches of golden grassland. The accompanying photos of verdant forests and fat cows are proffered as evidence that this farm is the modern Andean version of milk and honey and that the population of Granja Porcón in central Peru has reproduced the Promised Land on Earth. The author of the article goes on to describe the unusual economic and entrepreneurial success of the Granja Porcón, the entire population of which is Evangelical. The neighboring town, which "appears to suffer all the Biblical plagues," is quite evidently not Evangelical, but dominated by "popular" or practicing Catholics. This fabled story of Evangelical success and Catholic failure is repeated in many different regions of Latin America, most often aligning Catholics with harmful traditionalism and Evangelicals with progressive modernity. In the following, I show the importance of lived religious landscapes – those that incorporate evanescent humanity with the material landscape – in maintaining stories of religious difference.

5.3   Religious Pluralism in Peru

The history of shifting religious regimes in Peru reaches far beyond the Spanish conquests, but today's religious context is more closely related to the dramatic political and social changes brought about through the political relationships cultivated

---

[2] I acknowledge that this is a problematic assertion in the context of spiritualism (see, for instance, Holloway 2006), but even spiritualism will have landscapes that are linked to processes of identity formation or, from external perspectives, to identification.

[3] These include Sherman (1997), Annis (1987), Muratorio (1980), Coleman et al. (1993), Brusco (1995), and Gill (2004), among others.

between the Crown and the Catholic Church (see Spier 1994). The Catholic Church and the state maintained mutually beneficial relationships through independence including the identification of Catholicism as the official state religion, though some of the Catholic clergy was interested in promoting religious pluralism (Klaiber 1992). It was not until the liberals began to dominate politics that anticlericism was reflected in state policy. Liberal politics did open space for new associations like Protestantism, which was assumed to be a potential base for new "societies of ideas" (Barrera 1993: 59, author's translation).

Much of the early work of missionaries from every denomination was dedicated to clearing a path for the free practice of religion, a task which took substantial patience. Francisco Penzotti, a Methodist who worked for the American Bible Society (*sociedades bíblicas*), was arrested in both Arequipa and Lima for preaching and distributing bibles (Ugarte 1962). Although non-Catholic religion was still not tolerated in constitutional law, the public outcry over the popular minister's multiple arrests encouraged leniency on the part of the government (Klaiber 1999). By the end of the nineteenth century, the value of religious diversity emerged as an important consideration for the Peruvian state and a new social reality for the Peruvian people. Indeed, it is at this time that the outlines of today's familiar geographic patchworks of religious differentiation began to emerge, but not without strong reactions. In 1913, a violent attack on the mission of the Seventh Day Adventists in Platería, Puno, encouraged the passage of the Toleration Act of 1915 authorizing non-Catholic acts of worship. From 1945 through 1966, Evangelical churches were often prohibited the right to private assembly (Armas 1998: 120). It was not until the constitutional assembly of 1978–1979[4] that the division between church and state was formalized, recognizing the Catholic Church "…as an important element in the historical, cultural and moral formation of Peru," but clarifying that "the state may also establish different types of cooperation with other confessions" (Klaiber 1999: 260).

Even as the Catholic Church was being repositioned in Peruvian politics, its unique historical position guaranteed it the ability to reinterpret the process of secularization in a relatively positive light. Rather than relinquish control to the state, the church used the constitutional change as an opportunity to shore up its own power and reinforce its hierarchy. A 1980 agreement between the state of Peru and the Holy See in Rome strengthened the independence of the Catholic Church by clarifying that the state did not have control over apostolic appointments (Santolaria 2000). At the same time, the agreement enforced the unity and hierarchy of the church itself, noting that "…the representative parties would be the Roman Catholic Church, represented by the Holy See…, and not simply the Peruvian Episcopal Conference or certain local Catholic churches of Peru" (ibid, 63). The constitution of 1993 replicated – almost word for word – the 1979 constitutional agreement, thus reinforcing what Santolaria calls a "harmonious separation" between church and state (ibid, 62).

---

[4] Article 86 of the Constitution of 1979.

The resulting landscapes of religious affiliation are evidence of this history of repression, violence, and intolerance. Different areas fell under different religious influences because of the serendipity of missionary arrival and out of the assertion of minority religious rights. In contemporary Cusco, spheres of Evangelical influence are informally determined through the local Evangelical governing body, with Assemblies of God dominating some regions and *Iglesia Evangelica Peruana* for other regions. Collective decision-making between Evangelical churches through an umbrella governance organization helps mitigate any potential conflicts between different denominations, such that tensions over evangelization are more frequent with Catholic parishes than with Evangelical *hermanos* (brothers). The history of conflict and current arrangements begins to explain the patchwork pattern of a religious affiliation that seems characteristic of the rural areas in departments like Cusco, where so-called Catholic communities might exist alongside an informally segregated Evangelical community or where one pueblo assembles an elaborate fiesta for the patron saint while their more "modern" neighbors prepare for the secular *feria*.[5]

Today, there is little agreement as to precisely how many non-Catholics there are in Peru. Studies by Motte (2002) and Marzal (2000) suggest relatively modest growth in size or diversity of non-Catholic communities through the end of the twentieth century. However, Armas (1998) identified 13 non-Catholic churches in Peru in 1930, already located in 54 different locations, increasing to 26 churches by 1933.[6] The World Christian Database identifies 73 separate denominations in Peru as of 2000.[7] Of these, only six non-Catholic churches appear to have experienced a decrease in membership between 1970 and 2000, and these are historical Protestant denominations, such as Lutherans, Anglicans, and Wesleyans. In contrast, churches that normally fall under the broad category of *Iglesias Evangelicals,* including a wide range of Pentecostal, charismatic and neocharismatic, and other apocalyptic Christian denominations, have all enjoyed growth through the last decades of the twentieth century. Thus, despite concerns among Latin American scholars that rates of conversion might be overestimated (Cleary 2004), the popularity of non-Catholic Christianity appears to still be growing in Peru. As noted above, this growth has been accompanied by a vigorous neo-Weberian debate which considers how religious conversion might be leading to a new ethic of production. Though most cases are not as photogenic as that of the *Granja Porcon*, most development practitioners can offer their version of the valley or two villages where Evangelicals, eager to embrace the offerings of modernity, are contrasted with "traditional" Catholics.

It was in a similar storied rural landscape in the high provinces of Peru where, in 2002 and 2003, I conducted 9 months of fieldwork. The data described below was

---

[5] See for example Annis (1987) on Guatemala, Muratorio (1980) on Ecuador, and Beams (2001) on Peru.

[6] This is presumably a reference to the number of independent churches or groups of worship, though Armas does not clarify or provide a citation for his data.

[7] http://www.WorldChristianDatabase.org

conducted through ethnography, complemented by semi-structured interviews conducted with men and women of 43 households spread across the *comunidades campesinas* (communities) of two rural districts in the province of Canas, Cusco. I was interested in understanding the production of these mythical landscapes of Evangelical development, both materially and symbolically. What I found is that the symbolic production was equally, if not more, important to the perpetuation of this differentiation than were the material realities of economic income or capital possession,[8] and that landscape played an important role as a "surface" upon which these symbols could be solidified.

5.4 Miramiento and the Construction of Religious Difference

> Back in the time when this lake was made, Hanocca was marrying Yauri,[9] and at the wedding there was a very old person. This old 'girl' was given food before the wedding even took place, but she wasn't treated well. And she said, 'Do you still think that was I made just to serve you? Wipe your nose already!' She ate Hanocca and Yauri, and the saints all left… The *mamasuncha*[10] left up this side, and from that side the Virgin [Rosario], and the saints, who were angry, said "you have to find a way up without flying." So the Virgin Rosario turned into a woman. Part way up she had to pee and flooded the valley. After peeing she turned around and turned to stone. This is why there is a big rock on the hill on the way to Descanso. And this is how the lake came about.

5.4.1 The Story of the Creation of the Lake Narrated by Sra. Alvarez of Hanocca

The rural districts of Hanocca and Yauri and the main pueblos that bear the same name are anchored to the shores of one of the largest lakes in the high Andes of Peru. From Yauri, it is a short walk to the dirt highway that leads from Sicuani through the rest of the high provinces and, eventually, to Arequipa. The distance between the two pueblos is approximately 12 km along a road bounded by the lake on one side and the steep ridge of peaks rising up on the other. If a traveler were to continue from Hanocca past the pueblo of Yauri and along the broad, dramatic

---

[8] It is not possible to review the evidence here, but an in-depth survey of households revealed that perceptions of economic difference were primarily based on: (1) the higher proportion of Evangelicals who were migrants into the region and had converted to Evangelical faiths while working at mines and earning a wage which they were able to invest into their farms; (2) the geographic location of particular Evangelical annexes of the community, which required them to rely on animal husbandry rather than subsistence crops, thus focusing their production on trade at regional markets; (3) lack of spending on alcohol among Evangelicals; and (4) popular impressions that Evangelicals had more international links than Catholics.

[9] All places and persons have been given pseudonyms in this paper.

[10] This is likely a reference to the Virgin Asunta, another saint of Hanocca.

sweep of the glacial valley to the southeast, she could in a day's walk descend into the high and sparse grasslands of the department of Puno. A detour to the north leads to the asphalt highway that stretches across the boundary between the departments of Cusco and Puno. The lake serves the twin purpose of anchoring the two pueblos together while simultaneously offering a constant material reminder of their divisions. The story of the creation of the lake as narrated by Señora Rosa illustrates the importance of the landscape as a recorder of history and an active participant in the separation of the two ill-fated towns/lovers. It is also notable for the ease with which Catholic symbolism has been interwoven with *K'anchis*-inspired stories of landscape formation. In addition to these older stories that are read from the landscape, contemporary layers have been added to the embodied religious landscape that describe not rocks and *Apus* (mountain deities), but the changing religious composition of the region.

Hanocca and Yauri are situated within the boundaries of the *Iglesia Surandina* (church of the southern Andes), a regional alliance of the Catholic Church which coordinated the political and social activities of the five prelates stretching from the city of Cusco to Juli, Puno, during its height of activity in the 1970s and 1980s. Often considered a problem by the more conservative Lima Church,[11] the five bishops of the southern Andes embraced a project of liberation theology in "an uncommon moral leadership" (Klaiber 1992: 322; see also Riedel 1999; Olson 2006, 2008). In the 1970s, the priests and nuns of the zone led the "march for the land," an attempt to enforce the land redistribution issued under legislation passed in 1969 by the "revolutionary" military government of General Velasco. In the 1980s, they established vicariates to monitor human rights violations at the hands of the Shining Path and the government. Since the early 1970s then, the prelate of Sicuani (which covers the functioning of all of the high provinces of Cusco) has been largely dedicated to this project of liberation, developing a complex system of development-oriented "social teams" to begin addressing issues ranging from agriculture to education to the establishment of democratic institutions throughout the region. In many ways, the Catholic Church continues to structure the lives and livelihoods of Catholics and non-Catholics alike. Though there are churches and parish houses in both Hanocca and Yauri, the French priest lives in Hanocca and has a tremendous presence in political, social, and spiritual affairs there. The two nuns who live in Yauri are, by comparison, relatively hidden public figures in both districts. The clear center of the Catholic Church in this region is Hanocca.

The second largest religious organization in Hanocca and Yauri, the Evangelical Church of Perú (*Iglesia Evangelica Peruana,* or IEP), is likewise enmeshed in the social process of the two districts. Unlike other "traditional" and Evangelical protestant denominations, the local IEP was originally established in Yauri in the 1930s as a distinctly Peruvian and proudly independent Evangelical denomination. Its historical narrative reflects the themes of resistance to violence and subordination

---

[11] The bishop of one prelate was advised that the southern Andes should send representatives to episcopal meetings in Rome in order to defend themselves from charges of supporting leftist politics and movements.

that dominate the national discourses of the fight for religious freedom and parallel local indigenous uprisings against abusive landowners. Regional leaders are themselves *campesinos*. The IEP does not have a complex network of development structures and has minimal contact through the regional or national scales of the institution. Nonetheless, the values espoused by the IEP reflect the same concerns about cultural expression and public ethic as Evangelical movements in North America or Europe. The result is a complex position that eschews forms of "traditional" worship and some markers of indigenous identity while rejecting such modern inventions as rock music and evolution.

For most people in this region, the boundaries between Catholics and Evangelicals are as real and evident as the line that separates one *chakra* from the next. Just like other features of the landscape, it is common knowledge that in the community in Yauri, where the majority of households are Evangelical, the Catholics live in the upper reaches of the district. These lay religious geographies are often oversimplified, particularly as households themselves become religiously diverse when children or one partner converts to Catholicism or the IEP. Yet they also reflect well-known histories of social conflicts that accompanied the emergence of religious pluralism in the region and the processes related to intolerance and aggression that help to explain the geographic division of religious households.

One key to understanding the maintenance of religious difference is through *miramiento*, a concern raised frequently by both Evangelical and Catholic community members, and the power of which was most succinctly captured for me on one of my early trips to Yauri from Cusco City. I was visiting with a friend, "Lupe," and keeping her company in her yard while she washed her hair, and we both tried to warm ourselves the early morning sun. Lupe is the wife of the Evangelical *presbítero*, and the last time we had seen each other was in Cusco City when she was attending a theological workshop. As she braided her long hair into two plaits and finished dressing, she laughed at the layers of skirts that she put on. "I can't wear those other clothes that I wore in Cusco," she explained to me, referring to the "modern" green patterned skirt that I had seen her in several weeks prior. "*Hay miramiento.*"

The literal English translation of *miramiento* varies between a sense of envy and a desire to remain respectful, but this does not fully do justice to the meaning intended by Lupe, or in its common deployment by other residents of the two pueblos. Javier Marías, a Spanish novelist, complied a collection titled *Miramientos* (1997), in which it he interprets the photographs of various authors with the effect of highlighting what one critic deemed the "involuntary confession" of appearance.[12] For all the speaking these authors have done, it is the critical, transformative power of the gaze that invents them anew. This is not far from the intention of the word when employed by people in Hanocca and Yauri where it refers to the judgment expressed through "looks," "rumors," "snubbing," or "gossip." Far from a passive act of observation and

---

[12] Carlos Pojul, 16 January 1998 *ABC Literario* (http://www.javiermarias.es/PAGINASDECRITICAS/criticasmiramientos.html).

longing, *miramiento* is an act of judgment, sometimes contestation, and it pertains to patterns and the general power of a gaze in establishing social order and as such provides a vivid parallel to feminist approaches to landscape and the power of the gaze (Nash 1996; Rose 1993). In these Andean communities, deviations from accepted patterns of behavior can have a negative impact not only on friendships and livelihood but also on that of extended family. Though it is evident in a range of processes, here I focus on the role of *miramiento* in the performance, maintenance, and conscription of symbolic rituals that occupy public spaces of the two districts.

5.5   Maintaining/Containing Public Ritual

The multiple crosses planted on the peaks high above the town of Hanocca provide constant visual reminders of the enmeshment of Andean and Catholic traditions. Some crosses are very old according to the townspeople, although most of them had fallen into disrepair or had altogether disappeared before the parish priest resurrected them. They mark the major *Apus,* the sacred peaks that surround the lake. The parish priest makes a climb to each cross at least once a year, at which time the community members leave their offerings of potatoes, beans, and candles at the base of the cross. They do this, as well as make other *pagos a la Pachamama* (offerings to Mother Earth), in order to insure good harvest and protection from severe weather. In comparison to Hanocca, it is the absence of Catholic occupation of public space that is the most striking aspect of religious landscapes in Yauri. There are no permanent crosses on the hillsides. Members of the community recall crosses that were once maintained on the mountains around the pueblo, but the cross that once stood above one community eventually fell down due to disrepair.

The crosses are just one of several texts contained within the landscape that reinforce the impression that Hanocca is Catholic and Yauri is Evangelical. The Catholic Church at Hanocca is by far the largest structure in town, visible from virtually any vantage point. The walls that surround it only accentuate its size and dominance over the vacant plaza of the pueblo. In comparison, the Catholic Church of Yauri appears to dissolve into the background of the central plaza, which is dominated by a large, modern concrete municipal building that will stand three stories when completed. The walls surrounding the Yauri Church conceal the space within in a way that the Hanocca walls do not. The comparative invisibility of Catholic structures in Yauri might be associated with uninspired Catholic leadership, but this is not the case. The nuns who live in Yauri and the catechists and *animadores* (non-catechist laity) work effectively and energetically within their religious network and in the broader community. Their distance from the masculine and hierarchical structures of the Catholic Church often engenders unique religious and humanitarian service. Nor are the IEP churches imposing or dominant, either in their design or their use of space. They are not in the center of the pueblo or the community, and they are distinguishable from any other structure only by their tin roofs and names printed above the doorway. Adornments inside are likewise simple, with most activities oriented toward a writing surface at the front of the church and a table to be used by pastors, readers, or musicians. Overall, the impression is the same that one might have walking into the mayor's office – functional.

This unmarking of Catholic space is not restricted to the built environment, for it is in the control and restriction of ritualistic space that the power of *miramiento* is most evident. There are Catholic celebrations in Yauri, as there are in Hanocca, which focus on the celebration of a particular cross. The celebration of the Cross of Exaltación is held in early September in a community several hours walk from the pueblo of Yauri. It includes a night of vespers held in a small chapel originally founded by the Jesuits and which today houses an altar with a sacred rock. The celebration of the cross consists of a mass and parading of the cross, followed by food and drink supplied by the family who selected a year prior to fulfill the *cofradia*. The isolation of the chapel means that there is very little observation of the actual event for those not attending, though the passage of people through the central parts of the community is observed by neighbors. Catholic celebration of this cross and others elicits ambivalence or criticism on the part of Evangelicals. "Why would you want to worship a cross when it killed Jesus?" one IEP member asked me in clear disapproval. Others expressed that it simply did not matter whether or not Catholics worshiped a cross. There is no indication, as in other regions of the high provinces, that non-Catholics are actively destroying the crosses in Yauri. But Catholics are quick to point out the disapproval that Evangelicals express about the worship of the cross, explaining that, like the worship of saints, the practices at Exaltación are considered idolatry.

The active monitoring of the occupation of space by religious ritual is perhaps most evident by comparing responses to the Catholic fiestas held in both Pueblos. The celebration of Hanocca's patron saint day (*Dia de la Virgin de Asunta*) in August occupies virtually all physical spaces of the pueblo and includes a running of the bulls in addition to the religious rituals. During the fiesta, families assume the *cargo* of setting up elaborate altars around the square, where the statue of the *virgin* is paraded. The September celebration of the *Virgin de Rosario* similarly occupies the central plaza, but with more Andean forms of expression such as the *K'anchis* (dancers dressed in traditional costumes). In this fiesta, the drums, voices, and movements of the dancers effectively blend the spaces of the church and the plaza, moving fluidly between the two. It is a visual analogy to the many ways that the Catholic Church is indelibly scripted on the landscapes in the built environment, as well as the penetration of Catholicism into a range of cultural processes.

In contrast to the fiestas of the communities and pueblo of Hanocca, the Catholic celebrations in Yauri are decidedly restricted. An important fiesta dedicated to the patron saint of Yauri is held in a community that shares a boundary with the pueblo, where the Catholic chapel sits on a broad, flat piece of ground abutting the base of a steep hillside. The celebration of the mass began with K'anchis dancing in the narrow space beside the chapel. There were less than fifty people participating in the fiesta itself and at least as many observing from the hillside above or the road adjacent to the chapel property. The audience was thus substantially different from that of the fiestas in Hanocca, where observers were also participants. In Yauri, these observers were clearly not participants and watched and spoke among themselves throughout the celebration and the mass. It would be difficult to label this gaze indifferent or ambivalent, as either of these descriptions might indicate disinterest. There was no clapping or cheering from the observers, no shouting out of names, or trying to draw the attention of a dancer as happened so commonly in Hanocca celebrations.

Unlike Exaltación, this celebration took place in an area that was readily observed, and its effect was palpable. The fiesta was not only comparatively brief, but claustrophobic, for though the dancers were clearly energized and excited, they were also anxious to thread their way into the low walls surrounding the chapel. The *fiesta* in the pueblo celebrating the patron saint was similarly constricted as the majority of the worship takes place on the grounds of the church, behind walls. Catholics are quick to point out that Evangelicals disapprove the worship of saints, and in Yauri, there is also an undercurrent among Catholics questioning whether the worship of saints is indeed idolatry. And this is one reason that *miramiento* appears to have been particularly effective in restricting the spread of embodied Catholic landscape in Yauri. As in Hanocca, the Catholics of Yauri are sensitive to the *miramiento* of Evangelical brothers. They also express more doubts about honoring saints than the Catholics of Hanocca and express particular skepticism about more "traditional" Andean traditions such as the *pago a la pachamama*.

In the context of this awareness, the gaze of others can also engender doubt and make retiring behind church walls or to remote fiesta settings a comfortable option. Indeed, it is a rather common observation that Evangelicals throughout Latin America reject the Catholic embrace and acceptance of indigenous worldviews and practices (Martin 1990; Sherman 1997). But rather than suggesting that the Evangelicals of Yauri are opposed to the religious or spiritual "traditions" of the region, it is more accurate to interpret their influence as an attempt to reinterpret these traditions as part of an historical imaginary. During the celebration of the district's founding in 2002, the school children put on an elaborate dance, singing, and folklore show in the main plaza. Dressed in K'anchi style clothing, with hats and other adornments made of paper, the children enacted several well-known stories of ancient battles, mythical relationships, and dueling families complete with feigned drunkenness. IEP parents and community members were visibly supportive of the celebration in spite of the fact that they were similar in many ways to the dancing and storytelling that is part of Catholic fiestas. By placing these rituals in the context of a secular event organized by school children, their religious meaning is neutralized, and they become part of history rather than practiced culture or as a "lived religion" (e.g., Garrard-Burnett 1998).

5.6   Myth, Miramiento, and Embodied Religious Landscapes

These two communities demonstrate, in very different ways, how historical and contemporary processes of religious difference become embedded in lived religious landscapes. How, then, might we make sense of the work that goes into lived religious landscape? The settled landscape is not easy to separate into categories of "the dirt under our nails" or "the picture in our heads" (Olwig 2003). This example from the Andean highlands would suggest that religious landscape is not "unwittingly read as it is unwittingly written" (Duncan 1990: 19), but rather keenly read and both subtly and aggressively written through *miramiento.* Though there are certainly landscapes that remain obscured through "cultural amnesia" (ibid), contemporary religious landscapes in Latin America are often written and read with considerable wit and with a firm acknowledgement of the kinds of representations and spaces that are being recalled by their various authors. Returning to Price, the stories of the borderlands between Mexico and the USA are both reflective and constitutive of the landscape such that "…stories, storytelling, and storytellers can be agentic" (2004: 172). By telling the stories of insiders, we are privileged to a very different version of the landscapes of the border. Assuming stories to be less true than the material morphology of landscape risks obscuring important elements of landscape. In the case of the borderlands:

> Myth and history often work together to the point that there exists little productive distinction between them. Indeed, the idea that there is ever a clear separation between event and the representation of that event ("history" and "myth") is debatable. Myth and reality, as these coalesce around the slippery entity of the West, bear such a close relationship to one another that trying to separate the two would prove infinitely frustrating. (Price 2004: 56)

Landscapes that reinforce the developed Evangelical, whether through positive associations with fat cows and green forests or in reference to the degraded landscapes of Catholics, are grounded in histories like those of Hanocca and Yauri. But together, these multiple landscapes combine to keep alive the idea that the Andes can be another Switzerland, a particularly hopeful narrative given the historical neglect and violent stewardship that has plagued the region in the tenure of the modern Peruvian state. In her analysis of the production of landscapes of fear through tales of heart thieves and vampires, Jaroz (1994: 433) reminds us that landscapes can be found "in the realm between material reality and the human imagination – a part of both but having no exclusive existence in either the reality or the imagination." The myth of Evangelical development exists at a similar boundary, sometimes rooted in the material realities of religious change, but more often reflecting images of what we have come to believe we will find. But this does not make it somehow less real, for myths can often tell us more about the normative presumptions underpinning material facts by articulating "the existence of competing sets of ideological beliefs about what society is and how it ought to be" (Flood 1996: 11–12). The myth of Evangelical development works because it combines the morphology of embodied religious landscape with expectations for development, whether comprised of modern clothing or performed secularities. Branding the relationship between religion and development in Latin America as a "myth" does not deny the possibility of real material differences between Catholics and Evangelicals. Rather, it suggests that communities like Granja Porcón exist not just in the material landscapes of particular places but also as a mythical landscape that exists independent of its material inspiration.

If "knowledge, theories and concepts are not floating over the landscape but always in relation to it" (Jauhiainen 2003: 395), the myth of Evangelical development is indicative of religion as one network through which development ideas and practices become embodied in contemporary Latin American societies. The myth is powerful and persistent not just because it is descriptive, but because it is constitutive, as the examples above suggest. Tilley suggests that "[i]f stories are linked to regularly repeated spatial practices they become mutually supportive, and when a story becomes sediment in the landscape, the story and the place dialectically help to construct and reproduce each other" (c.f. Price 2004: 28).

5.7 Conclusion

In this chapter, I have explored the emergence of a myth of Evangelical development and its meanings in the context of two rural districts in Cusco, Peru. Though much of this work in Latin America presents important insights into the meanings of religious transformation, like the original thesis, space and place is most commonly thought of as an inert stage through which actors, religions, and capital moves, rather than as something produced through social process. I have argued the importance of capturing the reflexive relationships between the stories that are being told of religion and development and the histories of societal relationship that both inspire and are influenced by them. The role of *miramiento* in the establishment of religious boundaries and the control of ritualistic spaces suggests that the "insiders" of these places are both aware and actively constructive of the materiality and symbolism of embodied religious landscapes.

It is my suggestion that the myth of Evangelical development also describes important changes in the landscape and its constitution, which then serves as material evidence of the possibility of progress which, in this case, relies on putting particular forms of "culture" into the right place which signals its historical relevance, rather than reserving it a spot in future visions. The relationship between religion and development in Latin America is incomplete without attention to the emergence of the myth in particular places and its range of authors, and it is on this point that we might return to the prevalence of Weberian references in and among literature relating to religious change and development in Latin America. Hamilton, when commenting on Weber's thesis, writes that "[i]t is surely more fruitful to examine *The Protestant Ethic and the Spirit of Capitalism* not only as a part of Weber's vision of society but as an expression of the ideas prevailing in early twentieth-century Germany…" (Hamilton 2000: 171). The same might be said of the current myth of Evangelical development in Latin America and the landscapes that both "prove" and contradict its veracity. These powerful symbols communicate two Andean futures: one where traditional belief is lived and another where it is historicized.

It is not my intent in marking these landscapes as "mythical" to deny the material outcomes of religious intervention. Rather, myth provides a link between material processes and the symbolic function of religious landscapes. As in other explorations of the written and spoken landscape, my intent has been to arrive at a fuller understanding of the function and meaning of social change to people whose interpretations and meanings are obscured when searching for a morphology that is more "real" or tangible. How symbols and myths become entangled or coaxed apart from material changes is therefore critical to understanding the establishment, recognition, and contestation of religious landscapes. The myth of Evangelical development is one way that people are debating meanings of progress, tradition, and custom in the Andes. As such, it is not only describing what a developed landscape should look like, but is also helping to define the characteristics that are attributed to development and underdevelopment. It is a story, or as Massey (2006) argues, a "provocation" that insists that we ask about the social relations of its production.

Acknowledgements   This research for this study was funded by a dissertation improvement grant from the National Science Foundation, and support for writing was provided through a fellowship from the Center for Humanities and the Arts at the University of Colorado. Special thanks to Timothy Oakes, Anthony Bebbington, Rachel Silvey, and Peter Hopkins for their comments on earlier versions.

References

Annis, S. 1987. *God and production in a Guatemalan town*. Austin: University of Texas Press.

Armas, A.F. 1998. Las nuevas iglesias como formadoras de la conciencia ciudana en los Andes. *Cuestion de Estado* 23: 43–45.

Barrera, P. 1993. Evidencias de un Nuevo Protestantismo: el caso de la Iglesia Evangélica Peruana (IEP) Perspectiva teológica y pastoral. *Cristianismo y Sociedad* 115: 57–81.

Beams, D.E. 2001. *Ideology, agency and production in an Andean peasant Community: The collective struggle for self-sufficiency*. Unpublished dissertation, University of Kentucky, Lexington.

Brusco, E. 1995. *The reformation of machismo: Evangelical conversion and gender in Colombia*. Austin: University of Texas Press.

Casey, E. 1996. *How to get from space to place in a fairly short stretch of time*. Sante Fe: School of American Research Press.

Casey, E. 1993. *Getting back into place: Toward a renewed understanding of the place-world*. Bloomington: Indian University Press.

Cladis, M.S. 2008. Painting landscapes of religion in America: Four models of religion in democracy. *Journal of the American Academy of Religion* 76(4): 874–904.

Cleary, E.L. 2004. Shopping around: Questions about Latin American conversions. *International Bulletin of Missionary Research* 28(2): 50–54.

Coleman, K.M., E.E. Aguilar, J.M. Sandoval, and T.J. Steigenga. 1993. Protestantism in El Salvador: Conventional wisdom versus the survey evidence. In *Rethinking Protestantism in Latin America*, ed. V. Garrard-Burnett and D. Stoll, 111–142. Philadelphia: Temple University Press.

Dewsbury, J.D., and P. Cloke. 2009. Spiritual landscapes: Existence, performance and immanence. *Social and Cultural Geography* 10(6): 695–711.

Duncan, J. 1990. *The city as text: The politics of landscape interpretation in the Kandyan kingdom*. Cambridge: Cambridge University Press.

Dunn, K.M. 2005. Repetitive and troubling discourses of nationalism in the local politics of mosque development in Sydney, Australia. *Environment and Planning D: Society and Space* 23(1): 29–50.

Flood, C.G. 1996. *Political myth: A theoretical introduction*. New York/London: Garland Publishing Inc.

Garrard-Burnett, V. 1998. *Protestantism in Guatemala: Living in the New Jerusalem*. Austin: University of Texas Press.

Gill, A. 2004. Weber in Latin America: Is protestant growth enabling the consolidation of democratic capitalism? *Democratization* 11(4): 42–65.

Gökariksel, B. 2009. Beyond the officially sacred: Religion, secularism, and the body in the production of subjectivity. *Social & Cultural Geography* 10(6): 657–674.

Gökariksel, B., and A. Secor. 2010. Islamic-ness in the life of a commodity: Veiling-fashion in Turkey. *Transactions of the Institute of British Geographers* 35(3): 313–333.

Hamilton, A. 2000. Max Weber's Protestant ethic and the spirit of capitalism. In *The Cambridge Companion to Weber*, ed. T. Stephen, 151–172. New York/Cambridge: Cambridge University Press.

Holloway, J. 2006. Enchanted spaces: The séance, affect, and geographies of religion. *Annals of the Association of American Geographers* 96: 182–187.

Jaroz, L.J. 1994. Agents of power, landscapes of fear: The vampires and heart thieves of Madagascar. *Environment and Planning D: Society and Space* 12: 421–436.

Jauhiainen, J.S. 2003. Learning from Tartu – Towards post-postmodern landscapes. In *Landscape interfaces*, ed. H. Palang and G. Fry, 395–406. Dordrecht: Kluwer Academic Publishers.

Klaiber, J.L.S.J. 1992. *The Catholic Church in Peru 1821–1985: A social history*. Washington, DC: The Catholic University of America Press.

Klaiber, J.L.S.J. 1999. Peru. Evangelization and religious freedom. In *Religious freedom and evangelization in Latin America: The challenge of religious pluralism*, ed. P.E. Sigmund, 253–268. New York: Orbis Books.

Knott, K. 2005. *The location of religion: A spatial analysis*. London: Equinox.

Knott, K. 2009. From locality to location and back again: A spatial journey in the study of religion. *Religion* 39(2): 154–160.

Kong, L. 2010. Global shifts, theoretical shifts: Changing geographies of religion. *Progress in Human Geography* 34(6): 755–776.

Marias, J. 1997. *Miramientos*. Madrid: Ediciones Alfaguara.

Martin, D. 1990. *Tongues of fire: The explosion of Protestantism in Latin America*. Cambridge: Blackwell.

Marzal, M. 2000. Categorías y números en la religion del Perú hoy. In *La Religión en el Perú al filo del Milenio*, ed. M. Marzal, C. Romero, and J. Sánchez, 20–55. Lima: Pontifica Universidad Católica del Perú.

Massey, D. 2006. Landscape as a provocation: Reflections on moving mountains. *Journal of Material Culture* 11(1–2): 33–48.

Mitchell, D. 2003. Cultural landscapes: Just landscapes or landscapes of justice? *Progress in Human Geography* 27(6): 787–796.

Motte, D. 2002. *Una revolucion Silenciosa? El Impacto Social de las Nuevas Iglesias no Catolicas del Peru*. Cusco: Centro de Estudios Regionales Andinos Bartolome de las Casas.

Muratorio, B. 1980. Protestantism and capitalism revisited, in the rural highlands of Ecuador. *Journal of Peasant Studies* 8(1): 37–60.

Nash, C. 1996. Reclaiming vision: Looking at landscape and the body. *Gender, Place and Culture* 3(2): 149–170.

Olson, E. 2006. Development, transnational religion and the power of ideas in the High Provinces of Cusco, Peru. *Environment and Planning A* 38: 885–902.

Olson, E. 2008. Common belief, contested meanings: Development and faith-based organizational culture. *Tijdschrift voor Economische en Sociale Geografie* 99(4): 393–405.

Olwig, K. 2003. Forum – Landscape: The Lowenthal legacy. *Annals of the Association of American Geographers* 93(4): 871–877.

Peach, C., and R. Gale. 2003. Muslims, Hindus, and Sikhs in the new religious landscape of England. *Geographical Review* 93(4): 469–490.

Price, P.L. 2004. *Dry place: Landscapes of belonging and exclusion*. Minnesota: University of Minnesota Press.

Riedel, F. (ed.). 1999. *Una Iglesia en marcha con el Pueblo*. Sicuani: Prelatura de Sicuani and Centro de Estudios y Publicaciones (CEP).

Rocha, A. 2002. La Tierra Prometida. *Somos* 824: 34–39.

Rose, G. 1993. *Feminism and geography*. Cambridge: Polity Press.

Santolaria, J.J.R. 2000. Relaciones Iglesia-Estado: reflexiones sobre su marco jurídico. In *La Religión en el Perú al filo del Milenio*, ed. M. Marzal, C. Romero, and J. Sánchez, 59–86. Lima: Pontifica Universidad Católica del Perú.

Secor, A. 2002. The veil and urban space in Istanbul: Women's dress, mobility and Islamic knowledge. *Gender, Place and Culture* 9(1), 5–22.

Sherman, A.L. 1997. *The soul of development: Biblical Christianity and economic transformation in Guatemala*. Oxford: Oxford University Press.

Spier, F. 1994. *Religious Regimes in Peru. Religion and state development in a long-term perspective and the effects in the Andean village of Zurite*. Amsterdam: Amsterdam University Press.

Streib, H., A. Dinter, and K. Söderblom (eds.). 2008. *Lived religion – Conceptual, empirical and practical-theological approaches*. Leiden: Brill.

Trudeau, D. 2006. Politics of belonging in the construction of landscapes: Place-making, boundary-drawing, and exclusion. *Cultural Geographies* 13(3): 421–443.

Ugarte, R.V. 1962. *Historia de la Iglesia en el Perú*. Lima: Marius Burgos.

Watson, S. 2005. Symbolic spaces of difference: Contesting the eruv in Barnet, London and Tenafly, New Jersey. *Environment and Planning D: Society and Space* 23: 597–613.

Zelinsky, W. 2001. The uniqueness of the American religious landscape. *Geographical Review* 90(3): 565–585.

Chapter 6
"You can't know how they are inside": The Ambivalence of Veiling and Discourses of the Other in Turkey

Banu Gökarıksel and Anna Secor

6.1 Introduction

On a summer day in 2009, eight young- to middle-aged women sat around a conference table at a downtown hotel in the central Anatolian city of Konya. All of the women wore what in Turkey is called *tesettür* fashion (see Fig. 6.1): Their heads were covered with brightly colored, patterned scarves, and their clothes reflected a range of styles and interpretations of modest Islamic dress associated with a new "Islamic chic" (White 1999).[1] The following discussion ensued in response to the questions: "What is piety? Do you consider yourself pious?" The conversation quickly turns to a relatively uncommon form of veiling in Turkey: the *çarşaf*, a loose, usually black, garment that covers the body from head to toe (see Fig. 6.2). Sometimes, the *çarşaf* is cinched under the chin, allowing the wearer's face to show; other times, it is cinched under or over the nose.

> Elif: Piety is something that begins inside of a person.
>   Filiz: I don't pray strictly five times a day. I'd be lying if I said, "I pray five times a day, every day." I cannot do it. I know the basics of my religion; I know what is forbidden and what is allowed, what is a sin and what is a good deed. I don't do extreme things, I don't go

---

[1] *Tesettür* comes from an Arabic root and simply means "covering." It is an umbrella term that is deployed in different ways. Many of our interviewees use tesettür to refer to religiously appropriate modest dress. We are using this term to refer specifically to a certain style of covering in Turkey, one that became popular in the 1980s and has since evolved into a fashion industry (see Gökarıksel and Secor 2009, 2010a, b).

B. Gökarıksel(✉)
Department of Geography, University of North Carolina at Chapel Hill,
Chapel Hill, NC, USA
e-mail: banug@email.unc.edu

A. Secor
Department of Geography, University of Kentucky, Lexington, KY, USA

P. Hopkins et al. (eds.), *Religion and Place: Landscape, Politics and Piety*,
DOI 10.1007/978-94-007-4685-5_6, © Springer Science+Business Media Dordrecht 2013

Fig. 6.1 Two women in tesettür fashion, Istanbul, 2010 (Photo by authors)

to *tarikat* meetings. In our apartment building, there are two women who wear the çarşaf. They cover their bodies fully; they have separate spaces for women (*haremlik*) and men (*selamlik*); they don't talk to our husbands. But I can say hello to their husbands.

Moderator: Do they see you as religious? Do you see them as religious?

Filiz: I don't know what they think but I think they are religious according to their own beliefs. They live their faith in that way. But I don't feel comfortable with extremely covered women. They think differently, they cannot come [to my house] and sit down comfortably, with their gloves and all. They have very different, peculiar things [habits, thoughts].

Nalan: I'm personally against the çarşaf. It's not clear if it's a man or a woman underneath. We live in the Republic of Turkey, not in Arabia. Ultimately I have to see a person's hands and face. Everybody's faith is inside of her. It's impossible to know. I have friends who are *açık* [not covered] but fully perform their ritual daily prayers. A woman may not be covered but may fulfill all religious requirements. We can't say [because she's not covered] "she must not pray." Allah will investigate [who's praying]. I'm against extreme çarşaf.

Melike: As long as no one hurts anyone else….

Fig. 6.2 A woman in a çarşaf, Istanbul, 2009 (Photo by authors)

İlknur: There's a much higher chance that [çarşaf wearers] are suicide bombers.

Nalan: They exclude us, çarşaflı women do.[2] *We* feel that we're covered, not open. I think I'm fully covered. What matters is hiding the shape of your body. But they [çarşaflı women] don't see you [tesettürlü women] as covered.

İlknur: But people can see the shape of our bodies. They [çarşaflı women] can be suicide bombers.

Nalan: Someone was caught in the garden of a saint's, Şems-i Tebriz's, tomb in Konya. The person was caught with a gun under the çarşaf....The state has to step in, the çarşaf should be completely banned.

Elif's formulation of faith as an internal affair immediately situates dress as an ambivalent signifier of piety. Nalan, a 43-year-old housewife wearing a small headscarf that allows some of her hair to show, launches the discussion of çarşaf

---

[2] Çarşaflı is used to refer to the wearers of this garment in Turkey.

with reference to the participation of çarşaflı women in tarikats (illicit Muslim brotherhoods, or sects); others chime in with a litany of suspicions concerning who or what the çarşaf may be covering. Similarly to discussions in other focus groups, here the çarşaf is portrayed as alien, fanatical, and deceptive. Many women, like Nalan, feel that the more thorough veiling of the çarşaf represents an implicit criticism of tesettür fashion, which stands in distinction both to the more conservative çarşaf and to the dress styles of the secular public.[3] Just as the burqa and the face veil have been banned in some European countries, Nalan suggests that the çarşaf should be banned in Turkey. Indeed, Nalan's own style of headscarf is already subject to regulation in Turkey, where it is forbidden in schools and universities, courtrooms, and other officially secular spaces. While lifting this ban has been a major platform of Islamist mobilization, Nalan nonetheless turns to the idea of state regulation to ameliorate her fears of çarşaflı women. In this way, a question about piety stirs up a discussion with broadly political and geopolitical contours.

Connecting the çarşaf with militancy, danger, and foreign influence resonates with the discourses of threat and fear linked to veiling in Europe today (Nussbaum 2010; Scott 2007). While today the figure of the Afghani women in *burqa* has been invoked to bolster support for the US "War on Terror" (Abu-Lughod 2002) and various forms of veiling have been treated with suspicion in Europe and North America, historically the veil has been a direct target of colonial power. In the dialogue above, when İlknur, a 48-year-old housewife dressed in subdued colors and a loose headscarf, warns that a woman in çarşaf may be a suicide bomber, her comments not only reflect contemporary fears of terrorism but unwittingly recall the 1954–1962 French-Algerian war, when the French launched a violent campaign to unveil Algerian women with the justification that the enveloping garments were being used to transport guns and bombs for the resistance (MacMaster 2010; Yeğenoğlu 1998). Indeed, after 1923, the veil became a symbol of all that the revolutionary Republic of Turkey hoped to turn away from following the overthrow of the Ottoman Empire. In their project to secularize and modernize Turkish society, the early Republican elite associated veiling with backwardness and urged women to uncover their heads in public spaces (Arat 1997; Göle 1996). While a diversity of covering practices nonetheless persisted in Turkey for many decades, in the 1980s, a resurgence of enforcement of the official ban on headscarves in universities spawned a series of headscarf protests and catapulted the question of veiling into the national limelight (Olson 1985; Özdalga 1998). In the decades since, veiling styles have proliferated in Turkey as the practice has become increasingly popular in tandem with the rise of pro-Islamic political parties, Islamic entrepreneurialism, and consciously Muslim lifestyles (Adaş 2006; Gökarıksel and Secor 2009; Saktanber 2002; Tuğal 2009; White 2002; Yavuz 2003).

Thus, when Nalan suggests that the state needs to step in to regulate the çarşaf in the name of the *threat* posed by the unseen form (which can, she notes, even be a man),

---

[3] According to a national survey conducted by Ali Çarkoğlu and Binnaz Toprak in 2006, only 1.1% of women wore çarşaf and 11.4% wore tesettür (Çarkoğlu and Toprak 2006). They found that 48.8% of women wore some kind of veiling.

she is tapping into a discourse with broad and deep roots, one that puts covered women squarely at the center of geopolitical struggles. As feminist geographers have shown, global mappings of space and difference are lived and produced through embodied practices (Hyndman 2001; Marston 2004; Secor 2001; Sharp 2007; Staeheli et al. 2004). Similarly, recent work in geographies of religion has begun to look "beyond the officially sacred" to understand religion as both corporeal and quotidian (Gökarıksel 2009; Kong 2001, 2010). Geographers have argued that the body is the most intimate site where religious meanings are inscribed and beliefs are nurtured (Bailey et al 2007; Gökarıksel 2009; Holloway 2003a, b, 2006; Connell 2005). As the dialogue above demonstrates, feminist geopolitics and embodied approaches to religion intersect at the site of the veiled body. The çarşaflı becomes the other of tesettürlü women, who use this opposition to situate themselves in particular ways within a broader landscape of political, religious, and social difference.

Dress, as situated bodily practice (Entwistle 2000), is part of how the body is formed and represented in relation to religion and other markers, such as gender, age, and class (Arthur 1999; Domosh 2001; Tarlo 1996). Veiling[4] not only produces the body as a site of religious signification but also works to cultivate distinctions of piety and class (Gökarıksel and Secor 2012; Mahmood 2005). In Turkey, where a wide range of veiling styles have become available in the recent decades, women's diverse veiling practices have become loaded with ever shifting and contested meanings. More than any other style, the newly emergent tesettür fashion has become the flashpoint for controversies and political debates surrounding the role of Islam in Turkish society (Kılıçbay and Binark 2002; Saktanber 2006; Sandıkçı and Ger 2005, 2007, 2010). Islamist scholars and pundits condemn the sometimes showy and ever-tighter styles, the catwalk displays, and the increasing commodification that the tesettür industry promotes (Eygi 2005, 2009; *HaksözHaber* 2010). At the same time, tesettürlü women are subject to intense criticism from the secular public, which both lampoons the wearers of tesettür fashion for seeming hypocrisy while also stigmatizing them as a vanguard of a threatening Islamicization (Hakan 2008; *Milliyet* 2008; Tanyol 1999; *Yeni Şafak* 2008). Tesettürlü women thus occupy a questionable position both within the Islamic movement and the project of secular modernity.

In this chapter, we draw on our six focus group interviews with tesettür fashion consumers[5] to examine how tesettürlü women deploy the image of the fully covered

---

[4] We use the English word "veiling" to refer to a wide range of covering which includes headscarves, tesettür, and çarşaf.

[5] This research was supported by the National Science Foundation (BCS-0723986 and BCS-0722825), with the project title: "Collaborative Research: The veiling-fashion industry: transnational geographies of Islamism, capitalism, and identity." In 2009, we conducted six focus groups with the consumers of tesettür fashion in Istanbul and Konya. Organized along the lines of age and socio-economic status, the groups were each comprised of eight women who did not previously know one another. Fieldwork was conducted with the assistance of the Istanbul-based social research firm, Sosyal Araştırmalar Merkezi, who recruited participants from their databases. The authors are solely responsible for the content of this chapter.

çarşaflı women to position themselves within both Islamic and secular modernity in Turkey. In all of our focus group interviews, women mobilize the image of the çarşaflı woman to make a range of sometimes conflicting points. We find that this discourse of the çarşaf is part of how these participants situate themselves and assert their "distinction" (Bourdieu 1984). We begin by analyzing the ways in which our tesettürlü research participants question the religious signification of çarşaf. In their discussions, our participants both orientalize the çarşaf (with undertones of eroticism, danger, and exoticism) and assert that it is just as ambiguous as their own much-scrutinized tesettür. We argue that by questioning the relationship between faith and dress in the case of the çarşaf, tesettürlü women open up a discursive gap between inner piety and outward appearance. Tesettürlü women use this gap to destabilize the perceived moral position of the çarşaflı women. By othering the çarşaflı and creating an inner/outer distinction that throws the çarşaflı's piety into question, tesettürlü women produce a discourse in which they themselves can become the pious but modern, socially integrated, authentically Turkish citizen of the republic.

6.2   What Get-Ups Emerge from Under the Çarşaf!

Tesettürlü women employ various discursive strategies that open up the çarşaf's perceived religious signification to scrutiny. Central to these strategies is the distinction tesettürlü women make between the inner space of corporeal piety and its representation to the outer world by clothing. The gap between the two – discursively created and spatially formulated – allows tesettürlü women to locate ambiguities in the relationship between faith and çarşaf. For tesettürlü women, the çarşaf is a particularly potent delineator of the inner/outer boundary because it encloses an inner space much more effectively than their own clothing. The inner space that the çarşaf creates is not visible to and hardly knowable by the onlooker.[6] Therefore, tesettürlü women argue that the çarşaf can be deceptive. The pointed criticism of Yelda, a 25-year-old university student in Konya, quoted above is a typical phrasing of the çarşaf's potential to deceive: "What get-ups emerge from under the çarşaf!" Implicit in her remark is the common perception that çarşaf is supposed to signify advanced piety. Yet, the kinds of clothes that sometimes emerge (or have emerged) from under

---

[6] Scholars have also been interested in the inner space created by the çarşaf and other similar garments. For example, Papanek (1982) argues that the purdah in Pakistan provides "portable seclusion" to women, while Abu-Lughod (2002) likens the Afghan burqa to a "mobile home." Both emphasize that the veil carves out sanctified or protected space for women in public spaces, thus enabling women's mobility. In our focus groups, tesettürlü women did not view the çarşaf as enabling or increasing women's mobility in the context of Turkey. Their inquiries and criticisms about the çarşaf were driven more by suspicion and skepticism about the inner space the çarşaf created.

the çarşaf may belie any expectation of modesty. With this comment, she warns against taking outward appearance as a stable sign of what is inside.

The instability of veil's meaning is known well by tesettürlü women in Turkey where they are under constant scrutiny from secular and conservative Muslim publics alike. One of the most implacable criticisms of tesettürlü women's clothing and scarf styles has centered on the impossibility of knowing the real intent of their covering: "Is she wearing a headscarf because she is pious or because she wants to be fashionable?" (Eygi 2005, 2009; Barbarosoğlu 2002). Tesettürlü women, in turn, scrutinize the çarşaf and çarşaflı women. They describe the çarşaf as ideally representing inner piety to the outer world. In the focus group with younger tesettürlü women, the ideal link they see between çarşaf and piety is expressed:

Moderator: Okay, let me ask in a different way and then we'll stop talking about this. Is there a difference in terms of acceptance? Like when you see a woman in *çarşaf*, do people who see her think that she's religious?

Jale: Well, when we say "religious," we mean we know that she's doing at least one of the religious requirements in the best way possible.

Moderator: One of the requirements.

Esin: That's how it's evaluated when you look from the outside, that's what we say: "Oh she's really covered, she must be very religious." I personally do say that.

Songül: But you can't know how they are inside.

Esin: Of course not.

Songül: Sometimes we see just how they are inside, the kinds of things they can do.

Esin: Of course but listen, this is my opinion. That's how I evaluate it when I see it from the outside. I too have seen the contrary at the university, for example. You'd see a girl in *çarşaf*, for example and then at school, oh my God, she'd be wearing miniskirts. There are people like that.

Jale, a 30-year-old housewife, sees çarşaf as fulfilling one of the fundamental requirements of Islam in the best way possible. Likewise, Esin describes how she sees more covering as an indicator of more piety (see also Gökarıksel 2009). Esin is a 31-year-old woman who came to the interview with a distinctive look, wearing a green pashmina draped loosely around her head and neck, a black long-sleeved T-shirt, black pants, and Puma sneakers. Even as she admits to reading the çarşaf as a sign of advanced piety, she, like many other tesettürlü women in our research, stresses that the çarşaf is what appears on the outside. This emphasis on the çarşaf as the outer representation of piety opens up a discursive gap that allows the questioning of what is inside. Similarly to Songül, tesettürlü women of varying age and socioeconomic status in all of our focus groups asked the question of what is underneath the çarşaf over and over again. Their responses were often animated, emotive, and humorous in their emphasis on the surprise and even shock they felt between what they expected to see and what they actually saw emerging from beneath the çarşaf. Their stories about çarşaflı women were sometimes based on first-hand experience but were often heard from others. The common thread in these stories was the unveiling of the çarşaf (purposefully or accidentally, i.e., by the wind) to reveal a woman who was completely or nearly naked, or otherwise very provocatively dressed. One story repeatedly told in almost all focus groups, with

only minor changes to detail and context, was that of the çarşaf taken off to reveal
a bikini:

> Arzu: There's a women's beach. Last year a friend of mine called me to say, "let's go there."
> Moderator: Is it in Istanbul?
> Arzu: In Istanbul. We went there together. There was a table next to ours. Five-six
> çarşaflı women came [to that table]. They took off their çarşafs. Underneath I saw Kom
> [brand] bikinis and swimsuits. Their [bikinis and swimsuits] were so nicely put together
> that you would think, "Can they really wear such nice things?" But it's so different, she
> looks covered but there are very different things inside.

Arzu is a 43-year-old housewife who came to the focus group in Istanbul wearing
an overcoat and a small, black-and-white polka-dotted headscarf tied in the latest
fashion. She took her coat off when settling into her chair in the interview room
and sat in a short-sleeved T-shirt until the end of the discussion. She was among the
very few research participants to do so and the only one in her group. Most women
kept their coats on during the interview even though there were only women present
in the room. Her eyewitness account of çarşaflı women taking off their outer
garments to reveal beautiful bikinis similarly takes place in a women's only space.
The rationale of a women's beach is to provide an environment where there is no
exposure to the male gaze and women can be more relaxed about their dress and
behavior. Yet, even in such a protected space, Arzu finds the sight of a bikini emerging
under a çarşaf appalling.

Her shock and disapproval are based on the juxtaposition of two garments that
are supposed to be at the opposite ends of a spectrum: the çarşaf providing maximum
coverage and the bikini providing the bare minimum. For her and others who
told very similar stories, çarşaf and bikini are two extremes that are essentially
incongruous and should not be worn by the same woman under any circumstances.
Furthermore, by mentioning the brand name of the bikinis, Kom, Arzu deepens
the contradiction she sees between the çarşaf and the bikini. Kom is a fashionable
swimsuit and underwear brand name in Turkey and its advertisements often feature
internationally famous professional models striking sexy poses. Through this brand
name, Arzu associates the bikini not only with immodesty but also with a consumerist
middle-class lifestyle. Her surprise is partly because she did not expect such beautiful
and expensive bikinis to be worn by çarşaflı women, whom she and other women
in our focus groups frequently assumed to be of lower-class status. She turns to the
inner/outer distinction to make sense of the contradiction she sees between the
çarşaf and the bikini. Although the çarşaf projects an image of piety and modesty
to the outside world, what lies inside of it may be quite different. Her example both
confirms the çarşaf as a garment with tremendous religious and cultural sign value
and criticizes its wearers for betraying this value in the way they act and dress in
their inner spaces (underneath the çarşaf on the street or at women's only spaces).

Following Arzu's comments quoted above, the focus group discussion continued
to reflect on the meaning of the çarşaf. Others in the group went further than
Arzu to point to the paradox they saw in having a çarşaflı woman at the beach.
For Fazilet (a 44-year-old housewife) and Meral (a 46-year-old boutique manager), it
was puzzling for a çarşaflı woman even to go to the beach, let alone wear a bikini. Meral

voiced her criticism bluntly: "If a woman is devoted enough to wear a çarşaf, then she would not think of going to the beach." She invoked the concept of *nefis* to explain what she meant. Wearing the çarşaf, like tesettür, is about training the *nefis*, disciplining the body and its desires (Gökarıksel and Secor 2012); it is about reaching a level of devotion at which all inappropriate or contradictory desires are eliminated. At this ideal level, one's *nefis* no longer wants to go to the beach. While the çarşaf creates an outward appearance that signals to the public advanced levels of piety, tesettürlü women take Arzu's story as evidence that the çarşaflı women may not be further along the path of religiosity after all. On the contrary, they describe the çarşaf as creating an inner space where the real intent and the deepest feelings and desires of a woman can be hidden from view. As Mehtap, a 42-year-old housewife (who tied her scarf under the chin and left a strip of her hair showing) in the same group with Arzu, summed up, "[The çarşaflı women] project a [religiously] covered image to society but the bikinis underneath their çarşafs reveal their real desires."

In cases when an unveiling of the kind Arzu encountered does not happen, tesettürlü women address the difficulty of knowing what is really under the çarşaf by searching for clues in the eyes, face, shoes, or behavior of çarşaflı women. They explain that what remains visible gives away what is made invisible by the çarşaf. Makeup, high heels, and nail polish hint at what the onlooker can expect to emerge from under the çarşaf: a bikini or an excessively showy outfit. Tesettürlü women also scrutinize çarşaflı women's behavior to get a sense of whether, or to what extent, the çarşaf stands for the ethical conduct being a good Muslim involves. They give a series of examples of çarşaflı women gossiping about friends, treating others badly, being overly critical of neighbors, and shoplifting. In these examples, çarşaflı women engage in morally questionable practices and fail to be good Muslims. Thus, tesettürlü women draw attention to the discrepancy between the image of the çarşaf and the women who wear it as well as between what appears outwardly and what happens within the space enclosed by the çarşaf.

It is both ironic and significant that tesettürlü women's suspicions that the enclosure of the çarşaf masks transgressive desires and behaviors resonate with orientalist fantasies of Muslim women's sexuality. Sarah Graham-Brown argues that, in the nineteenth- and early twentieth-century Western fantasies of the harem, "The strict control of women's appearance and behavior in public was assumed to be the corollary of unbridled license within the harem" (Graham-Brown 1988: 503). Indeed, in women's frequent speculations about what might be under the çarşaf, more common than fears of guns or bombs were insinuations of eroticism: bikinis, fancy lingerie, or complete nakedness. Such images recall colonial fantasies; for example, Malek Alloula (1986) discusses French picture postcards of the Orient in which Muslim women are portrayed as at once covered and naked, as in the image of a completely veiled woman with her breasts exposed. In addition to destabilizing the çarşaf's meaning by raising questions about what it hides underneath, tesettürlü women also criticize the çarşaf's utility as the best covering style in the specific context of contemporary Turkey. This criticism is based on their understanding of the rationale of veiling in Islamic prescriptions. Tesettürlü women point out that at the heart of veiling is the notion that a woman should not draw attention to herself. They emphasize this concept and debate what kind of covering best fulfills this imperative in the present context[7]:

> Meral: There are closed minded people. Regardless of what else you may be wearing, when you put on a headscarf, they mark you. That's not such a big issue [or there is very little we can do about that]. But we pay attention to choose clothes that will not stir up any discussion.
>
> Fazilet: We try to fit in.
>
> Moderator: Not drawing the society's attention to yourself.
>
> Meral: Of course, we're talking about the society.
>
> Fazilet: Not to get reactions.
>
> Moderator: It's not about attracting men's attention, but it's about avoiding extremes.
>
> Meral: What's important for women, as well as for men, is not to be talked about. [The goal is to] avoid extremes, in this [tesettür] style or in other styles.
>
> Moderator: Is it possible to call what you've described "moderate"?
>
> Meral: No, when we say "moderate," we don't mean what some people mean when they use this term, [they mean] "softening the rules"….
>
> Moderator: Not to draw attention and criticism.
>
> Meral: Even in Fatih when a woman wearing the çarşaf or a face veil walks by, everyone, even covered women, turn around to look…. They look. There are a number of women who wear the çarşaf and face veils [in Fatih]. Fatih, as you know, is a place where such styles can be seen. But even there, people turn around to look at [çarşaflı women]. That's what I mean when I say a dress style should not draw attention, it should not become a topic of discussion. I should not let people say, "Look, she's extremely covered!" There should be nothing to say about me. That's what moderation is about. It's not about giving up your faith or lifestyle.

By focusing on how the çarşaf draws attention to its wearer, Meral argues that the çarşaf is completely contradictory to the logic of veiling in Islam. She contends that even in one of the most conservative neighborhoods of Istanbul, Fatih, the çarşaf stands out, whereas tesettür fashion (even the orange headscarf she wore to the interview) seamlessly blends in to the crowds. It is not common practice to wear the çarşaf in Turkey and it is even less common to wear a face veil. When a woman walks on the streets of Fatih in a çarşaf and a face veil, she provokes the gaze of passersby; people on the street begin talking about her and her dress. Rather than being inconspicuous as demanded by Islamic prescriptions, çarşaflı women attract the eye to themselves. Tesettürlü women, like Meral, accuse çarşaflı women of turning their piety into an ostentatious public display and, thereby, denying the very basic principles of modesty. Thus, they question çarşaflı women's understanding of the fundamental Islamic principles that govern veiling and present the çarşaf as a morally inappropriate garment in the current context of Turkey.

Through these various discursive strategies, tesettürlü women challenge the çarşaf as a garment that unquestionably signifies Islamic piety. Instead, they emphasize the particular inner/outer distinction created by the çarşaf and demonstrate that

---

[7] This line of thinking follows a strategy employed by some "Islamic feminists" who argue for the need to understand the underlying principles of Islamic prescriptions and to apply them to the present context (Mernissi 1987; Wadud 1999).

the çarşaf is a floating signifier very much like their own tesettür. By prying apart the çarşaf and opening this discursive gap between inner and outer, tesettürlü women are strategically working to *close* the gap between their own dress and its signification. Tesettürlü women claim that, in contrast to the çarşaflı, their bodies are relatively visible; they are not hiding anything, and what is underneath is nothing mysterious. While at other points in the focus groups they do reflect on the ambivalence of their clothing (Gökarıksel and Secor 2010b, 2012), when they place themselves in relation to the çarşaf, they are able to project an image that appears more uniform and harmonious than is usually the case. By opening up the gap of the çarşaf, they work to suture the wound of tesettür, its controversy and instability. At last, for a moment, it appears that in tesettür, the inner and the outer are not distinct; there is no gap and no space for ambiguity; the veil and its wearer are one.

6.3   Çarşaf Is Vulgar in the Republic of Turkey

What is at stake in all of these discursive strategies through which tesettürlü women work to distance the çarşaf – spiritually, socially, and spatially? In the previous section, we showed how the discursive gap that the discourse of the çarşaf opens up between inner and outer helps tesettürlü women momentarily step out of the controversial position that their own veiling practices place them within Turkey; by suggesting that the çarşaf, in its voluminous indistinction, may mask a lack of harmony between inner and outer states, they imply that their own mode of dress is in fact a less ambiguous signifier. But throughout this analysis, we have also shown that there is more going on than a mere questioning of the çarşaflı women's piety; there is also a process of othering that relies on orientalist tropes of threat, eroticism, and strangeness. We argue that it is through these kinds of stories that tesettürlü women claim for themselves the position that Turkey's secular elite has long denied them: that of the authentically Turkish, modern, and socially integrated citizen of the republic. Indeed, when Ilknur, the middle-aged housewife from Konya whom we also met in our opening dialogue, declares that "Çarşaf is vulgar in the Republic of Turkey," she is making a strong statement. By using the formal state appellation, "the Republic of Turkey" (*Türkiye Cumhuriyeti*), she lays emphasis on the republican, modernist character of the state and marks a distance between the çarşaf and such ideals. Implicit in this statement is the claim that her own more bourgeois mode of covering, tesettür fashion, can rightfully stake a place within the Republican vision.

The group of women passed around a picture of a model on a catwalk. The model wore black satin headscarf, a short black jacket, and a long, red, ruffled skirt with a dramatic slit that revealed her stocking legs and high heels. The eight women at the table, all from the lowest rungs of Istanbul's working class, shook their heads in amazement. "Ridiculous," said one. Another noted that maybe a covered woman "in high society, the kind that has golden faucets" might wear such a thing. Finally, another suggested that perhaps such a getup would be worn in Arab countries, where indoor and outerwear are dramatically distinct. This comment led Özge, a 29-year-old housewife wearing a large draping headscarf, cardigan, and long skirt, to share the following story:

> Inside [their outer covering] there is nothing at all. My father-in-law did the hajj and came back. He says, "How strange they [Arabs] are!" He says, "Now I was trying to buy something at the market, and this woman, wearing the çarşaf," he says, "bends over from the other side, and it opens like this." Apparently, it opened like this. How does the çarşaf open, what kind of a çarşaf is that? "She bent over," he says, "and she was completely naked," he says. "I can't believe it," he says. "I went and immediately performed my ablutions [ritual cleansing in Islam]." He says, "I didn't mean to look, she bent over in front of me. I was just trying going to buy something, I was looking at something, slippers or perfume," he says. I mean, they really dress that disgracefully, do you know?

In many ways, this story is an extreme example of the discourse of the çarşaf. Set in a market in Saudi Arabia, the story is as much about foreignness as it is about what might emerge from under the çarşaf. It begins from the idea that Arabs are different than Turks and that their dressing habits are not only strange but incomprehensible, even disgraceful. Under the çarşaf, this time we find absolutely nothing [*bomboş*], like a scene from an orientalist fantasy. There is no spiritual advantage for this fully covered woman in Mecca; underneath, she is naked, and her çarşaf magically whisks away to reveal this shocking absence of not only clothes but also piety. The good Turkish hajji can only perform his ablutions and perhaps find another market from which to buy a pair of slippers.

In our focus group discussions, the çarşaf was often depicted as foreign, as a garment not properly Turkish but instead imported into Turkey along with foreign strands of Islam from the Arabian peninsula and Iran.[8] In the following dialogue, the idea that the seemingly alien practices of a tarikat are *not* foreign is cause for incredulity:

> Ayşegül: I really can't stand them [tarikat members], who shout "hu hu." I was on the balcony once and I heard these chants, like "hu Allah, hu Allah…." There were all these women in çarşaf, chanting "hu Allah, hu Allah" and waving their heads about. You could see them from outside their window. They're from Samsun [on Turkey's Black Sea coast], can you believe it? I really didn't expect it of them.
> Gizem: I'm from Samsun, too. I've seen no such thing there.
> Nesrin: There's no such thing in Samsun.

What Ayşegül, a 48-year-old housewife dressed in a red headscarf, red tunic, and red pants, is describing is the *zikr*, a relatively common ritual among various Sufi sects, but one that is so strange, frightening, and foreign to her. She finds it unbelievable that these women are from Samsun. Indeed, two other participants chime in to distance such rituals from their *memleket*, their ancestral home on the Black Sea

---

[8] Ironically, perhaps, the popularity of both modes of covering, the çarşaf and tesettür fashion, is a recent phenomenon in Turkey. Perhaps the most "Turkish" mode of covering is what our participants refer to as "grandma" style: a simple, patterned scarf tied under the chin (Gökarıksel and Secor 2010b).

coast. By associating the çarşaf with tarikats, women further distanced the garment from mainstream practices of Sunni Islam in Turkey.

This sense that the çarşaf, in contrast to tesettür fashion, marks a lack of social integration is reflected in stories women told about relatives and neighbors who wear the garment. In the dialogue from Konya with which we opened this chapter, Filiz contemplates her çarşaflı neighbors who cannot speak to her husband, though she can speak to theirs. Filiz sees these women as unable to partake in common neighboring practices: "They think differently," she says, "they cannot come [to my house] and sit down comfortably, with their gloves and all." When tesettürlü women come into contact with çarşaflı women, they often see them as nonetheless maintaining a distance. In the following narrative, Jale, a 30-year-old housewife in Istanbul who attended the focus group wearing a buttoned-up, blue double-breasted overcoat and large purple headscarf, talks about her çarşaflı sisters-in-law:

> My sisters-in-law [elti, wives of her husband's brothers] wear the çarşaf, all three of them. You can't see their eyebrows either. You can only see this part of the face. But neither of my brothers-in-law [kayın, husband's brothers] nor my husband asked me to wear the çarşaf. That means, no one told them [my sisters-in-law] to wear it either, it was their choice. For example, they don't talk when my husband is there. Because women's voice is considered haram [forbidden]. They wear the çarşaf around each other's husbands or mine. They don't talk. For instance, during the holidays -- I mean I'm covered too and I chose to cover, knowing my religion, but I was so surprised! -- they only nod to mean, "Happy holidays" [Bayramın mübarek olsun]. The men understand that that's what they mean when they nod. So they reply, "Happy holidays to you too." They [the women] can't even say, "Happy holidays."

Jale makes a point of noting that the three women who married her husband's brothers have chosen the çarşaf without any pressure from the family. She clearly finds their habits regarding gender segregation extreme, including their choice not to speak to each other's husbands, even to say something as ritualized as "happy holidays." Jale interjects into her story that she is covered too, by choice and out of piety; nonetheless, she was unprepared for her sisters-in-law's religious understanding, in which even the female voice is forbidden, even within the family. Here, the çarşaf falls like a curtain not only marking off a kind of interiority but also creating a socio-spatial divide within the family.

The perceived lack of social integration of çarşaflı women was highly significant for tesettürlü women, many of whom expressed their own aspirations for public recognition and integration. Often, women talked about wanting to combat local and transnational stereotypes of veiled women through their own dress and behavior. For example, in a 2004 interview, a saleswoman at a major tesettür retail outlet discussed how, after the events of September 11, 2001, she chose hot pink-and-white polka-dotted headscarves and completely white attire for the salesclerks in an effort to improve the image of veiled women in society (Fig. 6.3). Through the consumption of veiling fashion, tesettürlü women may emphasize their femininity, their class status, and their moderation. Participants in our youngest focus group (18–25-year-olds) were especially concerned about their public image. In the following dialogue, Bahar, a 21-year-old fashion designer, talks about how she adapts her behavior with the specific goal of promoting a certain kind of image for covered women, not just in Turkey but abroad.

Fig. 6.3 Salesclerks with
pink uniforms in a tesettür
fashion shop, Istanbul, 2004
(Photo by authors)

Bahar: Religiosity has to do with ideas of religion. Some people live very isolated lives. It's because of them that people who live Islam are called narrow-minded. You shouldn't exaggerate [living Islam] by saying things like, "I'm religious so I won't watch TV," or "I'm not going to go there," or "I won't shake hands with a man." That's a bit fanatical [*yobazlık*], if you ask me. I try to lead a reserved life but people still say, "Look at the state she's in. Look how she lives. This is not Islam." I've seen this a lot.

Rabia: That's when people call you narrow-minded, if you live like that. And that's nothing anyone can stand.

...

Bahar: We had this German customer. Once when he was here, he shook everyone's hand and said "take care." He speaks very good Turkish. He was hesitant to try to shake my hand. You know, because he didn't know whether I would shake hands with him. Usually you nod and bow slightly, you see. But I have to adapt to the situation, both at work and in daily life too. If I hadn't offered my hand to that gentleman for him to shake, he could have had very different ideas about covered women, Turkey and Islam.

Rabia: And he could've passed those ideas on.

Bahar: So you have to act accordingly. It's not like I'm going to hug him or kid around with him because we've done business together. But people have to know how to act a certain way in order not to appear narrow-minded.... Moderation is very important, one shouldn't exaggerate. Everything has a time and a place.

Wearing the latest styles of tesettür fashion, Bahar sees herself as a kind of ambassador for "covered women, Turkey, and Islam." Faced with an awkward German customer, she forgoes her usual habit, the nod and slight bow that maintains a distance between an unrelated man and woman, and offers her hand as a gesture intended to signify that covered women in Turkey are moderate, worldly, and open-minded. Here is the flip side of the image of the fully shrouded, unspeaking, bomb-toting, and *zikr*-chanting çarşaflı woman. Indeed, by discursively situating the çarşaflı woman in this position (one well established by orientalist fantasies, old and new), tesettürlü women hope to escape their own inscription within that signifying chain, in which the veil is associated with threat, strangeness, and eroticism. Whereas tesettür-style veiling is often impugned as the banner of a transnational Islamist movement with roots outside of Turkey,[9] tesettürlü women posit the çarşaf to be the really foreign and threatening style of covering. Similarly, while tesettür is frequently depicted as preventing women's full participation in modern Turkish society by separating them physically and symbolically in public spaces, tesettürlü women argue that it is actually the carsaf that builds a social barrier between the çarşaflı women and the rest of society. By focusing on the peculiarity of çarşaflı women's behavior and daily conduct, tesettürlü women emphasize that the çarşaf creates socio-spatial gulfs even among neighbors and relatives. Through these stories in which the çarşaf becomes tesettür's other, tesettürlü women are able to narrate their own dress styles, conduct, and spatialities as authentically Turkish and modern. In doing so, they stake out a position for themselves – even if momentarily – at the very center of the republican culture of Turkey.

6.4 Conclusion

The veil is at once a quotidian practice of dress and a highly contested symbol. Without doubt, veiling practices are meant to signify a woman's relationship to Islam. Yet, in the very moment that the veil becomes such a symbol, a crack opens up. The excess of the signifier (the veil) over the signified (the pious Muslim woman) opens up a space of ambivalence, a *gap* that is constitutive of the most intimate spatiality: an interiority/exteriority defined by the space between dress and the body, between hand and glove so to speak. Although covered women explicitly seek to harmonize their inner and outer states (see Gökarıksel and Secor 2012), once

---

[9] See Robert Olson (2000) for a discussion of how the attempt of a parliamentarian, Merve Kavakçı, to take her oath of office wearing a headscarf in April 1999 caused an uproar that brought to the fore Iranian support for the Turkish pro-veiling movement. Recent books such as Bulut (2008) and Koloğlu (2008) discuss tesettür in Turkey as a phenomenon with strong links to the Arab Middle East and Iran.

Fig. 6.4 A woman in tesettür and a woman in çarşaf walking together, Istanbul, 2010 (Photo by authors)

this discursive division between inner and outer is broached, the ambivalence of the veil as a signifier becomes apparent. As one of our participants, Songül, put it, "…you can't know how they are inside." In the case of tesettürlü women's critique of the çarşaflı, the interior is suspected of being the site of all that the outer appearance is supposed to negate. Such a construct has roots in orientalist fantasies of the harem and the veil, but it also is part of how tesettürlü women themselves are scripted within Turkey. In their fashionable and sometimes form-fitting attire, tesettürlü women themselves are frequently accused of hypocrisy, immodesty, or lack of piety by secular and Islamic critics alike. It is because their own practices of dress are not absolved of this ambivalence – far from it – that tesettürlü women take pains to distinguish themselves from the çarşaflı. Tesettürlü women discursively position the çarşaflı as their other and emphasize the socio-spatial gap between them. However, in practice, the tesettürlü and çarşaflı may not be that distant from one another. For example, it is not unusual to have tesettürlü and çarşaflı women in the same family or to observe them walking side by side on the street (Fig. 6.4). Yet, in their discourse of the çarşaf (that we have traced across our focus groups), tesettürlü women amplify the distance between these two styles of veiling in their attempt to justify and stabilize their own position within Turkish society.

In this chapter, we have focused on the discursive rendering of the çarşaf among tesettürlü women in Turkey. We have not discussed in detail how tesettürlü women represent their own practices of dress (though we discuss this at length elsewhere, Gökarıksel and Secor 2010b, 2012), and we have not included the perspective of those who wear the çarşaf. Nothing of what we have argued is meant to signify what the çarşaf is or does for those who wear it; instead, we have explored what work a particular discourse of the çarşaf is doing within a particular segment of Turkey. In taking this approach, we have tried to demonstrate the complex geopolitics of veiling as an embodied religious practice. Discussions about neighbors, sisters-in-law, encounters on the street or at the beach, and stories told and retold – these ordinary renderings can in fact be read as producing a highly localized and intimate spatial politics. Tesettürlü women are not just maligning çarşaflı women out of ignorance or fear; they are in fact using the image of the çarşaf to help them grapple with questions of pressing concern to their everyday comportment and sociopolitical status: How is piety to be performed on the streets, in the work place, in the neighborhood, or at home? Who belongs within the Turkish public – and where is the "other" against whom such a claim to modernity and national belonging can be staked? Filtered through the discourse of the *other* veiled woman, these are fundamental questions of religion and politics in Turkey today.

References

Abu-Lughod, L. 2002. Do Muslim women really need saving? Anthropological reflections on cultural relativism and its others. *American Anthropologist* 104(3): 783–790.

Adaş, E.B. 2006. The making of entrepreneurial Islam and the Islamic spirit of capitalism. *Journal for Cultural Research* 10: 113–137.

Alloula, M. 1986. *The colonial harem.* Minneapolis: University of Minnesota Press.

Arat, Y. 1997. The project of modernity and women in Turkey. In *Rethinking modernity and national identity in Turkey*, ed. S. Bozdoğan and R. Kasaba, 95–112. Seattle: University of Washington Press.

Arthur, L. 1999. *Religion, dress and the body.* Oxford: Berg.

Bailey, A.R., D.C. Harvey, and C. Brace. 2007. Disciplining youthful Methodist bodies in nineteenth-century Cornwall. *Annals of the Association of American Geographers* 97: 142–157.

Barbarosoğlu, F. 2002. *Moda ve zihniyet* [Fashion and mentality]. Istanbul: Iz Yayıncılık.

Bourdieu, P. 1984. *Distinction: A social critique of the judgement of taste.* Cambridge, MA: Harvard University Press.

Bulut, F. 2008. *Kadın ve tesettür* [Women and tesettür]. Istanbul: Cumhuriyet Kitapları.

Çarkoğlu, A., and B. Toprak. 2006. *Değişen Türkiye'de din, toplum ve siyaset* [Religion, society and politics in changing Turkey]. Istanbul: TESEV.

Connell, J. 2005. Hillsong: A megachurch in the Sydney suburbs. *Australian Geographer* 36: 315–332.

Domosh, M. 2001. The 'women of New York:' A fashionable moral geography. *Environment and Planning D: Society and Space* 19(5): 573–592.

Entwistle, J. 2000. *The fashioned body: Fashion, dress and modern social theory.* Cambridge: Polity Press.

Eygi, M. 2005. Müslüman sosyete [Muslim high society]. *Milli Gazete*, 9 December. http://www.tumgazeteler.com/?a=1012437. Last accessed 22 Mar 2010.

Eygi, M. 2009. Müslüman zenginler [The Muslim rich]. *Milli Gazete,* 21 April. http://www.mehmetsevketeygi.com/habergoster.asp?id=759. Last accessed 22 Mar 2010.

Gökarıksel, B. 2009. Beyond the officially sacred: Religion, secularism and the body in the production of subjectivity. *Social and Cultural Geography* 10(6): 657–674.

Gökarıksel, B., and A. Secor. 2009. New transnational geographies of Islamism, capitalism, and subjectivity: The veiling-fashion industry in Turkey. *Area* 41: 6–18.

Gökarıksel, B., and A. Secor. 2010a. Islamic-ness in the life of a commodity: Veiling-fashion in Turkey. *Transactions of the Institute of British Geographers* 35: 313–333.

Gökarıksel, B., and A. Secor. 2010b. Between fashion and *tesettür*: Marketing and consuming veiling-fashion. *Journal of Middle East Women's Studies* 6: 118–148.

Gökarıksel, B., and A. Secor. 2012. Even I was tempted: The moral ambivalence and ethical practice of veiling-fashion in Turkey. *Annals of the Association of American Geographers* 102(4): 847–862.

Göle, N. 1996. *The forbidden modern: Civilization and veiling*. Ann Arbor: University of Michigan Press.

Graham-Brown, S. 1988. *Images of women: The portrayal of women in photography of the Middle East, 1860–1950*. London: Quartet.

Hakan, A. 2008. Dinsel maskaralık [Religious ridicule]. *Hürriyet* , 23 April.

HaksözHaber. 2010. Tesettür modası protesto edildi [Tesettür fashion was protested]. 12 April, http://haksozhaber.net/news_detail.php?id=13968. Accessed 17 Aug 2010.

Holloway, J. 2003a. Make-believe: Spiritual practice, embodiment, and sacred space. *Environment and Planning A* 35(11): 1961–1974.

Holloway, J. 2003b. Spiritual embodiment and sacred rural landscapes. In *Country visions*, ed. P. Cloke, 158–175. Harlow: Prentice Hall.

Holloway, J. 2006. Enchanted spaces: The séance, affect, and geographies of religion. *Annals of the Association of American Geographers* 96(1): 182–187.

Hyndman, J. 2001. Towards a feminist geopolitics. *The Canadian Geographer* 45: 210–222.

Kılıçbay, B., and M. Binark. 2002. Consumer culture, Islam and the politics of lifestyle: Fashion for veiling in contemporary Turkey. *European Journal of Communication* 17: 495–511.

Koloğlu, O. 2008. *Cilbabtan türbana: Türkiye'de örtünmenin serüveni* [From jilbab to türban: The history of covering in Turkey]. Istanbul: Pozitif.

Kong, L. 2001. Mapping 'new' geographies of religion: Politics and poetics in modernity. *Progress in Human Geography* 25(2): 211–233.

Kong, L. 2010. Global shifts, theoretical shifts: Changing geographies of religion. *Progress in Human Geography*. doi:10.1177/0309132510362602.

MacMaster, N. 2010. *Burning the veil: The Algerian War and the 'emancipation' of Muslim women, 1954–1962*. Manchester: Manchester University Press.

Mahmood, S. 2005. *Politics of piety: The Islamic revival and the feminist subject*. Princeton: Princeton University Press.

Marston, S.A. 2004. Space, culture, state: Uneven developments in political geography. *Political Geography* 23: 1–16.

Mernissi, F. 1987. *The veil and the male elite: A feminist interpretation of women's rights in Islam*. New York: Basic Books.

Milliyet. 2008. SHP: *Türban Türkiye'yi İslam devleti yapmak isteyenlerin simgesidir* [Türban is the symbol of those who want to make Turkey an Islamic state]. 28 January. http://www.milliyet.com.tr/2008/01/28/son/sonsiy16.asp. Last accessed 22 Mar 2010.

Nussbaum, M. 2010. *Veiled threats?* Opinionator, exclusive online commentary from the Times, 11 July. http://opinionator.blogs.nytimes.com/2010/07/11/veiled-threats/. Last accessed 16 Aug 2010.

Olson, E. 1985. Muslim identity and secularisms in contemporary Turkey: "The headscarf dispute". *Anthropological Quarterly* 58: 161–170.

Olson, R. 2000. Turkey–Iran relations, 1997 to 2000: The Kurdish and Islamist questions. *Third World Quarterly* 21: 871–890.

Özdalga, E. 1998. *The veiling issue, official secularism and popular Islam in modern Turkey*. Richmond: Curzon.

Papanek, H. 1982. Purdah in Pakistan: Seclusion and modern occupations for women. In *Separate worlds*, ed. H. Papanek and G. Minault, 190–216. Columbus: South Asia Books.

Saktanber, A. 2002. *Living Islam*. London: I.B. Tauris.

Saktanber, A. 2006. Women and the iconography of fear: Islamicization in post-Islamist Turkey. *Signs: Journal of Women in Culture and Society* 32(1): 21–31.

Sandıkçı, Ö., and G. Ger. 2005. Aesthetics, ethics and politics of the Turkish headscarf. In *Clothing as material culture*, ed. S. Küchler and D. Miller, 61–82. Oxford: Berg.

Sandıkçı, Ö., and G. Ger. 2007. Constructing and representing the Islamic consumer in Turkey. *Fashion Theory* 11: 189–210.

Sandıkçı, Ö., and G. Ger. 2010. Veiling in style: How does a stigmatized practice become fashionable? *Journal of Consumer Research* 37: 15–36.

Scott, J. 2007. *The politics of the veil*. Princeton: Princeton University Press.

Secor, A.J. 2001. Toward a feminist counter-geopolitics: Gender, space and Islamist politics in Istanbul. *Space and Polity* 5: 199–219.

Sharp, J. 2007. Geography and gender: Finding feminist political geographies. *Progress in Human Geography* 31: 381–387.

Staeheli, L.A., E. Kofman, and L.J. Peake (eds.). 2004. *Mapping women, making politics: Feminist perspectives on political geography*. New York/London: Routledge.

Tanyol, C. 1999. *Neden türban: Şeriat ve İrtica* [Why the headscarf? Sheriah and fundamentalism]. Istanbul: Gendaş Kültür.

Tarlo, E. 1996. *Clothing matters: Dress and identity in India*. Chicago: University of Chicago Press.

Tuğal, C. 2009. *Passive revolution: Absorbing the Islamic challenge to capitalism*. Stanford: Stanford University Press.

Wadud, A. 1999. *Qur'an and women: Rereading the sacred text from a woman's perspective*. Oxford: Oxford University Press.

White, J. 1999. Islamic chic. In *Istanbul between the global and the local*, ed. Ç. Keyder, 77–91. Lanham: Rowman and Littlefield.

White, J. 2002. *Islamist mobilization in Turkey: A study in vernacular politics*. Seattle: University of Washington Press.

Yavuz, H. 2003. *Islamic political identity in Turkey*. Oxford: Oxford University Press.

Yeğenoğlu, M. 1998. *Colonial fantasies: Towards a feminist reading of Orientalism*. Cambridge: Cambridge University Press.

Yeni Şafak. 2008. *Başsavcıya göre 'türban yeşil devrimin sancağı'* [Chief prosecutor: 'türban is the flag of the green revolution']. 7 March. http://yenisafak.com.tr/Politika/?i=126728. Last accessed 22 Mar 2010.

Chapter 7
Different Democracy? Arab Immigrants, Religion, and Democratic Citizenship

Lynn Staeheli and Caroline Nagel

7.1 Introduction

Religion and expressions of faith occupy an unsettled space in the public realm of modern democracies. The secularization thesis predicts that as societies modernize and daily life becomes more secure, religious observance will recede and become less important as a means of control and authority. Scholars debate the ordering, pathways, or 'requisites' of democracy, but a general picture emerges of modern democracies relying less on religion as a means of rule and more on the rational decisions of autonomous, public individuals known as citizens. A sort of gestalt emerges through these debates in which secularism, rationalism, modernization, economic development, and democracy reinforce each other. C. Wright Mills' (1959, pp. 32–33) comments are typical: 'Once the world was filled with the sacred – in thought, practice, and institutional form. After the Reformation and the Renaissance, the forces of modernization swept across the globe and secularization, a corollary historical process, loosened the dominance of the sacred. In due course, the sacred shall disappear altogether except, possibly, in the private realm.' The democratic public envisioned by Mills was decidedly secular, even if individuals continued to practise their faith in private.

   This vision – which may be rooted in normative expectations as much as in empirical experience – is one reason for current debates over the role of religion in public life and its implications for democracy. While some people are concerned about the increasing role of Christianity in public life (e.g. Goldberg 2006), debates

L. Staeheli (✉)
Department of Geography, Durham University, Durham, England, UK
e-mail: Lynn.staeheli@durham.ac.uk

C. Nagel
Department of Geography, University of South Caroline, Columbia, SC, USA
e-mail: cnagel@mailbox.sc.edu

P. Hopkins et al. (eds.), *Religion and Place: Landscape, Politics and Piety*,
DOI 10.1007/978-94-007-4685-5_7, © Springer Science+Business Media Dordrecht 2013

over Islam are perhaps most significant in this regard. Daniel Pipes, an academic and a board member of the US Institute of Peace, for instance, has written extensively and excoriatingly about Islam, generally arguing that it is incompatible with democracy. On April 17, 2008, his editorial the *Jerusalem Post* began: 'There's an impression that Muslims suffer disproportionately from the rule of dictators, tyrants, unelected presidents, kings, emirs, and various other strongmen – and it's accurate' (Pipes 2008). He concluded: 'Hard work can one day make Islam democratic. In the meanwhile, Islamism represents the world's leading anti-democratic force.'[1]

Pipes is not alone in his argument that Islam is incompatible with democracy as we know it. In the United States, conservative politicians and talk-show personalities regularly claim that Barack Obama is a Muslim and is therefore unsuitable for the US presidency. And in many European countries, legislators have either banned or attempted to ban headscarves and veils for Muslim women in public spaces. Proponents view these bans not as restrictions on Muslim women's democratic liberties but rather as a means of protecting women – and western societies more generally – from a repressive and aggressive faith. These happenings speak to a fear that Islam has somehow slipped through the door unnoticed and that it has, with the help of multicultural policies, taken root in western societies, undermining core societal values and norms. Debates about the presence of Islam in public life are often accompanied by assertions of the 'Judeo-Christian' values of western democracies, which are variously seen to include tolerance and respect for differences, gender egalitarianism, and non-violence. It is not clear, in this sense, whether critics of Islam fear the re-injection of religion into public life or whether it is the supposed foreignness of Islam and Muslims that is the problem.

In this chapter, we examine the debates over the relation between religion and democracy, and we explore, in particular, the tension between religious beliefs, values, and identities and the commitment to democratic practices and institutions. A number of expansive studies have examined the relationship between secularization and democracy in a comparative framework, either geographically or historically (e.g. Fish 2002; Bruce 2003; Norris and Inglehart 2004; Taylor 2007). Rather than following this approach, we enter the debates from the perspective of Arab migrants and their children to the USA and UK. We use their experiences as people marked

---

[1] After this chapter was written, a series of uprisings in North Africa and the Middle East heralded the 'Arab Spring' in 2011. In these uprisings, popular protest challenged – and in some cases toppled – long-entrenched, autocratic regimes. Western countries reacted with mixed gestures: supporting the right to protest and to demand greater accountability and democracy from regimes, but fearing instability in the region and the possible ascendance of political parties identified with Islam in equal measure. At the time this chapter went to press, the outcomes of the Arab Spring and the ways in which Islam would be interwoven with democratic practice were unclear. What was clear was the way the youth who led the protests demanded democracy as citizens of their countries. Observance of Friday prayers in the central squares of cities was a key feature of many of the protests, but protestors overwhelmingly demanded their rights as citizens of their countries, not as Muslims or even as citizens who happened to be Muslim.

by cultural, ethnic, and religious difference to interrogate the assumptions that are made about the ability of 'different' citizens to support democracy. Arab immigrants are good entrée to this topic precisely because so many of them are not religious but are often *assumed* to be. Furthermore, many people assume that Arabs are all Muslims; that they are not means their experiences allow us to pick apart the often incoherent ideas about religion, democracy, and difference that we suspect fuel many of the comments about the appropriate role of religion in putatively democratic societies, such as Britain and the USA.

7.2 Democracy and Religion

Many of the debates over the role of religion in public life and about the compatibility of democracy and religion draw from the assumption that democracies will be secular, at least in terms of the ways that societies are governed. They take an assumption from liberalism that democratic citizens will be rational, autonomous individuals who are capable of participating in decisions about how they will be governed. Sovereignty is therefore vested in rational citizens, rather than in a divinely appointed ruler. What currently seems to be an increasing prominence of religion in public life sits uncomfortably with the idea of secularism. Many of the debates about the role of religion in public life, however, do not distinguish between religion as a source of authority for rule as compared to a set of values, stances, and moral outlooks that shape people's lives and political actions. As such, the debates fuse – and perhaps *con*fuse – different ideas about the role religion does and should play in public life and about how differences can be accommodated in a democracy. In order to add some clarity to these debates, we address four issues pertaining to the relationship between religion and democracy in the West.

First, there is an assumption that democracies, as regimes of governing, will be secular. As noted previously, scholars examining the secularization thesis have pointed to the historical interaction between capitalist economic development, democratization, and the secularization of governance and authority in the West. Some western democracies, such as the United Kingdom, continue to have state religions, but the basis of sovereignty has shifted decisively from divinely sanctioned rulers to citizens who elect the governing regime (Bruce 2003). In other democracies that do not have a history of divinely appointed rulers, the separation of church and state is often fundamental to both the way the country is governed and to its identity. In the United States, the First Amendment to the Constitution prohibits the establishment of a state religion; in keeping with this constitutional principle, the protection afforded to religious minorities to worship freely and without state intrusion features prominently in national narratives. The principle of laïcité is equally fundamental to governance and national identity in the French Republic. It signifies, very basically, the prohibition on state recognition or funding of any religion but also speaks to a more general ethos that frowns upon the insertion of religious identities and beliefs into public discourse, institutions, and structures. As in the United States, democracy in France is not argued to be incompatible with religion; the key point is that state legitimacy derives from a democratic process, rather than a divine right.

For proponents of secularism and the secularization thesis, the growing prominence of Islam and Islamic governments – or, indeed, of other theologies and theocracies – is a worrying trend precisely because rule and governing seem to rely on religious authority, rather than on secular authority. Focusing specifically on Islam, however, a series of studies have examined the 'democraticness' of countries with different religious traditions and have concluded that Islam is negatively associated with democratic rule. In a major cross-national study, for instance, Bruce (2003, p. 206) argues that '…religious traditions do indeed vary in the sorts of politics they create, legitimate and sustain'. He argues that 'a crucial difference between Islam and Christianity can be seen in this simple fact of political history. Wherever they are found in significant numbers, Muslims always want either to take over the state or to secede from it – the goal being the imposition of the sharia' (pp. 234–5). His conclusion is that Islamic countries will always violate basic human and individual rights related to religious freedom, and he locates the problem in the sharia – the basic code of law rooted in the Qur'an and the Sunnah.

The thesis that Islam is, by its nature, antithetical to western, secular, liberal norms has received substantial airing in recent years, with Bernard Lewis' 1990 article 'The Roots of Muslim Rage', being a notable example. Huntington (1993) has famously (or perhaps infamously) spoken of a 'clash of civilizations' between western Judeo-Christian 'culture', which has produced secular democracy, and Islamic culture, which has increasingly turned to religious sources of governance and authority. The notion of civilizational struggle informs much contemporary political discourse, and it underlies many reactions to efforts to incorporate Muslims and Islam into mainstream political structures in the West. It thus came without surprise that Rowan Williams, the Archbishop of Canterbury, unleashed a firestorm of controversy in 2008 when he suggested it might be possible to combine some elements of sharia within the British civil law and justice system. His comments were interpreted as calling for a repositioning of parts of the judiciary – the part of the state that protects civil and democratic rights – from secular to religious control.

The second source of concern about the role of religion in democracy and public life also relates to sovereignty, but this time as it describes the individual citizen. Most theories of democracy, including liberal theory, conceptualize citizens as autonomous, rational individuals (Dahl 1989). These individuals are capable of participating in public debate, of making choices in the public interest, and also of assuming the responsibilities of citizenship. Over the years, the kinds of individuals deemed to be capable of such acts have been expanded in most countries to include men who do not hold property, women, and racial and ethnic minorities. Indeed, the expansion of citizenship is seen as a marker of democracy and of freedom. Yet religion continues to be a stumbling block to democratic expansion for two interrelated reasons: the presumed (in)ability of people guided by faith to make rational decisions as individuals, and the degree of loyalty to a democratically elected governing regime rather than a divinely appointed leader who may be in a distant country.

With respect to the first issue, individuals' relationship with their god[2] is central. If there is an unmediated relationship between the individual and his or her god, then faith can be seen as an individual, and presumably private, matter. But if the relationship is mediated by a divinely appointed figure, then the individual's relationship to the public can be directed or manipulated, and the individual fails to meet a criterion for autonomy (see Rasmussen and Brown 2005). Several faith traditions have been viewed with a degree of wariness in this regard, including Catholicism (at least historically) and Islam (Norris and Inglehart 2004). The concern about the lack of autonomy for individuals is complicated by the territoriality of the modern state system and the deterritorialized nature of many religions, again including Catholicism (even the name invokes universalism) and Islam. Fealty to religious leaders and institutions in this situation is often imagined as requiring reduced loyalty to the state. In the case of democratic states, this means that secular authority is undermined by religious authority, often located elsewhere. John F. Kennedy faced this complaint in his campaign for the US presidency, with questions as to whether, as a Catholic, he would be loyal to the US Constitution or to Rome and the Pope. While worries about Catholicism may have abated in the west, fears about Islam have not. The unity of the *ummah*, or a global community of believers, is argued by some to be the basis of a transnational movement that is unparalleled in human history (Bruce 2003; but see Bowen (2004) for a more nuanced account).

The potential challenge to the nation-state and the introduction of nonconforming beliefs underlies a third reason that religion, and particularly religions introduced through migration, are seen to challenge democracies. Democratic rule, it is argued, relies on democratic societies (Gould 1988; Laclau and Mouffe 1985; Walzer 1983). Indeed, some theories are less concerned with the institutions of governing and rule than they are with the democratic qualities of the civitas. To the extent that the state is important to these theories, it is because the state supports and enforces social relationships and is amenable to change in accordance with democratic principles and action, through what Benhabib (2006) calls 'democratic iterations'. The introduction of new religious beliefs and practices through migration has the potential to disrupt social relationships (Stark and Bainbridge 1987), even when the religion is practised in the home or in private spaces. This is because religion and faith instil *values* and *expectations* that are carried into the public realm, even when religious *identities* remain invisible. This is part of the reason that debates over veiling in public spaces are so contentious. In July 2010, for instance, the French Parliament debated 'The bill to forbid concealing one's face in public', which would impose fines on women wearing the niqab or burka in public spaces. The Parliament had previously passed a non-binding resolution that claimed the full veil was 'contrary to the values of the [French] Republic'. The French justice minister Michele Alliot-Marie

---

[2] We use the lower case 'god' when referring to a non-specific deity and the upper case 'God' when referring to a personal diety named 'God'. The latter appears most often in quotes from our respondents.

argued the new bill was not intended to stigmatize a particular religion but rather was necessary because 'Democracy thrives when it is open-faced'. Other MPs, however, argued that the bill represented 'nothing more than the fear of those who are different, who come from abroad, who do not share our values' (BBC 2010). These passages from the debate are significant in that even those MPs who opposed the ban still expressed fear that Muslims 'do not share our values'. Contemporary debates about Britishness share the same sense that the values associated with Islam rest uneasily with British values, thus putting the presumably democratic character of the public sphere at odds with a particular religion that is cast as having opposing, undemocratic values.

These issues related to the reproduction of the polity are compounded when religious difference is accompanied by racial or ethnic difference, as it often is in the west. A number of studies have examined the emergence of enclaves characterized by both racial and religious difference (e.g. Peach 2006; Philips 2008) and the intersections between racial, religious, national, and transnational identities (e.g. Dwyer 1999; Hopkins 2004; Ehrkamp 2006). As this research documents, a public narrative about self-segregation has emerged in many European cities in which racial and religious minorities are argued to withdraw from 'mainstream' society. In isolated communities, there are fears that extremism will grow and pose a threat to national values and social cohesion. While a number of studies challenge that argument, particularly as it relates to self-segregation (e.g. Phillips 2008), the public narrative seems unmoved. In that discourse, it often seems that it becomes easier – and perhaps more socially acceptable in an ostensibly secular society – to make claims about unwillingness to assimilate based on assumptions about religion rather than race. In this way, fears about racial and cultural change and a threat to national identity posed by a lack of social cohesion are aired through the language of religious difference, and about Islam in particular (Naber 2008; Shryock 2008).

The interlinked nature of these issues – national sovereignty, the autonomy of citizens, cultural change accompanying migration, and growing racial and ethnic difference – means that debates about the relationship between religion and democracy are slippery, sometimes invoking normative political ideals and sometimes incoherent but still deeply held fears. Often missing from these debates, however, are the voices of the people who are often cast as the challenge to democratic societies: migrants and religious minorities.

In the sections that follow, we explore the ways that Arab immigrants respond to concerns expressed by dominant groups about religious and ethnic difference and how they envision their membership in secular, democratic societies. Our account focuses on activists from Muslim and Christian backgrounds, and it highlights the diverse ways our study participants think about religious and ethnic identities and the proper role of religion in public life. Our study participants are sensitive to claims that are often made against Arabs and Muslims. For our respondents, the problem is not *their* ability to adhere to democratic norms but the ability of western societies to adhere to their own ideals and thereby to function as democratic societies.

7.3   Arab Immigrants in the USA and UK

Our analysis is based on interviews and focus groups with over 100 Arab immigrants and their offspring in cities in the USA and UK.[3] The majority of the respondents were identified through Arab or Muslim organizations, and we describe them as activists, though several of them describe their work as strictly non-political. The missions of the organizations varied quite widely and included fostering cultural awareness, (re)building cities and societies in their home countries, protection of civil liberties, fostering interfaith dialogue, and social service provision. Approximately one-third of the respondents were Christian; of the Christian respondents, all but one was in the United States. Many of them commented on the close relationship between Arab culture and Islam, but were also careful to point out that being Arab and being Muslim are two separate things, and that Arab as a category of ethnicity includes members of multiple faith groups. As such, these respondents provide an entrée into the entangled relationships between nation, culture, and religion as they shape democratic subjects.

This group of respondents is clearly not representative of the wide range of Arab immigrants or Muslims in the USA or UK, and we make no claims to that. Our in-depth interviews, however, allowed us to explore a number of issues related to integration, community building, and citizenship. In that context, many of the respondents talked about religion, its influence on public life, and on the quality of democracy in both the Middle East and the West. It is through these conversations that we were able to explore the query implied in the title of this chapter: is the 'problem' with religion in public life that it leads to a different kind of democracy than that implied by secularization thesis, or is it that democracies struggle to accommodate difference?

7.4   Democratic Citizens

We began conducting interviews with Arab activists in 2002, not long after the 9/11 attacks in the United States, when the faces of Osama bin Laden and his associates, almost all of them from Arab countries, were seen constantly on television. A few of our respondents had mobilized specifically in response to the attacks and the conflation between Arab/Muslim and 'terrorist'; most, however, had long been involved in community activism. These individuals were motivated by a sense that Arab immigrants need to be more involved in their societies of settlement, both to protect their rights and to fulfil their obligations toward their adopted countries. Respondents commonly described their work in terms of 'active citizenship', and

---

[3] This study has been described in greater detail elsewhere; see Nagel and Staeheli (2008) and Staeheli and Nagel (2006). All names used in this chapter are pseudonyms.

their explanations of active citizenship were compatible with the calls for an engaged citizenry coming from politicians and commentators, who had begun to fret about the erosion of social cohesion and civil society.

Probably the most striking element of our respondents' activism, in this sense, was how utterly 'mainstream' it seemed. People were involved, for instance, in voter registration drives, educational campaigns to raise awareness about cultural differences, meetings with candidates for elected office, lobbying governments or politicians, attempts to strengthen the political capacities of their communities, and the provision of social services to local communities. Only efforts to raise money for overseas philanthropies might raise an eyebrow, but even these focused almost exclusively on 'non-political' causes such as university scholarships and medical assistance to children and the disabled. Respondents employed a vocabulary of building bridges between people and developing tolerance and multicultural under-standing. Farida, a Palestinian woman living in London, for example, spoke eloquently about the need to connect with people and to build bridges 'horizontally and vertically, in civil society, the private sector, and government'. She envisioned a community of responsible, committed people who would work across frontiers, be they political, religious, or cultural.

In some ways, the rather mainstream nature of our respondents' activities was unsurprising, given that we identified most of our respondents through publicly accessible websites and phone directories, and we did not expect members of extreme groups to make themselves available to us for an interview. But however mainstream and mundane, our interviewees' activities stand in stark contrast to media coverage and public perceptions of Arabs and Muslims in Britain and the United States (Alsultany 2008; Joseph et al. 2008). That they were planted so firmly in the mainstream was an important point for our interviewees: it suggested that they, as Arabs and/or Muslims, did not have a problem with adhering to democratic norms and that American society was perhaps not living up to its democratic values and its tradition of inclusiveness.

These themes were especially prominent in our interviews with activists involved in civil rights issues. Many people linked their commitments to civil rights and democracy to the fact that they had left undemocratic regimes; some argued that commitment to democracy was why they cherished their new homes, while others noted they would be unable to return to their countries of origin because they would face persecution and arrest. Adam, a Palestinian, explained that Arabs migrate to countries such as the USA for a specific reason:

> They come here, knowing that in America, there is democracy. Democracy to them is a completely foreign thing. Not in all Arab countries, but in the majority of them, you have monarchies or dictatorships. So freedom or being free is the key of what brings them over here. They came here for the political freedom and the right to live at ease and not feel scared all the time.

These respondents were thus doubly committed to protection of civil rights that they felt were being eroded, particularly in the wake of 9/11 in the USA and 7/7 in the UK. Salwa, a Palestinian woman living in Orange County, California argued:

> People have left other countries because there is no freedom of speech, no freedom of expression, and so forth, to come to this country, and now they're finding that America is

starting to go where they were. We don't need to import those bad practices. We need to export the good practices that were here in the United States.

The leader of a civil rights organization in Detroit, Labib, had direct experience of the denial of civil liberties in the USA, but he noted that the problem predated the attacks in 2001 and 2005 and that the struggle for civil rights in the Muslim and Arab communities was not something new. He was subdued when he spoke of his experience of being detained, being denied access to a lawyer, and then being given a deportation order without being presented with the evidence against him:

> Yes, I know how it feels when you are victimized, and that is why I have a sense of passion. It's simple. My own experience going through an ordeal and knowing how it feels as a victim created a sense in me to be able to see things differently and yet to be more determined, not to lose hope, not to surrender, to believe more in the process, believe more in our values, that they will prevail at the end of the day. That's why I don't surrender to pressure easily.

After winning several court cases to force the government to either present the evidence or drop deportation proceedings, this man took American citizenship and invited some of the FBI agents involved in his case to his naturalization ceremony.

Not all respondents reacted with the kind of forgiveness demonstrated by Labib. Many were angry that *they* were seen as not understanding democracy or about how to behave as democratic citizens. They railed against the hypocrisy of the British and American governments failing to support democracy at home or within the Middle East. Hala, a Palestinian-Iraqi woman living in London, noted:

> First, democracy, as far as I understand it, is choosing a government that is well-intentioned and having people that are well informed, and you don't have either in America. Second, the idea of democracy in the Middle East: they wanted to bring Ahmed Chalabi as president of Iraq! You call this democratic? I'm sorry, but I don't consider this democratic, and I don't want them dictating to us that we need to be democratic when they behave that way.

Sam, whose parents fled Palestine and who now lives in San Francisco, was critical of the acquiescence of Americans to the denial of civil liberties across the board. He felt there was no room for dissent or for struggle and thereby no room for democracy in the US: 'It's really the neo-conservative agenda or nothing. I mean, you have neo-conservatives right now who are saying things like they are going after judges for judicial activism. They threaten judges. It's really kind of crazy right now in this country.' Democracy, in his mind, no longer existed in the USA, and it made no sense to blame that on the values of either Arabs or Muslims. The diminution of democracy was the result of a broader political agenda promoted by native-born American Christians.

Finally, Tareeq, born in Britain of Palestinian and Egyptian parents, challenged the idea that democracy was western and therefore somehow incompatible with Arabs or Muslims:

> Gordon Brown at the Fabian Society ... was talking about Britishness as these concepts of liberty and fairness, which I thought was ridiculous because all humans have these aspirations. All humans love liberty, all humans love freedom, and any sensible human being, whether they live in a democracy or not, is up for those kinds of principles.... I was in an anthropology class and somebody was talking about western cultural norms, and you know what they were? It was things like 'freedom' and 'responsibility'. What do you mean

they are western? We started the bloody postal system; the Greeks did I don't know what. The Iraqis invented bureaucracy and responsibility and accountability and law, in the first place, and now you tell us [Arabs] don't understand these things, and you do because you're western.

Tareeq, and others, struggled to understand why they were seen as somehow less capable of understanding democracy and rule of law, when they argued that the origin of such values was in the countries from which they came. Almost all of the people we interviewed mentioned the struggles their communities faced in being seen as democratic citizens. Despite this, most of our respondents argued that they would ultimately be accepted, because the communities shared values with Britain and the USA and because their members accepted their responsibilities and the need to be held accountable for their actions.

It was this belief in responsibility and accountability that led some respondents to express unease with the radical comments of some immigrant imams, a stance that seemed to align the respondents more closely with the presumed American and British mainstream than the stereotypes of Muslims and Arabs. Ramia, for instance, struggled with this issue but concluded: 'We have people in the Islamic community who don't actually represent Islam, but who come to a country where there is democracy and have the right to preach negative Islamic statements and be seen as representing other Muslims. I think it's right that the government is looking to restrict that kind of behaviour'. From her perspective, these people were hypocrites who took advantage of democratic freedoms to promote inaccurate representations of Islam, which in turn was used to justify actions on the part of governments that might be seen as limiting freedoms. Certainly, she worried, the actions of these radicals reinforced negative ideas about Islam and about the ability of Arab immigrants and Muslims to act as responsible, democratic citizens.

Yet many people argued it was difficult for Arabs and Muslims to act as democratic citizens in Britain and America because of their precarious position within those democracies, not because of their views about democracy or their religious beliefs. Many respondents noted that the history of living under repressive regimes made their communities reluctant to become involved in politics in Britain or the United States. Furthermore, that initial reluctance was reinforced by the scrutiny they were now under. What dismayed other respondents was that this fear made some mundane acts of citizenship, such as registering to vote, a source of worry for some people. Yasmin, a woman from Palestine now living in London, lamented:

There's no sense that the state is benign or that the state is there to look after people. When you feel that the state is benign or that it is there to serve the people, then you feel that you should be responsible to your community, that you should care about what is going on around you, that you should participate. I embrace citizenship because I have seen the state as benign, as giving me rights and providing. But this is not the case for many Arabs who come here.

In this way, she continued, the state was implicated in the low level of participation amongst Arab immigrants and their relatively shallow feeling of responsibility and citizenship; people's lack of participation, she worried, would reinforce the stereotype that Arabs and Muslims were not good citizens.

Yasmin was by no means unique in the importance she placed on acting responsibly. Our respondents spoke frequently about the responsibilities of citizenship, about the need to participate as active citizens and community members. There was little in their comments that suggested a view of democracy or of rights that differed from the views of commentators or politicians in the USA or UK, although there was one aspect of their conceptualizations of democracy that placed them squarely in the middle of heated political debate. This issue had to do with recognition as a democratic right, which places them in the middle of contemporary debates about multiculturalism.

As discussed above, most theories of democracy imagine that all citizens are equal; there is, however, considerable debate about what equal means and how it should be evaluated. Does, for instance, the principle of equality simply mean equal treatment before the law? Does it mean that everyone is the same, regardless of historical (or contemporary) disadvantages? Or does it mean that citizens are not burdened or encumbered by their differences? The argument made by some of our respondents is that they have an inalienable right to be different and to be accepted as equal, but different, citizens. Some respondents thus argued that the state and society is required to recognize difference and respect it. For Rafik, a Yemeni man living in Birmingham, recognition requires that the government 'realise that my culture, my faith, my needs, my entire presence and existence, need to be identified, respected, and given the support and service I need'. Some respondents thought this recognition could come through the inclusion of a category 'Arab' in government data, such as the census. Others thought it was necessary for Arabs and Muslims to be included in equality legislation and affirmative action policies. Still, others, including supporters of a registered political action committee (PAC) in Detroit, thought the key to gaining recognition was through their appointment in the civil service or by electing Muslims and Arabs to political office. Yet such efforts to gain recognition were waged through activities that are firmly in the mainstream of American and British politics.

7.5   Citizens: Faithful *and* Democratic?

If the activism and views of democracy expressed by our respondents were unremarkable – even vaguely uninteresting because they were so unremarkable – their views about the role of religion in public and in politics were more contentious. As Adam, mentioned earlier, remarked, this is not surprising: 'Arabs love politics. I think for Arabs, politics and religion are the two things they can talk about forever, and they argue about it even within themselves.' Several issues related to the intersections of faith, politics and democracy emerged in the interviews.

While some respondents did not discuss religion or dismissed it as irrelevant, most of our respondents argued that faith and spirituality shaped their political outlooks. Many of them – both Muslims and Christians – invoked God and their religious faith when explaining their activism, and they spoke of the importance of religion as a source of moral guidance in their public lives. One example is Boulos, a Palestinian Christian living in suburban Washington, who argued that it was more important to be moral and to follow the ethical code of the religion in your heart than it was to be law-abiding. As the president of an Arab-identified political action committee, he often found himself conflicted between the ideal and the practical in making political choices. Most other respondents, though, found the balance between moral values and practical politics to be far less of a struggle, emphasizing the compatibility between their faiths and western democratic institutions and norms. Our Muslim respondents, in particular, argued that their moral code and core beliefs were entirely consistent with democracy. One young Palestinian-American woman living in suburban Washington spoke eloquently of the compatibility of Islam and democracy, commenting 'It is almost as though Thomas Jefferson read the Qur'an'. Significantly, many Muslim respondents were also keen to point out the many overlaps between Islam and Christianity, especially in terms of their common commitment to social justice.

However, most of our respondents did not publicly identify themselves as Muslims or Christians, and only a few mobilized primarily on behalf of religiously defined communities. We did speak to a small number of activists who *were* active in Muslim or Christian organizations and who prioritized their Muslim identities over all others. But most of our respondents, despite being deeply attached to their religion and feeling the effects of their faith on their interactions with others, argued that faith was essentially a private matter. There were several interrelated reasons given for insisting on this. Asad, a Lebanese man living in Detroit, is a devout Muslim and he praised God several times in the interview, but he seemed to regard politics as a decidedly secular, if not venal, affair:

> This is the United States. It's a corporation, and you need to have shares. No one's going to give you the shares. You have to buy it by hard work, by accumulating strength, by forming institutions, by belonging to political parties and social clubs and to help the poor.

Democracy, as he understands it, is a rich blend of economics, interest group politics, responsibility, and social justice; it was only in the latter elements that moral values associated with faith seeped in. Respondents such as Asad explained that Arabs needed to battle the stereotypes that they are defined by religion and so tended to emphasize the 'cultural', rather than religious, basis of Arab identity. A common refrain in the interviews was that Arab culture is distinguishable more by language and history than by religion and that Arabs can be Muslims, Christians, and Jews.

Some of these individuals, moreover, had lived through (or fled from) the civil war in Lebanon and viewed any focus on religion as potentially divisive and as detracting from larger, more important issues. Mirroring wider debates taking place in the west, a number of respondents, as well, worried that some in the community were becoming too attached to more extreme versions of their faith. Latif, an Egyptian-born Muslim living in London, for example, worried that religion was starting to control people's behaviours, which he felt was not good. 'Religious belief is all right for myself', he argued, 'but if my belief starts to affect others, this is bad'.

And Yusef, an Iraqi also living in London, was concerned that religion was becoming a means of brainwashing people, and often, to turn people against each other:

> You can't have a peaceful, thriving, growing, creative society with people saying, you either believe what I believe or I'm going to kill you….I've been on hajj, I've been to Mecca twice. It's not like I'm the atheist, areligious, whatever. But I am secular and I believe that religion is manmade and was done to pacify the masses and has been misused and abused. It worries me when you see people being led with such conviction that they either turn everyone to Muslims or Christians or whatever, or else hell is awaiting!

For people such as Yusef, religion is a value system that commits him to particular views of social justice, and it is a view of justice that is perfectly aligned with democratic values. The issue for him was that some extremists – Muslim, Christian, or 'whatever' – were advocating rigid conformance to particular practices, rather than the divinely mandated responsibility to help people.

As seen in the quote above, activists like Yusef typically described their organizations and their own political outlooks as 'secular'. Secularism, as explained by these individuals, meant neither a public denial of one's faith nor personal rejection of religion but rather an insistence on the fair treatment of different religious groups and the removal of religious affiliation or identity as a basis of political decision making or claims making. They tended to see themselves acting as Arabs (or Arab Americans or British Arabs), rather than as people of faith, in order to get their message across. So, for instance, when one young Palestinian-American woman spoke of attending protests and meetings, she said that she presented herself as a Palestinian or as an American, not as a Muslim. It was not that she was ashamed of being a Muslim or thought that it would distract from her message; it was simply that she was participating as either an American or as a Palestinian, not as a Muslim. Religion, she and others argued, is a set of spiritual beliefs, not a nationality.

Some of these same respondents argued that it was the British and the Americans who were bringing religion into politics and policy; in confusing faith with nationality, they argued, many native-born Britons and Americans violated both the values of their countries and democratic norms. Sam, mentioned earlier, worried that the neoconservative movement in the USA, which is intertwined with the religious right, was curtailing dissent. Rafiya, a Yemeni woman living in Sheffield, called out conservatives in Britain who, she claimed, equated democracy, Christianity, and Englishness. She also discussed – with some degree of incredulity – the ways that many British people seemed to think that Muslim women who wore a veil somehow suppressed *Christian* women. Over and over, Muslim respondents commented on the inability – or unwillingness – of Americans and British people to understand that Christians, Muslims, and Jews worship the same god. Nazih, a second-generation Palestinian-Lebanese man from Detroit, shook his head with a mix of amazement and anger while commenting:

> Some people in this country think I don't believe in God because I call him Allah in Arabic. Allah is the Arabic word for God. So I say, 'Allahu akbar,' they say 'Oh my God, he's a terrorist.' That's the same exact god that Christians recognize. So for me, people can do what they want. I'm going to do what I believe is right for the community and for America, and that's it.

For him, arguments about the incompatibility of Islam and democracy reflected the ignorance of people making that claim, rather than a deep understanding of Islam, of democracy, or of what it meant to be an American.

7.6   Different Democracy or Democracy and Difference?

There is a great deal of discussion today about the 'resurgence' of religion worldwide and especially about the growth of more virulent and fundamentalist forms of religion. The increasing visibility of religion is often viewed as a backlash against the values of modernity and secularism and as an effort by those marginalized in a globalizing world to re-inject religious authority and identity into political life. For many proponents of liberal democracy, this can only lead to the erosion of democratic rights and of western values and norms. In many western contexts, these concerns are directed toward immigrant and minority groups, and especially toward Muslims, who are often viewed as implanting foreign – and even extreme – values into western societies and as manipulating an insistence on tolerance to their own advantage. Western governments, in turn, are increasingly inclined to indicate the limits of their acceptance of religious differences and to compel minorities to conform.

Political discourse, however, tends to ignore the ways that people of faith think about and act on the relationship between their religious beliefs and their participation in democratic societies. Our interviews with Arab-origin activists in the United States and Britain suggest that immigrants (and undoubtedly others) approach religion in multiple, complex ways that reflect their concerns and experiences with stigmatization, as well as their political aims and strategies. While respondents recognize western societies to be secular at one level, they also understand that western societies are not entirely devoid of religious identities and that, moreover, religious freedom is a central tenet of western liberalism. Islam, they argued, is as compatible as Christianity with democracy, but anti-democratic politics and practices within the West – some of them justified on religious grounds – have targeted and denigrated Arabs and Muslims, equating their culture and beliefs with terrorism.

At the same time, our respondents, for the most part, suggest that while religion informs their political beliefs and practices, it is not central to their activism; that is, they see themselves as participating as democratic citizens, not Muslim or Christian citizens. We did speak with individuals and organizations who take a different position and who do mobilize as Muslims on behalf of a Muslim community. Our point, though, is that we cannot assume that Islam is somehow inherently political – or that it is any more political than Christianity.

Vast literatures exist theorizing subaltern politics, radical democracies, and insurgent citizenships that would seem to challenge mainstream views of democracy. Surely, people who are marginalized on multiple social axes would come to form a different view of democracy. Our respondents, though, upheld rather mainstream views of democracy; their marginalization in dominant discourses, in this sense, had not led them to embrace radical visions of society (either democratic or anti-democratic) but instead to insist that dominant groups adhere more closely to their own professed norms. The people who spoke with us were at pains to highlight both the outlooks and values they shared with Americans and Britons and also to demand recognition of the differences between them. These differences, they argued, were not framed as differences in democratic outlooks or even differences that emerged through the experience of migration. Rather, they argued that cultural and religious differences can and should be respected in modern, democratic societies. The issue for them, therefore, was how democracy could recognize and accommodate these differences, rather than the need to forge a different democracy.

References

Alsultany, E. 2008. The prime-time plight of the Arab Muslim American after 9/11: Configurations of race and nation in TV dramas. In *Race and Arab Americans before and after 9/11*, ed. A. Jamal and N. Naber, 204–228. Syracuse: Syracuse University Press.

BBC. 2010. French MPs set to vote on Islamic full veil. 13 July. http://news.bbc.co.uk/1/hi/world/europe/10611398.stm. Last viewed 13 July 2010.

Benhabib, S. 2006. *Another cosmopolitanism*. Oxford: Oxford University Press.

Bowen, J. 2004. Beyond migration: Islam as a transnational public space. *Journal of Ethnic and Migration Studies* 30: 879–894.

Bruce, S. 2003. *Politics and religion*. Cambridge: Polity.

Dahl, R. 1989. *Democracy and its critics*. New Haven: Yale University Press.

Dwyer, C. 1999. Contradictions of community: Questions of identity for British Muslim women. *Environment and Planning A* 31: 53–68.

Ehrkamp, P. 2006. 'We Turks are no Germans': Assimilation discourses and the dialectical construction of identities in Germany. *Environment and Planning A* 38: 1673–1692.

Fish, M.S. 2002. Islam and authoritarianism. *World Politics* 55: 4–37.

Goldberg, M. 2006. *Kingdom coming: The rise of Christian nationalism*. New York: Norton.

Gould, C. 1988. *Rethinking democracy*. Cambridge: Cambridge University Press.

Hopkins, P. 2004. Young Muslim men in Scotland: Inclusions and exclusions. *Children's Geographies* 2(2): 257–272.

Huntington, S. 1993. The clash of civilizations? *Foreign Affairs* 72: 22–49.

Joseph, S., B. d'Harlingue, and A. Wong. 2008. Arab Americans and Muslim Americans in the *New York Times* before and after 9/11. In *Race and Arab Americans before and after 9/11*, ed. A. Jamal and N. Naber, 229–275. Syracuse: Syracuse University Press.

Laclau, E., and C. Mouffe. 1985. *Hegemony and socialist strategy*. London: Verso.

Mills, C.W. 1959. *The sociological imagination*. Oxford: Oxford University Press.

Naber, N. 2008. 'Look, Mohammed the Terrorist is coming!' Cultural racism, nation-based racism, and the intersectionality of oppression after 9/11. In *Race and Arab Americans before and after 9/11*, ed. A. Jamal and N. Naber, 276–304. Syracuse: Syracuse University Press.

Nagel, C., and L. Staeheli. 2008. Integration and the negotiation of 'here' and 'there': The case of British Arab activists. *Social and Cultural Geography* 9: 415–430.

Norris, P., and R. Inglehart. 2004. *Sacred and secular: Religion and politics worldwide*. Cambridge: Cambridge University Press.

Peach, C. 2006. Islam, ethnicity and South Asian religions in the London 2001 census. *Transactions of the Institute of British Geographers* 31: 353–370.

Philips, D. 2008. The problem with segregation: Exploring the racialisation of space in northern Pennine towns. In *New geographies of race and racism*, ed. C. Dwyer and C. Bressey, 179–192. Aldershot: Ashgate Publications.

Pipes, D. 2008. A democratic Islam? *Jerusalem Post* 17 April. Available at http://www.danielpipes. org/5517/a-democratic-islam. Last viewed 6 June 2010.

Rasmussen, C., and M. Brown. 2005. The body politic as spatial metaphor. *Citizenship Studies* 9: 469–484.

Shryock, A. 2008. The moral analogies of race: Arab American identity, color politics, and the limits of racialized citizenship. In *Race and Arab Americans before and after 9/11*, ed. A. Jamal and N. Naber, 81–113. Syracuse: Syracuse University Press.

Staeheli, L., and C. Nagel. 2006. Topographies of home and citizenship: Arab-American activists in the United States. *Environment and Planning A* 38: 1599–1614.

Stark, R., and W. Bainbridge. 1987. *A theory of religion*. New York: Lang.

Taylor, C. 2007. *A secular age*. Cambridge, MA: Belknap.

Walzer, M. 1983. *Spheres of justice*. New York: Basic Books.

Chapter 8
'It is not a shelter, it is a church!' Religious Organisations, the Public Sphere and Xenophobia in South Africa

Barbara Bompani

8.1 Introduction

South Africa presents an excellent opportunity to understand the evolution of the relationship between the state and religious organisations and their public role in a postcolonial context (cf. Greenstein et al. 1998). Prior to the end of the undemocratic regime of Apartheid, many Christian churches and religious organisations were broadly aligned with the anti-Apartheid movement and their strategy of state resistance during the liberation struggle (Gifford 1995). The years immediately following the first democratic election in April 1994 marked a period of consensus between the state, civil society and religious organisations. This period was characterised as one of 'critical solidarity' in the process of nation building as religious organisations eschewed the critical voice of the liberation struggle and aligned themselves with the ruling party, the African National Congress (ANC) (Bompani 2006). The general strategy of South African religious groups is similar to those of other civil society movements toward democracy, but there are also critical differences which, at various moments in the contemporary history of the nation, erupt in and through the humanitarian activities of faith-based communities.

The aim of this chapter is to examine some of the unique characteristics and situation of religious groups in the context of South Africa's most recent challenges to the nation-building process. The post-1994 consensus has slowly eroded in the face of governmental inefficiency, continuing inequality and social crises that belie the ideal of an inclusive, tolerant country based on respect for human rights that was both promised and expected. In response, it appears that a new trend is emerging and that religious leaders and religious organisations are to some extent reoccupying

B. Bompani (✉)
African Development, School of Social and Political Science,
University of Edinburgh, Edinburgh, Scotland, UK
e-mail: B.Bompani@ed.ac.uk

P. Hopkins et al. (eds.), *Religion and Place: Landscape, Politics and Piety*,
DOI 10.1007/978-94-007-4685-5_8, © Springer Science+Business Media Dordrecht 2013

the public sphere and redefining their public role by condemning government ineffectiveness in meeting the needs of the new democratic South Africa. This re-emergence was particularly notable in the response of religious organisations to the xenophobic violence that took place in 2008 and its aftermath.

In May and June 2008, South Africa was shaken as a wave of xenophobic violence spread across the country. Although violence against foreign nationals and other 'outsiders'[1] has been a long-standing feature of post-Apartheid South Africa (Nyamnjoh 2006), the intensity and scale of the May 2008 attacks was unprecedented. An isolated incidence of anti-foreigner violence in Alexandra township on 11 May quickly spread to other townships and informal settlements across the country. After 2 weeks and the deployment of the army, the violence subsided. In its wake, 62 people, including 21 South Africans, were dead; at least 670 wounded; dozens of women were raped; and at least 100,000 persons were displaced (Landau 2010; SAHRC 2010; IOM 2009). The government provided a slow response to curtail these incidents, and the lack of clear and proactive leadership hindered effective coordination between public and non-governmental agencies. For example, in an interview, a representative of the Institute of Islamic Services, Mr Hussein, explained that 'When the attacks started, the police used to bring the displaced people here and we would feed them and let them sleep here. Although the issue was in the news, the government was rather slow to react. They only reacted when the attacks had spread throughout South Africa and they started putting up refugee camps'.[2]

In contrast, religious organisations were amongst the first to respond to the humanitarian crisis, playing a vital role in helping victims obtain legal and psychological care, developing programmes of repatriation for some migrants, and enhancing programmes of reintegration and reconciliation for those who wished to remain in South Africa. Alongside their practical and material interventions, some religious organisations began to criticise the government's patchy responses to the crisis and to the issue of an extremely divided society, its inefficiency and lack of coordination, and its unwillingness to confront the roots of post-Apartheid South Africa's latent xenophobia. As Father Holdcroft from the Jesuit Refugees Service articulated, 'The [xenophobic] attacks got everyone by surprise and the government did not really have any plans and did not know what to do, so they went to the UNHCR … the government needs to have a clear policy and we are not getting any help from them in that regard … a clear policy from them would make our work easier'.[3] Against this background, and drawing upon research conducted between 2009 and 2010,[4] this chapter analyses the activities of the Central Methodist Mission (CMM) in inner-city Johannesburg as a means to show the re-appropriation of public space

[1] A few victims of the xenophobic attacks were actually South Africans, opening up a discussion around the construction of the identity of the 'outsider'.

[2] Interview with Mr Hussein, The Institute of Islamic Services, Pretoria, 18 May 2010.

[3] Interview with Father David Holdcroft, Jesuit Refugees Service, Pretoria, 18 May 2010.

[4] This research has been funded by the Development Trust Research Fund (DTRF) at the University of Edinburgh, and it would not have been possible without the valuable work of my research assistant, Tantenda Mukwedeya (PhD student at the University of the Witwatersrand).

by a religious organisation and its contestation with the South African state around issues of human rights, xenophobia and the defence of foreign nationals. The Zimbabwean community's fear of the unresolved xenophobic feelings in the country (Landau 2009), their lack of trust towards government agencies and the lack of concrete alternatives to the government drew many Zimbabwean citizens to this religious site, and it suddenly became a very contested place. The CMM shifted from being a religious site to a sort of improvised 'refugee camp' hosting around 3,000 refugees mainly from Zimbabwe and, in doing so, became the site of much contestation and controversy, occupying a very visible space in the media and within the public debate. The case helps to illustrate the various ways that religious organisations emerge as simultaneously essential to, yet often critical of, emerging democracies throughout Africa.

8.2   Religious Organisations: The Public Sphere and the State in South Africa

Being the great majority of South Africans are affiliated to a Christian denomination, Christian ideas and institutions have always been prominent in the public and political life of South Africa.[5] The transition to democracy in the 1990s has meant many things for various religious communities. While the Christian independent movement, and to a lesser extent the Pentecostal-charismatic churches (Googhew 2000),[6] has experienced a constant level of growth in membership since the end of the 1980s, mainline churches started to go through the opposite process (ibid.). The ecumenical movement, whose identity was closely knit to the anti-Apartheid era, has emerged considerably weaker. This has happened in part because senior leadership was lost to new institutions of the state or other secular organisations including business, to an extent because the shift from the register of resistance to the key of cooperation with government has proven very difficult, and in part because the identity of these organisations (once the Apartheid regime had been defeated) could no longer be the same and their reason for existence was no longer obvious.[7] The ecumenical character of the churches' struggle against Apartheid is contrasted by the weak collaboration amongst churches in the post-Apartheid period. According to some church leadership, the openness and collaboration between the churches and religious organisations of the liberation movement has thus been

---

[5] Christianity is by far the dominant religion in South Africa. More than 70% of the population declares to belong to a Christian denomination; see the South African census published in 2004, StatsSA. (2004). See also Elphick and Davenport (1998) (especially Introduction).

[6] Data from the South African State in Googhew (2000).

[7] Interview with Professor James Cochrane, Department of Religious Studies, University of Cape Town, 15 April 2001.

replaced with comparative isolation.[8] Mainline churches grew constantly in the first half of the twentieth century and kept growing in the 1960s and in the 1970s, though at a lower rate and with differences between ethnic groups. By the 1990s, however, mainline Christianity started to suffer a considerable decline in popularity and influence.[9] In this section, I briefly reflect on the reasons for this shift in the Christian religious landscape, before describing the work of the CMM in Johannesburg.

In South Africa, the churches' voice was particularly powerful in the struggle against Apartheid and was embodied in 'prophetic Christianity', a movement of Christian leaders that through the analysis of biblical values tried to promote social justice and active political participation. Based on respect of African values and on a commitment to interrogate society and to challenge the state,[10] prophetic Christianity represented an obstacle for the dominant racist party and for mainline theology, the latter of which had consistently refused to confront the state (Walshe 1991). During Apartheid, prophetic Christianity received 95% of its funding from overseas.[11] This money was used by an extensive network for assisting with the psychological, legal and material support of detainees and their families in the townships. Hundreds of clergy and Christian activists were detained, many were tortured and some were deported. The SACC building, Khotso House, as well as the Catholic Bishops' Conference (SACBC) Building, Khanya House, were damaged by bombs in 1988. There were pragmatic reasons behind the choice of using churches to channel money, for while political organisations were banned and political leaders exiled or imprisoned, religious organisations were able to preserve a certain level of autonomy and they were never completely repressed by the apparatus of the Apartheid State. A certain level of associational life has always been tolerated by the Apartheid regime (cf. Mayekiso 1996) especially in the case of religious organisations that were well connected to the international community. In the post-Apartheid era religious institutions and religious leaders withdrew considerably from the public arena. This was due to in part to the movement of leadership and trained people into bureaucratic or political institutions, to the lack of money from abroad and to the decline of membership inside mainline churches, due to

---

[8] An aspect many times lamented by people interviewed inside mainline churches.

[9] The Catholic Church is the historical denomination that lost the least number of members after the end of Apartheid.

[10] Interview with Archbishop Denis Hurley and my interview with Paddy Kearney, Diakonia organisation, both on the 12 of August 2000, Durban.

[11] A rare case in history in which money to support a liberation struggle was routed through international religious channels. For example, the Kagiso Trust, established in 1985 to channel funds from the European Community's (EC) to support victims of Apartheid, represents the unique case in which the EC has chosen to allocate funding through religious institutions. This is highly contested by part of the Church and by the South African government that tried to stop this partnership. See, for example, Tingle (1992). Money was also channelled by the World Council of Churches through the Programme to Combat Racism, which supported the non-violent aspect of the ANC struggle, such as education and public relations.

internal problems of redefinition of identity in the democratic context and the return to a denominational character and the abandoning of their interfaith and interdenominational work.

In the Apartheid era, prophetic Christianity never formulated alternative or independent solutions to the liberation struggle and never heralded a Christian third way to heal South African society. Christian efforts were fundamentally orientated into the broader liberation movement. It is not possible to speak of a Christian struggle but rather of Christian leaders and activists as part of the broader struggle for liberation. Prophetic Christianity in South Africa has never been synonymous with a strong and monolithic church. On the contrary, it emerges from ecumenical institutions such as Diakonia and the Institute for Contextual Theology, and from organisations like the Young Christian Students, within the different Christian denominations, Christian political leaders and activists might also have entered the movement independently without the support of the parish. The majority of members of prophetic Christianity were black South African Christians who were already active in the political struggle. This characteristic is important in understanding the complexity of Christian actors (and action) in the liberation struggle, although narratives tend to present the movement as homogenous (and ANC dominated). The relation between prophetic Christianity and the African National Congress in the Apartheid era determined the relations between churches and the political establishment in the post-Apartheid era and contributed to its support of the government's politics in the initial moment of national reconstruction.

There has been a change in churches' action in public life in more recent years, especially around issues of morality, justice and xenophobia, from the dominant position of alignment and co-optation towards a more independent and critical voice that has created a distance between churches and the government position. This period is marked by shifts within the churches, especially in the voice of their leadership, and it is characterised by a new wave of criticism towards government policy. More recently, since the end of the second Mbeki's presidency in 2008, churches began to publically attack the lack of personal morality amongst the leadership of the post-Apartheid government with pamphlets and sermons produced for their religious communities and through public speeches, press releases produced for the mass media. The Southern Africa Catholic Bishops' Conference, in a press release entitled 'Appeal to South African Leaders: Is your sexual morality making you a worthy role model for the youth?', commented on President Zuma's interpretation of polygamy:

> [The Southern Africa Catholic Bishops' Conference] expresses its strongest concern of the scandalous behaviour of leaders who shamelessly flout the norms of morality and decency, accepted and expected by the vast majority of people. In particular we deplore the attempts to excuse or even defend bad moral behaviour in the name of 'culture'. While we note President Zuma's expression of regret for engaging in 'unprotected sex', we are nonetheless appalled that for the second time in as many years he does not express regret or show remorse for his adultery. (SACBC's Press Release February 2010)

In February 2009, the newly formed opposition party Congress of the People (COPE) nominated a Methodist Bishop Mvume Dandala as the presidential candidate, symbolising a break from a political sphere increasingly perceived as amoral and untrustworthy. The dichotomy between religious/trustworthy and political/untrustworthy is sharp, yet they do not represent a strong interfaith and interdenominational alliance as was apparent during the struggle to end Apartheid. Thus, the re-emergence of religious voices in the public sphere is heterogeneous and marked by independent and differentiated responses.

An analysis of their action during and after the xenophobic attacks, for example, shows a lack of lasting partnerships or consensus (Phakathi 2010). Initially, during these attacks – and prior to the establishment of refugee camps – many of the foreign nationals turned to churches for protection, shelter, food and clothing because churches were publically recognised as 'safe' places. Appealing to their congregations, churches provided manpower and transport to distribute donated goods to refugee camps, and they were involved in the provision of medical supplies, doctors, counselling and emotional support in the camps. According to Phakathi's report, doctors from the His People Church provided medical assessments and medication at the Bramley Police Station where many foreigners were looking for protection. In Germiston City Hall, Bedford Chapel worked closely with Médecins Sans Frontières (MSF) to protect the well-being of displaced people. The Northfield Methodist Church organised security personnel in Benoni Town Hall. Other churches assisted in various ways displaced people in Johannesburg as well as in other places affected by xenophobic attacks (Phakathi 2010). For the first time, the moral authority of religious leaders, as well as a few other recognised figures inside the broader civil society cluster, was recognised and indeed sanctioned to serve as the primary mediator between the refugees, local communities and the South African government. As reverend Gift Moerane from the SACC said, 'We had to mediate and link between the government, both at a local and national level and the refugees. It became a problem that the refugees did not want to go back to their community and they did not want to have a dialogue with government officials. We were going to the refugee camps to talk to these people, we had to use influential religious leaders who were highly respected'.[12]

The work of some of these organisations goes far beyond the simple humanitarian intervention that the emergency of the xenophobic attacks in 2008 required. In the process of offering its own methods of protection and long-term assistance to 3,000 refugees, the Central Methodist Mission publically challenged the local government, the police and other critical voices, including the Southern Africa Methodist Church. In doing so, the church and Bishop Paul Verryn, who was the architect behind this project, were at the centre of public debates and media coverage at a local, national and Southern African (in Zimbabwe) level. If we accept that the public sphere is the 'common space in which the members of a society are deemed to meet through

[12] Interview with Rev. Gift Moerane, Ecumenical Secretary, South African Council of Churches (SACC), Khotso House, Johannesburg, 21 May 2010.

a variety of media...to be able to form a common mind about these' (Taylor 2007: 185), no other religious organisation since the demise of Apartheid in 1994 has been more successful in occupying this 'common place'.[13]

8.3   The Central Methodist Mission in Inner-City Johannesburg

The Central Methodist Mission in inner-city Johannesburg is a well-known institution in South Africa and across the border in Zimbabwe. There are multiple documentaries, blogs, Facebook groups and newspaper articles about the CMM and its hosting of international migrants and a small number of South African homeless people. Migrants know of the existence of this 'safe' space[14] even before leaving their own country. The church is an imposing, labyrinthine six-storey building. There are also two basement floors dubbed 'Soweto' by the church occupiers,[15] drawing a link with the symbolic, subversive and 'dangerous' township in South West Johannesburg (Bonner and Segal 1998). The two basement floors are mainly occupied by Zimbabwean Ndebele-speaking migrants, while the upper floors serve as temporary homes for Zimbabwean Shona migrants. Shona is the largest ethnic group in Zimbabwe (70% of the total population), Ndebele constitutes 25% of the entire population while Tonga, Venda and other small groups make up the rest (Ranger 1989). Though not empirically supported, tensions exist in the building regarding the suspected uneven distribution of goods between different ethnic groups, with Ndebele people suggesting that donated items never reach the basement. Newspapers, TV news and radio talks (especially the local station, Radio 702) reported episodes of violence inside the church between the Shona and the Ndebele. Although Bishop Verryn has always challenged these assertions, it was obvious that there were unresolved issues of difficult cohabitation between Ndebele and Shona

---

[13] This analysis moves away from strict interpretations of religion in the public sphere based on the seminal work of Habermas (1991, 2006). The way in which religious organisations occupy the public in developing countries is different from the Euro/Western-centric interpretations offered by Habermas and need to be contextualised. In Africa, where the level of organisation of civil society actors is quite weak for historical and economic reasons (see, e.g. Makumbe 1998), the role of religious organisations as public actors is vibrant and vital in ensuring a plurality of voices. Furthermore, in Africa, the separation between private and public spaces assumes different and less dichotomized meanings than in Euro/Western contexts. As Ellis posed it, there is a continuum between the visible and invisible world and between the public and the private sphere that deserves a deeper understanding (Ellis in Bompani and Frahm-Arp 2010). For a critique of Habermas's universalistic approach, see, for example, Meyer and Moors (2006).

[14] This strongly emerged from interviews and informal conversations with Zimbabweans at the church.

[15] Soweto represents a sort of mythological place in the rest of Africa for it is a political role in the struggle against Apartheid but also for the representation of the vast dangerous township; for example, a settlement in Nairobi, at the eastern fringes, is called Soweto. This is located in what was planned to have been Phase III of the Kayole, at the eastern fringes of Nairobi.

during a period of heightened tension in 2010.[16] A representative of the Southern African Centre for the Survivors of Torture (SACST), for example, explained that these conflicts reflect both very intimate and more political tensions:

> The tortured person leaves because of torture and because of the economic meltdown in Zimbabwe, the torturer also leaves and they meet at the central Methodist church and all of a sudden feelings of anger, pain and trauma comes back. We have heard cases of such tension and sometimes there are political debates as Zimbabwean African National Union (Patriotic Front) and Movement for Democratic Change supporters defend their parties and this sometimes ends up along ethnic lines for whatever reason. However no one reports these issues to the Bishop because they say he is not happy when they report these things, because he would love an environment where everybody exists peacefully and in harmony.[17]

The number of refugees at the Central Methodist Mission during 2010 was unknown, but it was estimated by the Church Refugee Ministry to be in the region of 3,000 persons by the beginning of 2010. Media reports have continued to estimate that there were more than 3,500 refugees staying in and just outside the church. One church staff member explained that they stopped registering refugees after the chaotic situation created by the xenophobic events.[18] In the first stage of my observation between May 2009 and January 2010, amongst the refugees, there were over 100 families of couples with their children and couples only. There were around 60 unaccompanied children, and there were also many pregnant and breastfeeding women.[19]

The church began to offer shelter to refugees, mostly from Zimbabwe, since 2005, following the deepening of its economic and political problems (Raftopoulos and Mlambo 2009). The church had previously been used to accommodate vulnerable and homeless South Africans. The church was led by Bishop Paul Verryn, a religious leader with a history of accommodating vulnerable people at his Soweto residence during the Apartheid era. The bishop was the person that pushed for the CMM to house vulnerable people at the scale we are witnessing today; the refugees have been accommodated by the initiative of Bishop Verryn,[20] and people recognise the refugees as 'the bishop's people'.[21] The CMM thus operates with two somewhat distinct organisational structures, with one focused on Church Ministry and the other on Refugee Ministry. The Church Ministry is formed by the regular church

---

[16] The same bishop addressed the issue of ethnic division in many sermons between May 2009 and January 2010 [fieldwork notes].

[17] Interview with Annah Moyo, Southern African Centre for the Survivors of Torture (SACST), 22 July 2009, Braamfontein, Johannesburg

[18] Interview with Leothere, French teacher and church steward, Central Methodist Church, 3 July 2009.

[19] These are data provided by the Church Refugee Ministry; they are more or less accurate although no updated records exist.

[20] Bishop Paul Verryn in the 1970s and in the 1980s was involved with the politically active South African Council of Churches (SACC) and lived in Soweto where he used to support and hide young comrades escaping from regime persecution.

[21] This idea strongly emerged through the Apartheid interviews with the church congregants and people living in the surrounding area or collaborating with the CMM (Johannesburg, July/August 2009; Johannesburg May/June 2010).

congregation with nine assisting reverends. Refugees are organised and administered under a Refugee Ministry Fellowship called the Ray of Hope Refugee Ministry.[22]

In the church, there were considerable numbers of projects and programmes that refugees were encouraged to attend. This was in line with the religious ethos (also called the bishop's rules) of the organisation: 'if one is unemployed, they must engage in some sort of empowering program like training, education courses'.[23] Whilst some of these programmes were organised for refugees, there were some that were organised by the refugees themselves with some support from the church. There were programmes on education and skills training, health and caring, amongst others. In terms of funding, all these activities were materially and financially supported by the church via the bishop. The church's main source of funding originated from donations.[24] During the xenophobic attacks in 2008, the CMM received overwhelming donations from individual well wishers and organisations that donated cash and in-kind where appropriate, including groups such as the Standard Bank, South African Airways (SAA), UNHCR and the Mormon Church, to name a few. The United Methodist Committee on Relief (UMCOR) has also been supporting CMM, and it is a major contributor to the ministry and work of Central Methodist Mission.[25] The Ray of Hope Refugee Ministry thus maintains its own bank account, retaining a degree of financial and programme independence from the Church Ministry.

At the time of this research, the CMM was collaborating with several local and international organisations in different areas. Médecins Sans Frontières was providing medical care from their clinic inside the main church building,[26] whilst Lawyers for Human Rights was continuously working with the church by providing legal services to migrants seeking asylum status or who were under arrest. The Refugee Ministry Centre was also working to document migrants at the church. The church was assisted by other groups, including the Council of Conciliation Mediation and Arbitration, the Legal Resource Centre, the Wits Law Clinic and the AIDS Law Project, and it was in partnership with UNICEF and the National Association of Child and Youth Care Workers and in collaboration with Jesuit Refugee Service. Other organisations also collaborated with the church by training people. The Centre for the Study of Violence and Reconciliation (CSVR) trained church dwellers from the refugee community about gender-based violence. The Southern African Centre for Survivors of Torture (SACST) also provided counselling services to the victims of violence and trauma.

---

[22] It has a loose leadership structure, but it is chaired by the bishop and has several subcommittees that are responsible for education, health and the different programmes undertaken at the church.

[23] Bishop Paul Verryn speaking at the Refugee Ministry meeting, Main Sanctuary, CMM, 10 July 2009.

[24] Interview with Bishop Verryn, CMM, Johannesburg, 21 July 2009.

[25] For further information, see http://new.gbgm-umc.org/umcor/newsroom/releases/archives09/journeytohope/

[26] Although it is open every day, this clinic does not make admissions. Patients in need of admission are assisted by the programme called Home Based Care, a programme that takes care of the seriously ill patients, and it is sort of a hospital ward. Volunteers run it from the refugee community.

In sum, the CMM was a very complex microcosm of ad hoc and planned humanitarian and development interventions, and these diverse influences presented diverse internal and external challenges. With every single metre of floor space occupied by refugees, tensions frequently arose amongst the dwellers. At the weekly meetings of the Refugee Ministry,[27] there were always complaints and denunciations of violence, abuse and stealing. Hygiene was a problem, although this was monitored by MSF.[28] Beyond the internal problems, the situation at the Central Methodist Mission also caused many different kinds of tensions and conflicts with the external environment and actors. The politics of becoming visible through refugee work impinged on the religious organisation.

8.4   Occupying the Public: Challenges Inside and Outside the Religious Site

Since 2008, all major events that affected this religious site have been scrupulously covered by newspapers, radio, TV and Internet sources. Indeed, migrants inside the church were well used to being interviewed and approached by journalists. On some occasions, migrants were paid for providing testimonies, and they expected some form of compensation from any other visitor to the church. In a context of extreme poverty and deprivation, inhabitants of the church were vigilant observers of who was approached for an interview – and therefore receiving some sort of compensation – and who was not. When I began openly trying to interview migrants in the building, I was immediately surrounded by other people who demanded to be interviewed and (hopefully, from their perspective) remunerated. This competition for involvement highlights the poverty of the migrants accommodated in the church and the underlying tensions heated by this poverty, especially Zimbabwean ethnic histories and a lack of space. It also illustrated just how in the spotlight the CMM was. Whilst not many academic researchers did work in the church, there had been visits by journalists and broadcasters who were, in practice, entering peoples' living spaces and dredging up difficult memories. For this reason, my research did not directly focus on migrants' opinions and perceptions unless they emerged from informal conversations and direct observation. Much of my attention revolved around the way this religious organisation was occupying the public sphere. As a critical voice inside the broader civil society umbrella, the CMM occupied a central, vibrant role in South Africa's public debate over the last few years, and it is this aspect that I wish to focus on for the remainder of this chapter by expanding upon

---

[27] These are weekly meetings in which refugees, members of external organisations and religious leaders meet to discuss the life, projects and events inside the CMM.

[28] For example, when South Africa was under a cholera epidemic towards the end of 2008, MSF set up a successful strategy to contain the spread of the illness in the overcrowded building. No death for cholera has been registered so far (data from the CMM documents archive).

three major aspects of CMM activities: (1) challenging the ability of the South African state (at a local as well as at a national level) in ensuring human and civil rights to foreign nationals, (2) raising public attention to international events like the crisis in Zimbabwe and the related issue of migration across borders and (3) generating a debate around issues of citizenship, inclusion and exclusion in the post-Apartheid nation-building project.

In South Africa in the post-Apartheid era, the charge of managing domestic migration and international migration, once migrants have negotiated the border, is largely the responsibility of local government. There are many challenges in developing effective responses to migration in Johannesburg, and since 1994, the local government has delivered little in this regard (Wa Kabwe-Segatti and Landau 2008). The CMM has been both vocal and visible in publically criticising these limitations. Until very recently, there has been little collaboration between the local government and the CMM. Although there have been discussions around alternative venues for the refugees, alternative forms of accommodation never materialised. As one migrant respondent explained, '[The government] started late last year, actually around November/December [2008], engaging with civil society and link up to find out how they can help with the refugees. What we have realised is that government does not know how to do things, so they want to partner with NGOs towards furthering those initiatives.'[29]

The church has also appealed to the council for water and electricity exemption without success. In March 2009, Gauteng local government Member of the Executive Council Qedani Dorothy Mahlangu[30] publicly said that Bishop Paul Verryn was exposing refugees at the church to more danger, asserting, 'We are not condoning what he is doing. We condemn it'. However, despite criticising the bishop, Mahlangu promised continued cooperation with him: 'The City of Johannesburg will continue to partner with the Central Methodist Church. We have been approached by the Church. They want to get a building. We are currently processing the issues of them leasing a building.'[31] A representative from the City Council expressed different sentiments: 'We know it is not a shelter; it is a church [...] The City tries to coordinate some of the moves like shifting people to shelters, especially children. But at the moment the Church does not let them go'.[32] In fact, the vision of how the refugees

---

[29] Interview with Annah Moyo, Southern African Centre for the Survivors of Torture (SACST), Johannesburg, 27 July 2009. We observed similar points of view from other interviewees, for example, Ms Geina Mahlatshana, community development worker, and Mr Dawood Moosa, Migrants Help Desk, City of Johannesburg.

[30] When we tried to contact the MEC for Health and Social Development, Ms Qedani Dorothy Mahlangu requesting an interview, the secretary kept asking to phone again later or to send other emails. This happened between July and October 2009. We never interviewed her. Also, Ms Loretta Modise, Office of the Premier (Private Office), and Ms Tuli from the Central Johannesburg Migration Desk refused to be interviewed.

[31] Internet source: www.polity.org.za/article/zim-refugees-shoud-not-stay-in-joburg-church---mec-2009–03–13

[32] Interview with Mr Dawood Mosa, operations manager for the City of Johannesburg Migrant Help Desk, Johannesburg, 06 August 2009.

should be redistributed to better-equipped accommodation varies from the church to the local government. Whilst the local government proposed to split small groups of refugees amongst different available shelters, the bishop opposed this proposal due to his interpretation of community links and well-being:

> People are not boxes, you can't just pick up a group of people and dump them somewhere without recognising that intrinsic to the functioning of the human being is the creation of friendship, community, connection, networking and all that kind of stuff and unfortunately the people in the building have done that. They have turned themselves into community; there are all sorts of things.[33]

This attempt to redistribute the refugees around Johannesburg has also been opposed by two other factors. Firstly, whilst the local government publically attacked the bishop's decisions, it never proposed realistic alternatives to the refugee crisis. Secondly, the great majority of the Zimbabwean refugees did lack trust in South African institutions and felt 'safe' and protected only within the church. Many refused to move to new shelters whilst others came back soon after being moved.

Another major issue that contributed to the visibility of the church in the public was its vociferous critique of the police's technique of detention and intimidation of migrants, the aim which was keeping public areas in inner-city Johannesburg free of refugees. There is sentiment that the South African police force did not do all it could or should have to stem the initial waves of violence, and this has led to a fractious relationship between police authorities, the CMM and refugees. At the very beginning of February 2008, for example, the building was raided by members of the South African Police Service (SAPS) from the Johannesburg metropolitan police office. Up to 1,500 refugees living on the church premises were arrested in a late-night raid to round up illegal immigrants. Bishop Verryn and several refugees complained that they were verbally and physically abused during the raid. The bishop, speaking to the *Mail and Guardian,* said he was verbally abused and shoved by police officers when he asked them why they were breaking down doors and assaulting refugees.[34]

In July 2009, about 350 Zimbabwean refugees who were sleeping in the area surrounding the building because the church was too full to accommodate were arrested for 'loitering'. The arrests were part of the city's pre-World Cup clean-up drive 'Operation Chachamela' (walking on burning coals).[35] As the bishop said:

> For instance you will remember the 358 people who were arrested in the streets for loitering at the beginning of this month [July 2009] so yesterday we had a meeting with all the people. Two things have come up, we will be going to the constitutional court to have struck from the books anything referring to loitering. Because it just seems to be an instrument that

---

[33] Interview with Bishop Verryn, CMM, 21 July 2009.

[34] Mail and Guardian online. 6 February 2008. Refugees return to raided church amid legal wrangles. Online source: www.mg.co.za/article/2008–02–06-refugees-return-to-raided-church-amid-legal-wrangles

[35] Interview with Bianca Tolbom, doctors without borders (MSF), Johannesburg, 22 July 2009.

is used by the police to harass people, very much like the old pass [Apartheid] laws. Then the second thing is we want an interdict against the police so that they may not continue doing this.[36]

In November 2009, the Central Methodist Church, supported by the Legal Resource Centre, Lawyers for Human Rights and the AIDS Law Clinic, turned to the High Court to declare arrests for loitering as unconstitutional. However, a group of shopkeepers around the building publically complained about the high number of refugees who were occupying public spaces around the church building due to the excessive overcrowding, and they took the bishop to court with the case still pending in 2010 at the time of the research. The shop owners complained about the dirt on the street and about security because customers could not freely walk into their shops. On one occasion, the church bought some mobile toilets, and the shops complained that the smell was bad, so they were removed from one street to another until Capello (a coffee shop close to the church) also complained, and the toilets were removed altogether. The shops have closed off neighbouring streets by putting up a fence to separate the church from the shopping area. At the time of writing, this section is closed from 6 p.m. until dawn, which is problematic as this is the section that refugees will occupy in the evening if they are unable to find space inside the church. Captain Dorego's, a restaurant in neighbouring small street, has been particularly opposed to the church, claiming that since the number of Zimbabweans raised after the xenophobic attacks, he experienced a 3% loss in his profit.[37]

Internal tensions were also generated. When Zimbabwean migrants turned to the church, this materially affected the running and organisation of the existing religious community as well as of the religious site itself. This generated a very public debate between the bishop and the church congregants about the compatibility of the two missions of the church, one focused on serving refugees and the other on Christian worship. The religious community, constituted by those who attended the service on a Sunday, was divided on the issue of accommodating refugees in their building. As the church steward said, 'some of the church members are not happy and criticize the Bishop whilst some glorify him, so there is this division in the church'.[38] He added that 'Some of the church members are not happy about the state of the building because a lot of people are staying here, even in the sanctuary where we have services'.[39] A community development workers explained, 'the church goers who go on Sunday are uncomfortable of the situation because there have been reports of muggings around that area but we do not have evidence if the muggers are in the church or not'.[40] During a conversation, the bishop mentioned his

---

[36] Interview with Bishop Paul Verryn, Central Methodist Mission, 21 July 2009.

[37] Interview with Paul DeKlerk – manager and co-owner of Captain Dorego's restaurant, Johannesburg, 27 July 2009.

[38] Interview with Leothere, French teacher and church steward, Central Methodist Church, 3 July 2009.

[39] Ibid.

[40] Interview with Geina Mahaltshana, community development worker, Johannesburg, 04 August 2009.

first experience from xenophobia in Johannesburg was from the congregation itself, when a few refugees were living in the garage and not in the main building: 'The Braamfontein congregation wanted to see me and I arrived and I have never been disrespected as profoundly as I was. They shouted and it was so obscene. I felt like a piece of dirt that had walked into the congregation'.[41]

All these forms of public contestation reached a head in January 2010 when Bishop Paul Verryn was suspended by the Methodist Church of Southern Africa (MCSA). The Methodist Church of Southern Africa's refusal to disclose the reasons for Verryn's suspension fuelled a speculation about the reasons behind it, and refugees, mass media and political parties expressed different opinions.[42] After weeks of confusion, the Central Methodist Church lawyers from the Legal Resources Centre (LRC) revealed that bishop was charged with instituting a legal proceeding (to have an independent guardian appointed to oversee the welfare of the 56 children living in the church) without the authority of the presiding bishop in the Methodist Church of Southern Africa or the executive secretary.[43] These unaccompanied minors were brought to the Soweto Community Centre under the bishop's supervision. Verryn was also charged with making media statements after being instructed not to do so. This was followed by a substantial local, national and international campaign, driven largely through blogs, chatrooms and Facebook, in support of the bishop, once again propelling the church, and the Methodist Church more broadly, into the public eye. On Thursday 29 April 2010, the result of the arbitration process was released – the decision to charge Verryn under the church's laws to discipline and suspend him was set aside, and he was effectively reinstated to his position in the CMM. Since February 2010, partly due to the bishop's court case and the fear that the church would soon close to refugees and partly for the spreading fear of a new wave of xenophobic attacks after the World Cup,[44] the number of refugees at the church has decreased considerably.[45] Some were looking for different accommodation, often leaving Johannesburg for other urban areas, while others opted for a return to Zimbabwe where the political situation seemed to be improving somewhat (Cheesman and Tendi 2010).

---

[41] Conversation with Bishop Verryn in front of the CMM building, Johannesburg, 30 July 2009.

[42] See, for example, http://www.mg.co.za/article/2010–01–29-paul-verryn-what-went-wrong
http://www.news24.com/Content/SouthAfrica/News/1059/411f07caf1bd44a1b66a4f17b0b74b7
c/22–01–2010–10–09/DA_Give_Verryn_some_credit and conversation with Mr Munya in front of the CMM, February 2010 [research assistant].

[43] Facebook support group: http://www.facebook.com/search/?post_form_id=29dd090f32bb92f73
8826879c1fb54fe&q=fre&init=quick&ref=search_preload#!/paulverryn?ref=search Facebook CMM fan page: http://www.facebook.com/pages/Central-Methodist-Church-and-Bishop-Paul-Verryn/16161293029.

[44] These are more than rumours that circulate amongst immigrants. Many have been approached by South African announcing new and more rigorous xenophobic attacks after the World Cup. For similar information, see the *Mail & Guardian* (May 21, 2010) 'Hate attacks may rise again' p. 14.

[45] Conversation with Reason Beremauro, PhD student working at the Methodist Church, Johannesburg, 24 May 2010.

8.5   Conclusion

The diminishing trust towards the South African state in terms of service delivery and the implementation of the promises embedded in the post-1994 nation-building project coincides with the diminishing capacity of the South African state to continue to construct a sense of belonging as well as of believing.[46] Along with these new concerns, we need to analyse new actors and the new spaces that are emerging in response. As Meyer and Moors (2006) stated, the public place is not a bounded entity but rather an evolving space subjected to continuous reconstruction and contestation and it is important to understand these dynamics. A new phase in the post-Apartheid era is emerging, and this is very different from the first 15 years of democracy in the country. The overwhelming enthusiasm of the first democratic decade and trust in the capacity of the state to fill the poverty gap and redistribute resources that perpetuated the alliance between the ANC government and civil society now seems to be replaced with a clear rupture and new contestations and differing visions. In this uncovered public space, religion is returning as a reservoir of cultural autonomy, as well as of moral authority (Cochrane in Bompani and Frahm-Arp 2010). Although religious organisations in post-Apartheid South Africa are not displaying the same level of collaboration and unified action as they did in the struggle, religion nonetheless needs to be understood as a powerful factor in the motivation of individuals and it generates capacities and strengths (ibid.). The ability of one church in inner-city Johannesburg to accommodate so many people, raise awareness and stimulate debate – both positive and negative – is testament to this.

In the often-dramatic interactions between migrants, locals and the South African state,[47] the Central Methodist Mission offered a 'safe' or at least safer place than the alternative of relying on a benign – and sometimes hostile – state. This case once again highlighted the role played by religious practices and religious institutions in positively helping internal dynamics amongst migrants, in keeping a sense of familiarity and relationship with their homelands ('I was a Christian in Zimbabwe and I am a Christian in South Africa'[48]) and with it the creation of a sense of protection in a foreign context (Landau 2009; Hansen et al. 2009). Migrants knew of the existence of this 'safe' place already before leaving Zimbabwe and through the visibility that this church received in the media. This place for many migrants became the only 'safe' alternative given the lack of possible solutions offered by the state and other groups within society.

---

[46] Drawing from Grace Davie's explanation of secularisation and churches in the United Kingdom, see Davie (1994).

[47] From this research in the CMM and from several research projects pursued by the African Centre for Migration and Society , the University of the Witwatersrand in Johannesburg, it emerged that migrants frequently experienced xenophobia from state agencies like in hospitals, from the police and at public offices. For more information on the issue, see, for example, Neocosmos (2008).

[48] My conversation with Joe, young Zimbabwean at the CMM, Johannesburg, 20 July 2009.

Embracing the cause and defence of these migrants, however, for the CMM meant embracing the politics of becoming visible, a turn which threatened at various times the well-being of the church community as well as the migrants. In coming out from the 'private' space of the religious community, religious organisations become subject to the expectations and demands of a range of other actors, as we have seen in this chapter. As Meyer and Moors, in their analysis of religion in the public in non-western contexts, argue, 'processes of mass mediation impinge on religious organisations as well as on individual experiences, and have major implications for the role and place of religion in society' (Meyer and Moors 2006, p. 6). What this example illustrates is the often precarious position of religious organisations which offer services that, for political, cultural, social or economic reasons, are not offered by the state. In the case of CMM, the services provided were essential for the state to be able to retain an image of progressive nationhood, but they were as an uneasy reminder of an underlying problem that the state has little capacity to solve. At various moments, the tensions within the church and with the local community erupted into the public sphere, focusing attention on the effectiveness or failure of the church activities, rather than the absence of state responsibility. The case also illustrates that in light of this dynamic process following Apartheid, religion and religious institutions are re-emerging as new public actors in South Africa. How the new focus on moral authority will shape the public sphere remains to be seen.

References

Bompani, B. 2006. Mandela mania: Mainline churches in post-Apartheid South Africa. *Third World Quarterly* 27(6): 1137–1149.

Bonner, P., and L. Segal. 1998. *Soweto: A history*. Cape Town: Maskew Miller Longman.

Cheesman, N., and B.M. Tendi. 2010. Power-sharing in comparative perspective: The dynamics of 'unity government' in Kenya and Zimbabwe. *The Journal of Modern African Studies* 48: 203–299.

Cochrane, J. 2010. Health and the uses of religion: Recovering the political proper? In *Development and politics from below. Exploring religious spaces in the African state*, ed. B. Bompani and A. Frahm-Arp. London: Palgrave-MacMillan.

Davie, G. 1994. *Religion in Britain since 1945: Believing without belonging*. Oxford: Blackwell Publishers.

Ellis, S. 2010. Development and invisible worlds. In *Development and politics from below. Exploring religious spaces in the African state*, ed. B. Bompani and A. Frahm-Arp. London: Palgrave-MacMillan.

Elphick, R., and R. Davenport (eds.). 1998. *Christianity in South Africa: A political, social and cultural history*. Cape Town: David Philip.

Gifford, P. (ed.). 1995. *The Christian churches and the democratisation of Africa*. Leiden: Brill Press.

Googhew, D. 2000. Growth and decline in South Africa's churches, 1960–1991. *Journal of Religion in Africa* 3(3): 344–369.

Greenstein, R., V. Heinrich, and K. Naidoo. 1998. *Civil society and the state in South Africa: Past legacies, present realities and future prospects*. Johannesburg: Community Agency for Social Enquiry and Sangoco.

Habermas, J. 1991. *The structural transformation of the public sphere. An inquiry into a category of bourgeois society*. Cambridge, MA: MIT Press.

Habermas, J. 2006. Religion in the public sphere. *European Journal of Philosophy* 14(1): 1–25.

Hansen, B.T., C. Jeannerat, and S. Samadia. 2009. Introduction: Portable spirits and itinerant people: Religion and migration in South Africa in a comparative perspective. *African Studies* 68(2): 187–196.

IOM. 2009. *Towards tolerance, law, and dignity: Addressing violence against foreign nationals in South Africa*. International Organization for Migration (IOM), Regional Office for Southern Africa; Internet source: www.iom.org.za.

Landau, L. 2009. Living within and beyond Johannesburg: Exclusion, religion and emerging forms of being. *African Studies* 68(2): 197–214.

Landau, L. 2010. Loving the Alien? Citizenship, law and the future in South Africa's demonic society. *African Affairs* 109(435): 213–230.

Makumbe, J. 1998. Is there a civil society in Africa? *International Affairs* 74(2): 305–317.

Mayekiso, M. 1996. *Township politics: Civic struggle for a New South Africa*. New York: Monthly Review Press.

Meyer, B., and A. Moors. 2006. Introduction. In *Religion, mass media and the public space*, ed. B. Meyer and A. Moors. Bloomington: Indiana University Press.

Neocosmos, M. 2008. The politics of fear and the fear of politics: Reflections on xenophobic violence in South Africa. *Journal of Asian and African Studies* 43(6): 586–594.

Nyamnjoh, F.B. 2006. *Insiders and outsiders. Citizenship and xenophobia in contemporary Southern Africa*. London: Zed Books.

Phakathi, S. 2010. The response of churches to the May 2008 xenophobic violence. In *South African Civil Society and Xenophobia*, ed. D. Everatt. Collection of case studies and reports available on CD.

Raftopoulos, B., and A. Mlambo (eds.). 2009. *Becoming Zimbabwe. A history from the pre-colonial period to 2008*. Hararw: Weaver Press.

Ranger, T. 1989. Missionaries, migrants and the Manyika: The invention of ethnicity in Zimbabwe. In *The creation of tribalism in Southern Africa*, ed. L. Vail. Berkeley: University of California Press.

SACBC's Press Release. 12 February 2010. *Appeal to South African leaders: Is your sexual morality making you a worthy role model for the youth?* Source available at: www.sacbc.org.za/Site/index.php?option=com_content&view=article&id=410&Itemid=100.

SAHRC. 2010. Report on the SAHRC investigation into issues of rule of law, justice and impunity arising out of the 2008 public violence against non-nationals. Pretoria.

StatsSA. 2004. *Census 2001 by province, gender, religion (derived) and population group*. Pretoria: Statistics SA.

Taylor, C. 2007. *A secular age*. Boston: Harvard University Press.

Tingle, R. 1992. *Revolution or reconciliation? Struggle in the church in South Africa*. London: Christian Studies Centre.

Wa Kabwe-Segatti, A., and L. Landau (eds.). 2008. *Migration in post-apartheid South Africa. Challenges and questions to policy-makers*. Paris: Agence Française de Dèvelopment.

Walshe, P. 1991. South Africa: Prophetic Christianity and the liberation movement. *The Journal of Modern African Studies* 29(1): 27–60.

Chapter 9
Homo Religiosus? Religion and Immigrant Subjectivities*

David Ley and Justin Tse

9.1 Introduction

> In everyday life, as in the social sciences, there is an ever greater demand for a *hermeneutics of the stranger* (Beck 2010: 179).
> I was a stranger and you invited me in. (Matthew 25: 35)

It is surely the best of times to be a geographer of religion and belief systems. We have moved from the blasé end of everything era—the so-called end of history with the termination of the Cold War, the imputed end of geography with globalisation's level playing fields and the putative end of religion with the seemingly irrepressible advance of secularisation—to a period that is both politically and culturally charged in its preoccupation with religious difference and intellectually reawakened to critical questions of faith and interfaith relations in national and global society. No less important, the geography of religion has itself undergone transformation from an exercise largely of description and classification to a more ambitious programme of interpretation and explanation (Kong 2001; Duncan 2004; Yorgason and della Dora 2009).

Our approach to the geography of religion here will come from an interest in the place of religion in international migration and from the viewpoint of authors who are sympathetic to religious worldviews. The argument will be developed on the basis of the religion we know best, Christianity as it has evolved in Euro-America.

*An earlier draft of this chapter was prepared by Ley as the keynote address to the Geography of Religion and Belief Systems Specialty Group at the Association of American Geographers conference in Washington, DC in April 2010. This version benefited from lively discussion at the GORABS session and a critical reading by Reinhard Henkel. It also includes significant additions by Justin Tse.

D. Ley (✉) • J. Tse
Department of Geography, University of British Columbia, Vancouver, BC, Canada
e-mail: dley@geog.ubc.ca

P. Hopkins et al. (eds.), *Religion and Place: Landscape, Politics and Piety*,
DOI 10.1007/978-94-007-4685-5_9, © Springer Science+Business Media Dordrecht 2013

While this vantage point is selective in its subject matter, it is broad enough to generate significant questions, especially in light of recent migration trends and consequences.[1]

The transformation in the significance of religion in practice as well as in theory is by now a familiar thesis and may be illustrated by the following events we witnessed. In 1996, a large research proposal was submitted to the government of Canada to establish an immigration research centre in Vancouver as part of a larger national network. Each proposal was to recognise and selectively incorporate from around 100 items of immigration policy of interest to government. Not a single item among the 100, *not one*, addressed immigrant religion. In 2002, a second submission was required for funding renewal for an additional research term. Again, there was a government prospectus identifying policy fields for recognition; among these bulleted items, the topic of immigrant religion was now prominent.

This is simply one indicator of a broader trend highlighted by Kong (2010) who counted eight different journals in human geography and related fields that had recently run special issues on religion. The geography of religion has moved to front stage in such fields as population and immigration studies (Bramadat and Koenig 2009), social and cultural geography (Yorgason and della Dora 2009) and not least geopolitics (Agnew 2006). Implicit in this transformation has been a longer-term shift from description to explanation and from the classification of landscape forms and distribution maps to a more challenging intellectual agenda of interpretation and explanation (cf. Henkel 2005). But that step into process and meaning requires, we will argue, an interrogation of the ontological and epistemological presuppositions of religious phenomena as social facts.[2]

National and international political anxieties may be one driver of this new agenda, but more basic conceptual work is also going on. In this chapter, after first reviewing the changing social geography of immigrant religions, we discuss contributions to conceptual innovation and in particular two significant and demanding books challenging the social science of religion from the perspectives of theology and religious philosophy. Finally, we experiment in an interpretation of immigrant subjectivity and religious adherence that tries to project the thinking of these two books from the position they advocate—that is, a position that argues for a theological reading of the migrant. We specify the separate existence of *homo religiosus* (Eliade 1959), the shy cousin of that better-known extrovert, *homo economicus*. From an understanding of the immigrant lifeworld and following the prompting of theological knowledge, we aim to account for the vitality of the immigrant church. In response to Ulrich Beck's (2010) challenge, this task will aim to provide a *religious* hermeneutics of the immigrant as stranger.

---

[1] For a thoughtful consideration of the reflexive dimensions of religious research in terms of the author's own religious identity, see the argument (and references) in Olson (2009) and Bailey et al. (2009).

[2] For a more philosophical approach to these issues, see Dewsbury and Cloke (2009).

9.2   Description: Geographies of Immigrant Religion

For a cultural field where we might expect tradition and stability to dominate, the social geographies of religion are shifting with surprising speed. As older Christian denominations in the global north founder in membership, newer streams of Pentecostalism and Evangelicalism are advancing on the world stage, incorporating conservative theology with contemporary expressive worship and sometimes significant forms of public discipleship, both in Catholic as well as Protestant traditions. These newer movements are concentrated in the global south (Jenkins 2006). Among the broadly defined family of global Pentecostals, for example, estimated at 250 million, while 20 million are in the United States, the largest grouping is the estimated 72 million Pentecostals in China (Martin 2002; Thomas 2009), a portentous statistic whose implications we have scarcely considered.

Indeed, the momentum in global Christianity is now concentrated in the emerging societies of the developing world. The renewal of Catholicism in Latin America depends on charismatic and liberation theology movements engaged in service delivery and justice and righteousness initiatives among the church of the poor (Olson 2006; Holden and Jacobson 2009). It is Latin American and Southeast Asian candidates who increasingly fill the seminaries and the pulpits of the Catholic Church in North America. In global Anglicanism, numerical primacy has also shifted to the global south. Nigeria has more members of the denomination than any other country, while in terms of religious attendance, there are more regular churchgoing Anglicans in the small nation of Uganda than in England.

Global immigration flows are carrying those effervescent religious beliefs and practices into the spiritually more somnolent countries of the north. Working against the conceptual grain of godless Europe, the historian Philip Jenkins (2007), in his book *God's Continent*, has many illustrations of the renewal of congregational life in Europe as a result of immigration from the global south. Evangelicals, charismatics and Pentecostals doubled in number in Europe from 1970 to 2000. In part, these groups represent home-grown renewal efforts: in west central London, for example, the two evangelical power houses of All Souls, Langham Place and Holy Trinity Brompton are Anglican mother churches with satellite congregations and a surprisingly broad range of social as well as spiritual ministries. Holy Trinity Brompton pioneered the Alpha course, an out-of-church programme introducing the foundations of Christianity to a society with limited religious literacy. Alpha has now diffused to millions of participants through Europe and the English-speaking world and has been described by the archbishop of Paris as one of Protestantism's two biggest gifts to Catholicism.

Despite such evidence of indigenous renewal, Jenkins (2007) suggests that the strongest infusion of Christian spiritual energy has come from immigrants. He notes that Africans lead four of the ten largest churches in Britain, typically with a charismatic or Pentecostal style of worship. The English Church Census of 2005 showed that non-white church attendance was growing, exceeding its share of the population by two or three times; 44% of churchgoers in London were Black; and a further 14% were other non-white worshippers (Evangelical Alliance 2006). Even among Evangelicals and Pentecostals, growth is occurring primarily among non-white groups. This is not just an English phenomenon. Throughout Europe, immigrants, sometimes students, have founded transnational churches that have grown rapidly. In Hamburg, a Ghanaian started a church in 1992 that now has a dozen offshoots elsewhere in Germany and some 60 plants back in Ghana, all in little more than a decade; in Ukraine, a congregation established by a Nigerian student in 1994 has planted 150 daughter congregations, spreading to Russia and other European countries (Jenkins 2007).

It is a similar story in the United States, although the mainstream culture is certainly more supportive of religious expression. While there is considerable variation in the religious experience of new immigrants (Levitt 2007), old truths are being reworked. The *Religion and the New Immigrants* project funded by the Pew Charitable Trusts has chronicled the transformative impact of diverse immigrant religions in seven principal gateway cities (Ebaugh and Chafetz 2000; Miller et al. 2001; Foley and Hoge 2007). Immigration is redefining in particular the profile of American Catholicism. Despite our stereotype of the Irish and Italian basis of an American Catholicism marginalised by an Anglo-Saxon Protestant majority (Hauerwas 1990), a large survey in 2007 estimated that close to half of adult American Catholics aged 18–40 are now Latino and that this growing ethnic population over time is diluting the Protestant ascendancy in the United States (Pew 2008). Moreover, more than half of Catholic Latinos describe themselves as charismatic, introducing spontaneity and more expressive spirituality to formal liturgies and providing social services to their congregations.[3] While immigrants are also the major adherents of non-western religions, the survey indicated that three-quarters of immigrants to the USA are Christian, a figure only slightly below that of the native-born and a proportion that has been steady for 30 years.

Canadian data also show the transformative effects of immigrant religions (Bramadat and Koenig 2009). In recent years, immigrants with Christian affiliations have fallen to less than half of total landings, while non-western religions are claimed by a third of new Canadians, and this share has been steadily rising (Kunz 2009). Among the native-born in contrast, non-western religions account for only about 5% of the population. But a clear transition is underway; Catholic affiliation, primed by immigration, rose slightly between 1991 and 2001, while Protestant numbers fell, and non-western religions grew between 80 and 130% during the decade, fastest among Muslims.

Growing religious diversity has led to varying national responses by the state, from secular assimilationism in France to the attempt to accommodate religious diversity within a multicultural paradigm in Canada. In contrast to the recent Swiss referendum that banned the construction of minarets on mosques (Traynor 2009), one sign of a more conciliatory environment in Canada is the successful sitcom, *Little Mosque on the Prairie,* now in its fourth season, which attempts to naturalise everyday Muslim family life in the apple pie context of the small prairie town. Learning perhaps from this pedagogy, Prince George, a small city in British Columbia,

---

[3] One example among many of the new Catholicism is the Cathedral of Christ the Light in Oakland (California), where services are held in an equal mix of English, Vietnamese and Spanish.

has approached construction of its first mosque as a place-marketing strategy to attract immigrant Muslims, notably professionals and entrepreneurs (Armstrong 2009). Elsewhere in Canada, however, relations between immigrant religious groups and a secular public sphere are less happy, describable in Quebec's language of 'reasonable accommodation' rather than the open-armed welcome promised in Prince George. Indeed, geographers have noted that Muslim migrants have sometimes experienced undue discrimination and struggle to express their identity in Canada (D'Addario et al. 2008), an experience common throughout western countries (see Dwyer 1999; Dunn 2004; Hopkins 2007).

Prince George has seemingly made a discovery emphasised by the sociologist of religion, Warner (2000: 273), that '*religion is typically salient for immigrants*'. We are reminded of interviews with immigrants in Vancouver where migration has sharpened a formerly misty or even opaque religious lens (Ley 2010). Mr. and Mrs. Yip told us:

> And when we were leaving Hong Kong we were in the peak of our profession or business… That's why we were too busy and we find too little time giving to the family and the kids at that time. So when we came over to Canada, and we first get away from that fast living we maintain the family life. This is the first priority we need to have, otherwise it ruins the meaning of coming to Canada if we put all the time into working and still neglecting our kids. We find we can adjust so well here. This is what I think because God changed my point of value… (now) we have the religion, and have a change in mind what is the priority in life.

Writing of the same immigration wave in Toronto, Lee (1991) found that 'the number of new converts is phenomenal'. In the United States, too, immigrant Chinese conversion to Christianity is a substantial current trend (Yang 1998; Zhang 2006). Equally notable is the intensity of belief (Chen 2006). So is the conversion rate and depth of conviction of Korean immigrants (Kim and Kim 2001). Whereas 25% of Koreans profess Christianity in their homeland, 50% of migrants to North America are Christian, and once landed, that figure rises to 75% among the population resident in North America (Warner 2001; Min 2002).[4] As church historian Timothy Smith (1978) once observed, immigration is a 'theologizing experience', establishing a new map of meaning following uprooting and relocation.

This description of the growing significance of immigrant religion provides the backdrop against which we turn to recent conceptual thinking on religious subjectivities. The more abstract conceptual discussion will provide tools to return to the vitality of the immigrant church in the final section, moving beyond description to interpretation.

9.3   Conceptualisation: Approaching Religious Belief

Of course, immigrant religion had not been ignored in earlier versions of the geography of religion. Landscape descriptions of ethnic churches, pilgrimage sites and even cemeteries were the remit of a cultural geography that saw its task to be the

---

[4] For further examples of the vitality of immigrant religion, see Samers (2010: 284–5).

description, classification and mapping of material cultural forms. So, too, social geographers mapped religious adherence from the census and other data bases; particularly notable are the several atlases of religion published in the United States in recent years. Such atlases are significant achievements to be sure, but their maps offer an incomplete scholarly project (Ley 2002). The movement beyond pattern to process has been evident in human geography for several decades. An early advocate was the social geographer, Jones (1972), with his celebrated complaint that 'atlases of social data are rather like cases of butterflies—very pretty and telling us something, but the butterflies are dead'. So too cultural landscapes are no longer regarded simply as the inert containers of unproblematised religious forms; they may also be a means of reproducing not only spiritual values but also, as Jim Duncan has shown, social and political hierarchies (Duncan 2004).

However, moving beyond form and distribution introduces the challenging task of interpretation and explanation. What categories are appropriate in making sense of religious meaning? Bailey et al. (2009) offer an important lesson as they reflexively ponder their interaction with a Methodist archive in the West of England.[5] The problem the authors recognise is that 'we ourselves are figuratively, literally, theoretically and spiritually in motion through the archive that we have constructed' (2009: 255). In an almost perfectly executed but fully unanticipated experiment, the authors looked at the Methodist archive of nineteenth-century religious practices from three different personal perspectives on Christian life and spirituality. These varying standpoints led to different selections and emphases in their use of the archive. In a significant conclusion, they acknowledge that collegial commentary on their own differences toward the archive led to a refining of the overall research product.

But their deliberations led to a deeper question than the positionality of individual researchers, important though this is. In their conclusion, the authors note that 'Methodism, and religion more generally, broke out of our frames of reference, resisted the narratives we sought to impose, and forced us to look with fresh eyes' (2009: 266). One researcher acknowledged that 'for me, religion is always social' and 'no more special than that' (2009: 260). But the translation of religious experience to social facts and no more imposes some categorical violence upon a religious experience claiming to be much more than social. The three co-authors wisely consider this, wondering 'whether it is possible, within the epistemological and methodological terms of social science, to study religious phenomena without subjecting them to reductionist arguments' (2009: 257). Stump (2008: 370) is equally aware of these dangers, noting 'reductionist interpretations that cast religious concerns purely in terms of material benefits miss [the] compelling character of religious belief as a factor in human behavior'.

These are powerful insights and they bring us to a door opened from the other side by theologians, who know more than a thing or two about hermeneutics from their long-standing focus on the meaning of religious texts. Here, we consider two

---

[5] Such reflexivity was a central theme of the humanistic geography of the 1970s and 1980s; perhaps the first statement on reflexivity appeared in Anne Buttimer's *Values in Geography* (1974). Significantly, Buttimer was writing at that time from within the context of a Catholic order.

major theological works that make a bold attempt to engage social science. Both are large, demanding books with ambitious objectives that proceed from a historically rooted Catholic tradition. *A Secular Age* is the bridge-building work of Taylor (2007), political philosopher, scholar of religion and recent winner of the Templeton Prize. Taylor's objective is to trace and critique the *experience* of secularism in everyday life as it has evolved through the modern period. A more prophetic and provocative volume is *Theology and Social Theory: Beyond Secular Reason* by theologian, Milbank (2006). Milbank offers an ambitious synthesis of different themes in the meeting of Christianity and secular social science in order to recuperate a *theological* reading of religious phenomena that escapes precisely those reductionist arguments identified by Bailey and his co-authors.[6]

Both authors write as social democrats in public policy. Taylor has run for parliament in Canada for the New Democratic Party, while Milbank is motivated by a desire to re-energise socialist hope against European neo-liberalism, for he regards socialism as Christianity's 'modern child' (2006: xiv).[7] A progressive politics is important for both authors.

Each book argues for the historicism of social science as it engages Christian belief. The social science of religion is not some objective scientific view from nowhere debunking arbitrary and malleable religious phenomena as this relationship has sometimes been cast. From a genealogy of the origins of the sociology of religion, Milbank (2006: 4) provocatively suggests that 'theology encounters in sociology not only a theology, and indeed a church in disguise, but a theology and a church dedicated to promoting a certain secular consensus'. Taylor (2007: 428) also presses the point that secular social science is not a superior and neutral vantage point; any claim for neutrality in the treatment of religion in the academy is 'bogus', for suspicion of religion has been internalised in the taken-for-granted world of the academy (2007: 560). The lifeworld of scholarship is value-impregnated, and such embedded values as materialism and sceptical detachment are sufficiently naturalised that they only become visible in open discussion with other viewpoints—like the reflexive exchanges of the three authors who engaged each other's concealed presuppositions as they worked with the Methodist archive. Both Taylor and Milbank deconstruct a social science that regards religion as an exception, a residual presence of 'sacred archipelagos' in an ocean of secular normality (Wilford 2009). Milbank is characteristically vigorous in his rebuttal: 'all twentieth-century sociology of religion can be exposed as a secular policing of the sublime' (2006:106).

---

[6] The books have a related, perhaps a common, project, although Taylor has a more accessible and conciliatory style. In the conclusion of *A Secular Age,* Taylor claims that his study is complementary to Milbank's. What he achieves for vernacular and everyday society, Milbank undertakes as an intellectual history.

[7] His 'Radical Orthodoxy' school has formed a putative political party, the 'Red Tories', in the United Kingdom and Canada led by theologian Philip Blond (see Hauerwas 2000a). Red Tories marry a traditionalist emphasis on the family with a communitarian ethic that is socialist in economic policy.

   The authors take their discussion further than deconstructing a sociology of religion that takes its marching orders from materialist ideologies. Taylor (2007) rejects the critique of secularisation as a single, accomplished project. He observes what he calls the 'nova effect', the splintering and recombination of both religious and materialist world views into a postmodern bricolage. He notes too how religious renewal represents spiritual experience as a new charismatic movement displaces the sclerosis of institutional religion. The continuing cycle of religious renewal and forgetfulness repeats the historic story of Judaeo-Christian religion in the Bible, where in cycles sometimes lasting several centuries, a new awakening followed periods of spiritual backsliding and syncretism. So too the Reformation and Counter-Reformation achieved a fresh valuing of the immediacy of the divine, displacing the institutional mediation and hypocrisy of the medieval church. Is the age of secularisation, we might ask, merely another such period of lapsed religiosity to be succeeded by a new charismatic awakening? And might the Pentecostal-Evangelical movement provide the outline of that renewal?

   Milbank (2006) squarely addresses appropriate categories for understanding religion. A typical social science model treats religion as a social fact to be explained by other social facts, but such a move abstracts religion from the theological context that gives it shape and meaning. Consider again those atlases of religion with their choropleth maps of religious affiliation. The exercise of mapping is an abstraction that removes church membership from any religious context, dumbing it down to homogenous responses that are counted and may then be correlated against other social facts, such as social class or regional location (Ley 2002). Here, Milbank's sharp critique gains traction, for the only conversion on view is the conversion of a religious act into a social fact. This is what he means when he speaks of the policing of religious life, the reduction of its mysteries to material visualisation, in our case to numbers and spatial distributions, with the search for covariances against other social facts.[8] He is arguing against such categorical violence, the imposition of modernity's iron cage over religious experience.

   Milbank's argument resonates with Asad's (2003) critique of secular approaches to Islam, which contends that many western readings impose a nineteenth-century liberal Protestant view that reduces Islam to a belief system without taking into account Islamic theological praxis. Masuzawa (2005) argues that these impositions tend usually to be Eurocentric forms of Orientalism, creating fantasies about eastern religions (see also Milbank 2006: 88). What is being resisted in such critiques is the imperial colonisation of the sacred by the secular—or to put it in starker geographical terms, the continued colonisation of the religiously vibrant global south by the assumptions of the global north.

   What is Milbank's solution? He argues that one cannot abstract religious life from its own belief system; personal and social religious life is embedded *within* the system of belief and practice, not outside it (2006: 90–1, 122). As Hauerwas (2000b)

---

[8] Compare Grace Davie's (1994) criticism of the inadequacy of church membership data in assessing the prevalence of 'believing without belonging'.

contends, categories for examining religious practice must therefore be drawn from the theology in question because religion is practised by a community of believers. To abstract practice from a praxis-oriented community is to commit epistemic violence on the religion. This position is close to Roger Stump's assessment: 'If adherents themselves, reflexively or not, understand and legitimise their own thoughts and actions in relation to their religious system, additional models or assumptions seeking explanation from nonreligious factors may be neither necessary nor useful' (Stump 2008: 371). In the final part of this chapter, we will experiment with this approach, returning to the vitality of immigrant religious practice with an account not from sociological reasoning (cf. Warner 2000) but rather shaped in terms of religious language and categories. This may be unfamiliar to readers, but is it any different from an argument that might follow neoclassical, Marxist or Foucauldian language and categories? Indeed, perhaps what *is* odd is that such an exposition should be unusual in the first place, an indication of the marginalisation of religious culture and meanings that Taylor and Milbank identify in the social science canon.[9]

9.4 Interpretation: The Vitality of the Immigrant Church

Milbank (2006) observes how the will to power is an influential position in some versions of contemporary social science, both as the voice of scientific authority and also in the preoccupation with power as a category. In contrast, he adds, Christianity expounds an ethic of weakness. Paradigmatically, Jesus, the Son of God, assumed the frailty of human form and was constantly in the company of the weak and the outcast, the sick, the poor and those marginalised by race, class, gender and age. But the rich and the powerful—including a worldly religious establishment—commonly opposed him, seeking to preserve their power and privilege. Their hubris blocked acceptance of his message of hope, discipleship and reconciliation with God. Even though each of us desires (in our own terms) what Taylor calls 'fullness' in life (2007: 769–70), the goals and standing of the rich and the powerful easily blind their spiritual vision and lead to their preoccupation with worldly goals. The Biblical parable of the rich fool is directed squarely against such a personality, so absorbed in material acquisition that he is blind to spiritual life (Luke 12: 15–21). This is a persistent theme in Jesus' teaching: 'The good news is preached to the poor' (Matthew 11:5); 'But many who are first will be last, and the last first' (Mark 10:31); unequivocally, 'Woe to you who are rich' (Luke 6:24); and in the famous analogy, 'It is easier for a camel to pass through the eye of a needle than for a rich man to enter the kingdom of God' (Mark 10:25).[10]

---

[9] 'Indeed, the exclusion/irrelevance of religion is often part of the unnoticed background of social science, history, philosophy, psychology' (Taylor 2007: 429). Stump makes a similar point from within the geography of religion: 'the influences of secularisation on social scientists themselves may have contributed as well to the de-emphasising of the study of religion' (Stump 2008: 369).

[10] See Ringma (2009) for a brief review of key Biblical texts.

So we would expect from a theological perspective to find the church to be primarily the church of the poor, and so it is in global terms, with the ascendancy of the global south and the erosion of religious faith in the richer global north. We would expect too in North America to find the church well represented among the marginalised.[11] And so it is. The black church like the Latino church is earnest in its mission, advancing both axes of the Cross, vertically, seeking the divine, and also horizontally, oriented to faith-based social justice (*Economist* 2009; Day 2001).

If the poor are marginalised from worldly gain, the immigrant confronts multidimensional marginality, palpable enough that care and hospitality for the foreigner or stranger is a frequent Biblical injunction (e.g. Matthew 25:35; Hebrews 13:2), for the stranger is disoriented and vulnerable in the new world in which she finds herself. Consider the phenomenological essay on the subjectivity of the stranger by Schuetz (1944), inspired by his own experience as a refugee in the United States after fleeing fascist Europe. For the stranger, social and cultural life are disorienting, experienced not 'as a protecting shelter at all but as a labyrinth in which he has lost all sense of his bearings' (507). In his radical disengagement from the space in which he finds himself, writes Schuetz, the immigrant 'is a man without a history' (1944:502), anticipating Oscar Handlin's (1951) characterisation a few years later of the European peasant in America as *The Uprooted*.

The vulnerability of the immigrant goes beyond social and cultural illegibility, amplified by a failure to speak the dominant language. Economically, downward mobility is a common experience at least in the early years of settlement but sometimes for much longer. Such downgrading involves not only material assets but also status and reputation. The multiple stressors of immigrant life may also include isolation from family members, with transnational family fragmentation separating members across continental borders. It is this broader category of 'the poor', including status as well as material poverty, that theologian Green (1994) discerns in his reading of allusions by Jesus to 'the poor'. So, too, poverty for international migrants in the twentieth and twenty-first centuries is not simply material deprivation; it is also about the stripping away of status.

We are not speaking abstractly here about the immigrant condition, but from the evidence of interviews with immigrants who came to Canada from middle-class, even upper middle-class, backgrounds in East Asia in the 1980s and 1990s (Ley 2010). This overseas Chinese population landed in Canada and found themselves in scarcely anticipated conditions of vulnerability. Many spoke no English or very poor English, and the simplest everyday tasks became a demanding project. Economic failure is pervasive among a cohort whose visa depended on their economic success in their countries of origin. Consider these dire economic experiences:

> I have been very depressed since we came here…We failed in everything we tried. We bought a commercial property, a retail store, but we were deceived. When we invested in a restaurant we lost the money…the business failed we lost all of our money. I invested $100,000 but we lost it all in two years.

---

[11] *The Guardian's* correspondent, Madeleine Bunting (2009), contrasts the poor immigrant Bible readers on her London bus with the middle-class movement to place anti-Christian advertisements on the same bus fleet.

So too:

> We had to adjust to the situation of being unemployed. We had to start our business from scratch. We could hardly face it…We just tried to make enough to cover our expenses…It's more stressful here…We really don't know what to do, we are kind of, at a loss, we are confused.

Or again:

> Lots of my friends started business here in a new environment. But they don't know the rules of the game and use Hong Kong knowledge, and it doesn't work in this place. They have no local knowledge and most of their investments are failures.

This was an abiding outcome. When the instructor in an English class for overseas Chinese immigrants asked how many had lost significant sums of money in Canada, all 30 adults in the class raised their hands.

Economic failure blights family life, but the loss of face hits men worse. An insightful retired businessman shared his assessment of his cohort of Hong Kong and Taiwanese immigrants:

> …95 % of male immigrants feel upset, feel embarrassed, feel very bad… around 35–50… men in this age usually feel upset because they have lost their self-confidence… their job, lost their respect.

A church elder confirmed that immigrant men 'feel ashamed that they have no real status in this society'. In such circumstances, it was very easy for men to return to East Asia, replenishing both their economic and symbolic capital in the business regime where they had previously known success. But family fragmentation, the dreaded condition of the astronaut family, brought fresh stresses to both the lone husband in East Asia and the exiled wife and children in Canada (Lam 1994; Waters 2002). Offshore wealth scarcely made good the costs of emotional separation: 'Don't tell me I have a big house', protested an astronaut husband briefly reunited with his family in Vancouver, 'this is a house of tears' (Ley 2010).

Reviewing the early years of this middle-class migration in Toronto, Lee (1991) had noted that 'immigration for most people approximates a real life crisis'. Our Vancouver interviews both with immigrants and the pastors and elders of Chinese and Korean churches amply confirmed this assessment (Ley 2008). Heightened isolation and pervasive anxieties shaped immigrant subjectivities. A pastor told us:

> When they first arrive in Canada, they feel very much alone and scared. The Church offers a community that will embrace them where they are at, Christian or non-Christian. The church offers cooked meals, places to stay… advice on the educational system… The church becomes their home.

Counselling by the church, other voluntary organisations and medical practitioners is a critical service to address both chronic and acute stress. It is a skilled practice, for overseas Chinese culture typically denies mental health problems like depression, and the counselling must be offered in culture-specific terms (Shen et al. 2006; Chen et al. 2010). One pastor told us:

> Some [immigrants] are in real need because they contemplate suicide and come from broken families… There are many cases in which the fathers are being depressed or stressed because they can no longer properly be the head of the family household…

A distinctive phenomenology of place accompanied such everyday struggles. In interviews, the church was described as 'a home away from home', 'a safe place to grow and feel accepted', 'a non-threatening place' and 'a refuge', away from the daily trials outside, 'where many are lonely and stressed'. The sharpness of this emotional distinction between inside and outside was marked, providing a particular spatial profile to Beck's 'hermeneutics of the stranger'. Moreover, forced detachment from the world of mainstream Canada created a condition akin to the Biblical profile of Christian life as lived in creative tension with the world. The apostle Peter wrote that his readers in principle should be 'aliens and strangers in the world' (1 Peter 2:11), while elsewhere, we read that Christians have a citizenship in another country and thus are 'aliens and strangers on earth…looking for a country of their own' (Hebrews 11: 14). Such 'resident alien' detachment does not mean indifference or non-participation in society as is clear from the example of Jesus himself, but it does mean a different calculus of claims and accountability and a separate teleology of spiritual hopes and disciplines (Hauerwas and Willimon 1989). Here, we are drawing close to the Christian prototype of the pilgrim or spiritual traveller, exemplified in *Pilgrim's Progress,* where one is a stranger passing through the world, avoiding its enticing distractions, en route to a spiritual destination. While this ideal type is rarely lived out, the enforced separation of the immigrant from worldly convention and comfort comes much closer to such detachment than the experience of many non-migrants. So the early years of immigrant settlement serve as a transitional liminal period, a time of disrupted habits, 'betwixt and between' the comforts of living in 'normal' society (Turner 2002). Consider one respondent's acknowledgement of such liminality as a motive for spiritual growth (Tse 2011):

> From being a powerful person, I became powerless… I looked back to see that God wanted me [to come] here. If I stayed in Hong Kong, I would be powerful, powerful, powerful, going up, but God wanted to make me powerless. I needed to be humble… I belong to God. He leads me. Good thing I have religion. If not, I would have gone mad.

Like Victor Turner's view of the liminality of pilgrimage, the immigrant's space and time apart facilitate an intensification of religious practice and commitment. Voluntary or involuntary non-incorporation into mainstream society provides opportunity for spiritual development.

The vitality of the immigrant church emerges in these conditions of liminality. Turner (2002) proposed that religious liminality is accompanied by such characteristics as a relative absence of property and status, simplicity, selflessness, homogeneity, *communitas* and a strong sense of the sacred and the spiritual. Here is a picture of the New Testament church community in its early years as it aimed to follow the radical prescriptions of Jesus' teaching. Totality is another of Turner's characteristics of the liminal period, and the church as the spatial expression of immigrant liminality has affinities with what Erving Goffman called a total institution. *Communitas* defines a period of intense development of bonding social capital. 'Birds of a feather', we were told in one Korean-Canadian church, 'don't just bond together, they stick together like crazy glue'.

Such traits of liminality are consistent with our interviews both of current Chinese and Korean churches of new immigrants (Ley 2008) and an earlier oral history of the young German immigrant churches in the 1950s and 1960s (Beattie and Ley 2003). *Communitas* was expressed in the warmth of the welcome to new members:

> As a whole, the German community looked after each other and I think during the first ten years this was the great strength of the churches…[including] emotional needs, spiritual needs and physical needs..

This memory from the 1950s was repeated by a current leader in a Korean church:

> The longer-established immigrants tend to help a lot of the recent immigrants. They show love and concern for the new immigrants.

Help is practical, addressing basic needs: housing, schooling, social services and sometimes employment.[12] 'We are a walking yellow pages to them', declared a Chinese-Canadian pastor. Mentoring for the practicalities of everyday life often occurs in weekly fellowship or care groups: 'our members from a care group will advise them how to apply for the social insurance card, how to open a bank account, recommend them a family doctor, etc.' Retired and longer-established immigrants are often prominent in volunteering, thereby building up the stock of social capital; in one Chinese-Canadian church, a retiree has prepared 50 different immigrants to take their driving test. Language services are another practical gift; one relatively small Chinese-Canadian congregation offers 16 h a week of English instruction.

There is a plethora of special interest events and activities to draw in the congregation several times a week (Ley 2008). In addition to Sunday worship are services:

> like English conversation classes on weekday evenings. Bible studies are in almost every part of the city, in people's homes of course. We also have programmes for the children, activities like sports, music and summer camps. There are areas like choirs and men and women's groups that are open to anyone.

The attributes of a quasi-total institution are revealed in the expenditure not only of time and talents but also of personal finances. Considerable sacrifices were made for major church events, including a building programme. A German-Canadian deacon remembered how in the 1960s:

> When the church was built, the people they stayed in basement suites, many of them instead of buying a home so that the church could be up… I spent eight months working on the church from the start…giving my job up for the construction of the church.

Similar commitment is being repeated as members of a Chinese-Canadian church are currently remortgaging their houses to raise money for a new church property.

The vitality of the immigrant church, then, is intensified through a period of liminality, its partial detachment, whether voluntary or involuntary, from the worldly pursuits of the society in which it is embedded. Reincorporation may well occur at

---

[12] See Huamei Han's detailed study of the deepening encounter of a Chinese immigrant couple with an evangelical Mandarin-language church in Toronto whose services met a wide range of their needs (Han 2009).

a later date, as the assimilation of church members economically and socially moves them from an ontology of weakness and apartness to an ontology of strength and integration. Then like the New Testament church of Ephesus addressed in the Book of Revelation, they may face the charge that they have lost their first love (Revelation 2:4). Tse (2011), for example, found in an established Cantonese-speaking church in Vancouver that some migrants from Hong Kong in the 1990s saw themselves as superior to newer migrants from Mainland China 15 years later.[13] Habits that bred exclusivity, such as speaking Cantonese instead of Mandarin as well as constantly invoking their experience of religious education in Hong Kong, led those who were recently in a liminal status themselves to establish a Chinese church in which it was difficult for newer Mainland migrants to integrate. A Hongkonger man married to a woman from Guangzhou expressed his frustration at the situation:

> Coming up is the Mandarin-speaking people. We need to work on that…But the church leaders have problems…I see quite a few people that speak Mandarin that they came and then left because they don't have that kind of support…I put this subject to some of the council members and with some sharp force: they said it's not easy to start Mandarin services because the people don't commit, and it takes a long time to nurture them.

This respondent is frustrated because church leaders—migrants themselves—seem to avoid caring for newer migrants because of cultural stereotypes that accompany the privileged Hongkonger dialect and educational pedigree.

9.5 Conclusion

In this chapter, we have sought to establish the existence of, and provide a particular identity to, *homo religiosus*. In undertaking a geography of religion that moves beyond the description of cultural landscapes and spatial distributions to their interpretation, engagement with the everyday meanings and world views of faith communities is necessary, where we can learn the rules of action. We have taken the advice of Charles Taylor, John Milbank and also several geographers that conventional social science may be a difficult starting point for such enquiry because our positionality makes us querulous about the status of the spiritual, which we seek to convert to the social and then interpret through other social variables. Such reductionism, in Milbank's terms, polices and contains religious belief in inappropriate categories. Weber's iron cage of modernity has compressed and distorted the realm of spirituality. At the same time, Milbank's (possibly) rhetorical desire to marginalise secular social science in the study of religion seems excessive. Our own study, for example, has benefitted from Victor Turner's concept of liminality. What *is* required is a degree of humility in approaching the spiritual with the recognition that spiritual experience cannot be adequately reduced to social facts and that theological accounts need to be part of the interpretive frame.

---

[13] Compare the cultural divisions between Gentile and Jewish Christians that the apostle Paul sought energetically to suture in his Biblical letters.

Examining the resilient faith of immigrant congregations, we have suggested that the vitality and high levels of affiliation in immigrant churches are accountable by referring to the theological bases of their faith and in particular to the great reversal that proclaims the spiritual advantage of worldly weakness. Withdrawal from the blinders of worldly advantage aids spiritual development, and in the liminal experience of immigrant dispossession, conditions exist for an estrangement from worldly habits and desires and an efflorescence of religious practice. 'What good will it be for a man if he gains the whole world, yet forfeits his soul?' (Matthew 16:26). In losing much through displacement, the immigrant as stranger to the world is in a potentially favoured position to gain spiritual wealth.

References

Agnew, J. 2006. Religion and geopolitics. *Geopolitics* 11: 183–191.

Armstrong, J. 2009. Building diversity: City pins big hopes on new mosque. *Globe and Mail*, 10 June, A1, A7.

Asad, T. 2003. *Formations of the secular: Christianity, Islam, modernity*. Stanford: Stanford University Press.

Bailey, A., C. Brace, and D.C. Harvey. 2009. Three geographers in an archive: Positions, predilections and passing comment on transient lives. *Transactions of the Institute of British Geographers* 34: 254–269.

Beattie, L., and D. Ley. 2003. The German immigrant church in Vancouver: Service provision and identity formation. *Die Erde* 134: 3–22.

Beck, U. 2010. Remapping social inequalities in an age of climate change: For a cosmopolitan renewal of sociology. *Global Networks* 10(2): 165–181.

Bramadat, P., and M. Koenig (eds.). 2009. *International migration and the governance of religious diversity*. Montreal: McGill-Queens University Press.

Bunting, M. 2009. Religions have the power to bring a passion for social justice to politics, *The Guardian*, 12 January.

Buttimer, A. 1974. *Values in geography*. Washington, DC: AAG Commission on College Geography, Resource paper 24.

Chen, C. 2006. *Getting saved in America: Taiwanese immigration and religious experience*. Princeton/Oxford: Princeton University Press.

Chen, A., et al. 2010. Mental health service use by Chinese immigrants with severe and persistent mental illness. *Canadian Journal of Psychiatry* 55(1): 35–42.

D'Addario, S., Kowalski, J., Leime, M., and Preston, V. 2008. *Finding home: Exploring Muslim settlement in the Toronto CMA*. CERIS Working Paper no. 68. Toronto: The Ontario Metropolis Centre.

Davie, G. 1994. *Religion in Britain since 1945: Believing without belonging*. Oxford: Blackwell.

Day, K. 2001. Putting it together in the African-American churches: faith, economic development and civil rights. In *Religion and social policy*, ed. P. Nesbitt, 181–195. Walnut Creek: AltaMira Press.

Dewsbury, J., and P. Cloke. 2009. Spiritual landscapes: Existence, performance and immanence. *Social and Cultural Geography* 10(6): 695–711.

Duncan, J.S. 2004. *The city as text: The politics of landscape interpretation in the Kandyan kingdom*, 2nd ed. Cambridge: Cambridge University Press.

Dunn, K. 2004. Islam in Sydney: contesting the discourse of absence. *Australian Geographer* 35: 333–353.

Dwyer, C. 1999. Veiled meanings: Young British Muslim women and the negotiation of differences. *Gender, Place, and Culture* 6: 5–26.

Ebaugh, H., and J. Chafetz. 2000. *Religion and the new immigrants*. Walnut Creek: AltaMira Press.

Economist. 2009. Latinos and religion: Separated brothers, *The Economist*, 18 July, 31.

Eliade, M. 1959. *The sacred and the profane: The nature of religion*. San Diego: Harcourt Brace Jovanovich.

Evangelical Alliance. 2006. Data compiled from *Religious Trends 6*, Findings of the 2005 English Church Census. www.eauk.org/resources/info/statistics/2005englishchurchcensus.cfm. Accessed 22 February 2010

Foley, M., and D. Hoge. 2007. *Religion and the new immigrants: How faith communities form our newest citizens*. New York: OUP.

Green, J.B. 1994. Good news to whom? Jesus and the "poor" in the Gospel of Luke. In *Jesus of Nazareth, Lord and Christ: Essays on the historical Jesus and new Testament Christology*, ed. J.B. Green and M. Turner, 59–74. Grand Rapids: William B. Eerdmans.

Han, H. 2009. Institutionalized inclusion: A case study of support for immigrants in English learning. *TESOL Quarterly* 43(4): 643–668.

Handlin, O. 1951. *The uprooted*. Boston: Little Brown.

Hauerwas, S. 1990. The importance of being Catholic: A protestant view. *First Things*, March.

Hauerwas, S. 2000a. *A better hope: Resources for a church confronting democracy, postmodernism, and capitalism*. Grand Rapids: Brazos.

Hauerwas, S. 2000b. *With the grain of the universe: The church's witness and natural theology*. Grand Rapids: Brazos.

Hauerwas, S., and W. Willimon. 1989. *Resident aliens: Life in the Christian colony*. Nashville: Abingdon.

Henkel, R. 2005. Geography of religion—Rediscovering a subdiscipline. *Hrvatski Geografski Glasnik* 67: 5–25.

Holden, W., and D. Jacobson. 2009. Ecclesial opposition to nonferrous mining in Guatemala: Neoliberalism meets the church of the poor in a shattered society. *The Canadian Geographer* 53(2): 145–164.

Hopkins, P.E. 2007. Global events, national politics, local lives: Young Muslim men in Scotland. *Environment and Planning A* 39: 1119–1133.

Jenkins, P. 2006. *The new faces of Christianity: Believing the Bible in the global South*. New York: Oxford University Press.

Jenkins, P. 2007. *God's continent: Christianity, Islam and Europe's religious crisis*. New York: Oxford University Press.

Jones, E. 1972. The nature and scope of social geography. In *Social geography*, 11–23. Bletchley: The Open University.

Kim, K.C., and S. Kim. 2001. The ethnic roles of Korean immigrant churches in the United States. In *Korean Americans and their religion*, ed. H.-Y. Kwon, K.C. Kim, and R.S. Warner, 71–94. University Park: Pennsylvania State University Press.

Kong, L. 2001. Mapping 'new' geographies of religion: Politics and poetics in modernity. *Progress in Human Geography* 25(2): 211–233.

Kong, L. 2010. Global shifts, theoretical shifts: Changing geographies of religion. *Progress in Human Geography* 34(1): 1–22.

Kunz, J. 2009. Religious diversity in a multicultural Canada: *quo vadis? Horizons* 12(2): 6–13.

Lam, L. 1994. Searching for a safe haven: The migration and settlement of Hong Kong Chinese immigrants in Toronto. In *Reluctant Exiles?* ed. R. Skeldon, 163–179. Armonk: M. E. Sharpe.

Lee, F. 1991. Chinese Christian churches in metro Toronto. *Canada and Hong Kong Update* 11: 9–10.

Levitt, P. 2007. *God needs no passport: Immigrants and the changing American landscape*. New York: The New Press.

Ley, D. 2002. Mapping the metaphysical, plotting the pious; four new atlases of religion. *Church History* 71(1): 143–151.

Ley, D. 2008. The immigrant church as an urban service hub. *Urban Studies* 45(10): 2057–2074.

Ley, D. 2010. *Millionaire migrants: Trans-Pacific life lines*. Oxford: Blackwell-Wiley.

Martin, D. 2002. *Pentecostalism: The world their parish*. Oxford: Blackwell.

Masuzawa, T. 2005. *The invention of world religions, or how European universalism was preserved in the language of pluralism*. Chicago: University of Chicago Press.

Milbank, J. 2006. *Theology and social theory: Beyond secular reason*, 2nd ed. Oxford: Blackwell.

Miller, D.E., J. Miller, and G. Dyrness. 2001. *Immigrant religion in the city of Angels*. Los Angeles: Center for Religion and Civic Culture, University of Southern California.

Min, P.G. 2002. A literature review with a focus on major themes. In *Religions in Asian America: Building faith communities*, ed. P.G. Min and J.H. Kim, 15–36. Walnut Creek: AltaMira.

Olson, E. 2006. Development, transnational religion, and the power of ideas in the high provinces of Cusco, Peru. *Environment and Planning A* 38: 885–902.

Olson, E. 2009. 'What kind of Catholic are you?' Reflexivity, religion and activism in the Peruvian Andes. *Fieldwork in Religion* 3(2): 103–121.

Pew. 2008. *US religious landscape survey*. Washington, DC: The Pew Forum on Religion and Public Life.

Ringma, C. 2009. Liberation theologians speak to evangelicals: A theology and praxis of serving the poor. *Crux* 45(2): 13–21.

Samers, M. 2010. *Migration*. New York: Routledge.

Schuetz, A. 1944. The stranger: An essay in social psychology. *The American Journal of Sociology* 49(6): 499–507.

Shen, E., et al. 2006. Clinical observations of a Cantonese cognitive-behavioral treatment program for Chinese immigrants. *Psychotherapy: Theory, Research, Practice, Training* 43(4): 518–530.

Smith, T. 1978. Religion and ethnicity in America. *The American Historical Review* 83: 1155–1185.

Stump, R. 2008. *The geography of religion: Faith, place and space*. Lanham: Rowman & Littlefield.

Taylor, C. 2007. *A secular age*. Cambridge, MA: Harvard University Press.

Thomas, S. 2009. Global trends in religious identity. *Horizons* 10(2): 14–18.

Traynor, I. 2009. Swiss vote to ban construction of minarets on mosques. *The Guardian*, 29 November. www.guardian.co.uk/world/2009/nov/29/switzerland-bans-mosque-minarets. Accessed 22 February 2010.

Tse, J. 2011. Making a Cantonese-Christian family: Quotidian habits of language and background in a transnational Hongkonger church. *Population, Space, and Place: A Journal of Population Geography*, 17(6): 756–768.

Turner, V. 2002. Liminality and communitas. In *A reader in the anthropology of religion*, ed. M. Lambek, 358–374. Malden: Blackwell.

Warner, R.S. 2000. Religion and new (post-1965) immigrants: Some principles drawn from field research. *American Studies* 41(2–3): 267–286.

Warner, R.S. 2001. The Korean immigrant church as case and model. In *Korean Americans and their religion*, ed. H.-Y. Kwon, K.C. Kim, and R.S. Warner, 25–52. University Park: Pennsylvania State University Press.

Waters, J. 2002. Flexible families? Astronaut households and the experiences of lone mothers in Vancouver, BC. *Social and Cultural Geography* 3(2): 117–134.

Wilford, J. 2009. Sacred archipelagos: Geographies of secularization. *Progress in Human Geography* 33(1): 1–21.

Yang, F. 1998. Chinese conversions to evangelical Christianity: The importance of social and cultural contexts. *Sociology of Religion* 59: 237–257.

Yorgason, E., and V. Dora della. 2009. Editorial: Geography, religion, and the emerging paradigms: problematizing the dialogue. *Social and Cultural Geography* 10(6): 629–637.

Zhang, X. 2006. How religious organizations influence Chinese conversion to evangelical Protestantism in the United States. *Sociology of Religion* 67(2): 149–159.

Chapter 10
'There's just no space for me there': Christian Feminists in the UK and the Performance of Space and Religion

Giselle Vincett

10.1 Introduction

Christian feminists hold together a dual identity which some others may see as problematic. Hampson (2002[1996]), for example, claims Christianity cannot be rescued from its misogyny (209), yet women remain the majority of church attenders (Brierley 2006: 5.8). If Christianity is misogynous, or if women perceive it as such, how does that affect women and their relationship with God? How do they remain religious, and why? What do religious feminist religious practices look like? How do women engage with aspects of religion that are excluding to them? This chapter is based upon a larger study which sought to answer these questions. Here, I look at the spatial positioning of Christian feminists within and without British liberal churches. I argue that their position is marginal and examine how their position affects women's sense of community with the churches, their theology and their ideas of what constitutes 'church', as well as the tactics women employ to ameliorate, negotiate and subvert their marginal position.

In this chapter, I shall first provide a quick overview of the literatures which I am using to build up a multilayered approach to the analysis of the position of Christian feminist women. I go on to discuss the background of the research upon which this chapter is based and my research methods. I then draw upon data from my empirical research to show how women are both displaced from Christianity and the churches and some ways in which they attempt to either cope with or revalue their marginality. Finally, I show how my research with feminist Christian women has broader implications for Christianity in the UK.

G. Vincett (✉)
School of Geography, Politics and Sociology, Newcastle University,
Newcastle upon Tyne, England, UK

University of Birmingham, Woodbrooke
e-mail: gvincett@gmail.com

P. Hopkins et al. (eds.), *Religion and Place: Landscape, Politics and Piety*,   167
DOI 10.1007/978-94-007-4685-5_10, © Springer Science+Business Media Dordrecht 2013

10.2   Locating Women

Feminist geography has allowed a picture of the 'place' of women in different spaces to be built up.[1] Massey (1994) has shown how the history of women and work is different depending on geographical and social contexts. Similarly, Rose summarized the work of feminist geographers showing how 'events of the everyday are bound into the power structures which limit and confine women' (1993: 17). She has outlined how spaces which have been constructed or represented as 'masculine' (i.e. *the public*) often hide other, more marginalized constructions, and how these alternative constructions may 'erupt into' the dominant constructions of space (37), particularly in relation to how women may make 'fragile' 'the masculine claim to public space' (37). Following Kim Knott's work on religion and place (2005a, b), I use a spatial lens to look at the 'place' of women in liberal UK churches and to examine how women (re)negotiate and/or subvert their positioning in and out of those spaces. For example, though there is no official place for women behind the altar in the Roman Catholic Church, women have simply created their own spaces where they can ritualize outside of the control of Rome. Meanwhile, the process of women moving into the ministry in the Church of England (the Anglican Church) has meant a corresponding physical movement from the pews to the pulpit and behind the altar. A spatial methodology allows me to analyse these issues and more.

Lefebvre (1991[1974]) showed how space is neither static, nor is it independent from everyday life. Instead, space is embedded in the social, and space may be subverted or re-conceived. Lefebvre acknowledges that space does not simply exist physically—as in the built environment—but that it also lives in the imagination and in text. It is the ability of actors to imagine new spaces or restructure existing space, which Lefebvre argues, engenders new spatial practices and positionings. An understanding of space as social, or relational, allows for an understanding that space is not simply 'there' but is enacted or performed ('produced' in Lefebvrian terms), embodied and imagined.

That space is produced or enacted has been taken up by Massey, who argues that space is (1) interrelational; (2) 'the sphere in which distinct trajectories coexist; as the sphere therefore of coexisting heterogeneity'; and (3) 'always under construction …always in the process of being made. It is never finished; never closed' (2005: 9). Despite her emphasis on 'the event of place', Massey recognizes that space always includes the past, or what she calls, the 'there and thens', which exist underneath the 'here and nows' (139). These different constructions, uses and interpretations of

---

[1] I am aware that geographers have made various distinctions between 'space' and 'place', but also that feminist geographers have critiqued this division as gendered (see, e.g. Rose 1993; McDowell 1999), so that 'space' has been treated as abstract yet dynamic (and hence implicitly 'male') and 'place' has been treated as local, passive and associated with nature (and hence implicitly 'female'). Since I have no wish to uphold such hierarchical and falsely dualistic distinctions, I have here treated the concepts as interrelated spheres that interact with one another and cannot easily be teased apart. In general, I follow the lead of my informants who use the terms almost interchangeably.

space are part of what Massey means when she points to the 'coexisting heterogeneity' of space. Class, race and gender are other differences in space and point to what Massey calls the 'power geometry' (130) of space. For the feminist women in my research, these points are especially relevant, as I shall show.

Feminist geographers in particular have developed the idea that different bodies experience and use space in different ways. Differences in the sexed body affect the ways space is 'conceived (in language), represented (e.g. in the built environment), and ultimately reproduced for human identity and becoming' (Knott 2005a: 17). Here I follow Knott in understanding the body 'to be formative for conceptual development, social relations, and the imagination of both in relation to space' (19) and the divine.

Until recently, the body was assumed to be a 'fixed, material entity subject to the empirical rules of biological science, existing prior to the mutability and flux of cultural change and diversity and characterized by unchangeable inner necessities' (Csordas 1994: 1). Since the 1970s, however, feminists and others have shown that the body can instead be thought of as the 'epitome of [historical and cultural] flux' (2). Butler argues that 'gender' and 'sex' cannot be teased apart as if they were independent, but that both are culturally constructed. She insists that the 'substantive effect of gender is performatively produced' (1990: 24). That is, we learn gender practices socially which are then inscribed and reinscribed upon and by us through practices of repeated performance.

However, McGuire (1988, 1990) argues that the body is 'part of the grounding of our human experience in reality. The "lived" body is our vehicle for perceiving and interpreting our world' (1990: 284), and as such is part of our self-identity, but also that 'the human body is both a biological and cultural product' (285). The body then is the means by which we exist in the world. However, we experience our body, sexuality and identity as a social being located within a particular cultural context with its dominant values and norms. Wherever we are (in space), we negotiate that space and relate to others primarily with our bodies (our voices, touch, mobility). Therefore, when Butler (1990) claims that women 'perform' womanhood (as above), the body is part of that performance. Relevant to the purposes of this chapter, Csordas (1994) takes the argument further and insists that 'the kind of body that members of a culture endow themselves with' affects how they 'come into relation with the kind of deity they posit to themselves' (3). My research shows that women's bodies are ' often the conflicting site of both giving in to, as well as resisting, dominant constructions' (Thapan 1997: 11) and that shifting notions of the body and space affect how feminist women experience church (both institutional and particular) and the divine and how they perform their religiosity.

10.3   Research Context

This chapter is based upon semi-structured interviews and participant observation with feminist Christian women in England and Wales and is part of a larger study of religious feminists examining how women hold together these sometimes conflicting self-identities and how their identity affects their beliefs, ritualizing and everyday lives. As part of the study, I conducted 50 semiformal, qualitative, interviews with feminist women about half of whom were Christians from a variety of liberal denominations.[2] I conducted participant observation with a Christian feminist ritual group consisting of about 15 women, and observed email lists and other computer-mediated spaces such as web forums. I also included and analysed texts written by informants. Women from a variety of backgrounds were interviewed, including grass-roots practitioners, liturgical leaders, writers and academics.

As with most women in the UK who identify as 'feminist', the majority of participants in this study were white, middle class and well educated, most having at least one degree in higher education. These women all have active religious lives—though they may or may not attend church—and belonged (in various ways) to liberal Christian denominations. Participants ranged in age from their late teens to their 70s, though most were in their 40s and 50s. This age range and spread conforms with other research, such as Brierley's study (2006) of UK denominations, which also shows a majority in the age range of 45–64 across all liberal denominations (5.6).

Below I will first outline how feminist Christian women feel displaced by traditional spaces and social structures in the church (both institutional and particular). I consider how such 'displacement' has consequences for a woman's sense of self, community and the divine, and I show how participants devise spatial tactics which enable them to hold together their dual identity of being a feminist Christian. I explore how these tactics involve the contestation of received or given spaces and their subversion or recolonization and the construction of new spaces, both physical and figurative.[3]

10.4   Displacement of Women in Christianity

Since its early days, Christianity has been highly oriented around the built environment and has used these environments to reflect and help construct Christian community, ideology and theology. Churches are spaces in which it is possible to leave the world of the profane (including the natural world) outside the door and interact with the divine in a sacred place. A Christian entering a church may literally close the door on the secular and be separated out from it. As Smith has written, 'When one enters a temple, one enters marked-off space' (2005[1987]: 33). More than this, churches are also places that consciously leave their stamp on the surrounding space (i.e. the landscape). As Christianity spread, the effect of building a church was to Christianize

---

[2] The Christian informants in my study came from the Church of England (Anglican), Roman Catholic, Methodist, Baptist, Unitarian and United Reformed churches.

[3] By 'received' or 'given' space I mean spaces such as churches which have histories of particular ideologies and symbol systems, which the people who use such spaces inherit and must engage with on some level whether through acceptance and continuance or through subversion and change.

the landscape. Even now, for regular, active church members, churches are places that leave a powerful stamp on their psyches. Churches thus exist as both material spaces and figurative or psychological ones.

Put another way, 'a particular place …enfolds its social, physical and cultural history within it' (Knott 2005b: 161). If one's experiences in a place are positive, one's sense of that place is likely to be positive also. For a Christian, what one *does* in church, that is, ritual, forms a large part of this experience, and herein lies a serious issue for women who until recently in Britain were largely excluded from leading liturgy and from public participation in the space of the sanctuary. Ruether explains that 'the roots of this injunction lie in the perception of women as impure and hence to be excluded from the sacred male space' (1990: 9).[4] Not only are churches spaces that are 'marked off' from the profane or everyday world outside, but within a church are spaces that are further marked off, and these are traditionally marked off from *women*.

Women's exclusion from sacred space is bound up with their embodiment. One participant, Amy (Church of England), related this story:

> [One woman] brought up that one of the original objections to women being priests was 'well, she might be menstruating while she's celebrating the Eucharist'. That wasn't something I'd been aware of, but then left me feeling completely off-balance because I was about to go and help officiate with the Eucharist, [pause] and I was menstruating! And I was quite unbalanced by it.

Women have been told that their embodiment is irreconcilable with the space of the sanctuary—indeed, that it has the potential to pollute that sacred space. The force of this long-term injunction has repercussions for women and their sense of self and relationship with the divine even in those churches which now ordain women. Amy's anecdote illustrates the feeling amongst women that still runs as an undercurrent in many Christian denominations that they and their bodily functions are 'unclean'. As Christina (Church of England) put it, '[women] are being treated as if they are people of lesser value in the church'. Space, as Knott writes, 'is thoroughly enmeshed in embodiment' (2005b: 166). If women's experience is that their bodies are denigrated and rejected as profane by the churches, they will literally feel displaced.

Churches are both particular built places *and* symbolic, abstract spaces that represent the Christian community and church institution as a whole; a particular church is never isolated from the larger church. Even a small, independent house church cannot be isolated from the history of Christianity or the worldwide community of Christians. By extension, because traditional Christian ritual tends to be formalized and regularized, what one does ritually in a particular church can be extended to include church in general. When I spoke with Brenda (Church of England), she was just on the point of graduating from ministerial training. Hers is a clear example of how painful ritual experience can transcend particular location:

---

[4] Ruether and others have shown how women have been conflated with the natural or material world (and opposed to the male who has been associated with the cerebral and spiritual).

[There was an incident] just before Christmas…when I spoke up about feeling excluded and marginalized by a Book of Common Prayer Eucharist, and [one fellow student] told me that women who wanted to have language inclusivized were just bitter and twisted… I felt physically hurt by that for three or four days really.

I asked Brenda what that experience did to her sense of community with the church, to which she replied, 'It's not very positive [long pause]. And I know I'm going to a church where I'll have to celebrate the Book of Common Prayer Eucharist on the first Sunday of each month.'

Christian feminist women thus often felt as though they were interlopers in church spaces, second-class citizens as it were. Church space becomes conflated with male, patriarchal imagery for God within which women have no place. As Wendy (Catholic convert from Church of England) put it, 'the problem of course is that however much you love your church, there is always this problem that it embodies this male imagery, and it is very difficult to know how to handle that'. Thus, the physical structure and imagery of a traditional church is 'read' by women as being a male space. It is difficult to conceive of how to symbolically re-conceptualize that space in a way that includes women. As places that were predominantly designed and constructed by men for men (at least in terms of the sanctuary), women must mould themselves into church space as foreign bodies.[5]

Women's exclusion from the space of the church can be hard to reconcile with the message of Christianity, which preaches that the church is meant to enfold all comers in its familial structure. This can be marvellously inclusive, and it can promote radical equality; unfortunately, however, it does not reflect the experience of the majority of my Christian feminist participants. If we accept that space is social, the exclusion of women from certain social roles and relationships in the church (e.g. liturgical leadership), along with their implicit ability to 'pollute' the space of the church and, hence, the potential for relationship with God within it, really forces women out of the space of the church. This leaves women without a ritual place that is safe and positive for them—they are, as I have said, displaced persons.

The result, for many participants, was a painful yearning for church and God. Megan, an artist and Ph.D. student (Church of England) related this powerful story:

I felt I needed to go to church. I kept going up to St. John's, which is an Anglican church. During this time I used to run, and I used to run up there and I can remember going up to the door and banging on it and thinking, 'I want to come in here, how do I get in?' And that sounds silly because all I had to do was come on a Sunday, but to me there was more going on there. You know? It wasn't necessarily about going through the doors, it was about something in me wanting to get into this space—and how did I do that?

Later she said, 'I can't go to church anymore, but I'd love to go to church'.

---

[5] Only one participant specifically mentioned attending a church in which the built environment could reflect her egalitarian, liberation theology. Julie's Catholic Church is a twentieth century 'in-the-round' church, a built environment conceived on an egalitarian ideology. It is perhaps this egalitarian space that helps Julie cope with the difficulties she identifies in Catholic hierarchy and language.

Similarly, the story of Frances illustrates both the displacement of women in/from the church and the tactics which women have employed in order to remain in church space and to continue their (public) relationship with God. Frances, who in her 70s was one of my older participants (Church of England), has always had a 'strong vocation involving God', but despite years of training (and retraining) for ministry was never allowed 'in': 'at the end of it all, we were back to square one, because they weren't going to ordain us'. The space behind the sanctuary rail was closed to Frances and women of her generation. Space is thus 'utilised, often ingeniously, by dominant groups in the exercise of power. It is often used to contain, even to obliterate others. Spaces, through the construction and manipulation of boundaries, are used to include and exclude' (Knott 2005a: 26). Indeed, Frances understands her exclusion as 'the men just were not seeing you… they just were not seeing you as a person at all'.

Finally, Frances gave up on being ordained. 'I ended up getting married [to a clergyman] because the alternatives that the church was offering were just insulting. …That was okay, because now I was normal to the men, now I was just a knowledgeable wife, and we were looked upon by the church as a useful package'. She adds, 'I guess I tried to do my theology through my husband's job'. In this way, though Frances appeared to acquiesce to the dominant order (what Knott calls 'ironic collusion' 2005a: 127), actually she manipulated church space in the only way she saw as open, 'hoping to produce cracks in the system and make [church] spaces suitable for habitation' (Knott 2005a: 27). Frances' worth to the church depended on being her husband's wife. This was made clear when he died:

> The church just has *no* idea of the reality of life for a [priest's] widow. You know, that you have to move house suddenly, you have to move communities, you have to re-establish yourself, and all of this when you really need stability. And of course, if I'd decided to go be ordained then, I'd have had to be retrained *again*.

Not only was Frances barred from the sanctuary, the only space in which she could theologize or help mediate the sacred (the pews and the vicarage) still depended on her husband's legitimizing presence. Frances' final exclusion from church space following the death of her husband (and hence her legitimating function) underlines the way in which women have been forced into *private* spaces in order to develop their spirituality and relationship with God. Below, I examine how the exclusion of women from public worship places affects their sense of God and their sense of solidarity with God (both negatively and positively) and how it forces women into a split spiritual life (i.e. what is possible in public and what in private).

10.5 Placing God

The power geometries inherent in the hierarchy of the churches and the histories of particular spaces displace women from church spaces. This displacement puts those women who wish to remain in, or engage with, the churches on the margins looking in. However, the church is supposed to be a place where God lives—it is God's 'house'; the question is, then, what happens to women's sense of God when they are marginalized and displaced from 'his' [sic] house?

Gill (Church of England from Scots Presbyterian) felt so 'othered' by the Presbyterian, uncompromising God and church of her childhood that even though she continued to practice occasionally as an Anglican, she was left without a sense of God or church which could include her: 'I feel bereft, really', she said, 'I'm left with the feeling that I don't know what life is for. And I feel quite despondent about it quite a lot of the time'.

Gill's latter feminist questioning of God and church undid her sense of community and God. She thus ends up in a metaphorical space which may be characterized as a broken space: a space which is broken from normal social existence, where even the woman who exists within it feels nullified (i.e. does not really exist). Nelle Morton once asked, 'What if, when you take the sexism out of God language, you have nothing left? What then?' (1985: 223) Morton articulates an often unspoken fear of feminist women that if they begin to question church structures, language, and so forth, that they will be left with nothing: no community, no faith, no sense of God at all.

For those participants who felt most 'displaced' by the church, such as Gill, the longing for the divine and for a religious community is virtually palpable and seems almost to take form. Gill has indeed been left with 'nothing' in a 'nowhere space'. Deconstruction of her childhood ideas of God and the sexist structures of the church has left her with nothing with which to replace them. Even though she has read alternative theologies of God, she feels so shut out from God and the church that she cannot find her way back in.

Other women, though they felt marginalized by the institution of the church, did not feel marginalized by God. Instead, God was imagined as a large and inclusive space. As Brenda put it, 'I'm aware that there's a place that I'm in touch with that—that is…resting with God. That doesn't have an image, and it doesn't necessarily have words. It's really a place'. Similarly, Phillipa (Catholic) says,

> I kind of imagine and feel God not as an image, but as a silence and a space. A place to be still and uncluttered; a friendly space; a space to be me and be with myself and think and fly. …You know, I sometimes sit with a cup of tea and look out the window and watch the birds. It's that freedom of flying that I imagine God to be.[6]

And Joan (Catholic) said,

> I often image God as space. I experience that as freedom—deep or wide inner space. There's deep peace in that, and love, and it's simple. There is nothing between you and God, you are yourself, free from restraints, and free to be yourself. It's a creative freedom.

---

[6] Since the time of our interview, Phillipa has stopped attending her Catholic Church, in part because of her dismay at Catholic sexual abuse scandals. She still occasionally attends a Church of England Cathedral and is involved with the Catholic Women's Network, which she views as her church community.

It is interesting that here, though the women have ended up with a similar 'nothingness' to Gill, they are nevertheless able to conceive of the nothingness as positive and relational, as both completely Other than themselves and yet as inclusive. Rather than a nothingness which closes in upon them, this nothingness is open and liberating. This then is one way that women construct a relationship with God and an understanding of God which accepts God as *intimately* Other. That this God is 'inclusive', that is, genderless or gender inclusive, is a tactic which enables participants to remain within the church and insists upon a theology which includes others. As Phillipa put it, 'I am a woman, I want to be a woman, and this is how I am. And there needs to be space [in God] for me to feel that my gender and the way I am is respected'. Amy described this need as 'desperately trying to hold on to some sense of inclusivity there in the very male dominated Trinity'. A God who promotes such a feeling in women is a God in whom women feel they have a place: that there is space in God for women. It also says that that space for women reflects something essential about the nature of God: that God is inclusive and relational.

As with Phillipa above, several participants mentioned 'flying' when trying to describe God. Caroline's words (Methodist), for example, were strikingly similar to Phillipa's: 'I'm also very fond of the eagle [as an image for God], the sort of soaring bird'. Embedded in the flying metaphor is a relational and embodied view of (God as) space. Flying negates the idea that space is simple nothingness, and shifts the focus to an understanding of the intimate relations of bird and wind (here, self and God). The soaring bird rides the wind. Its flight is a relationship not of 'power over', or opposition, but of 'power with'. The bird is not cut off from the earth, or embodiment, because although the image is not 'grounded', the bird is embodied, and in its relation with the wind it gives form to the unembodied. This is a sense of self-in-process, a sense of self-in-relation with God—not a self totally reliant on the Other, but a self *with* the Other. Ultimately, participants' images of God as space, where they are not constructed negatively, are about freedom: 'freedom to be a human being' (Phillipa) and to construct one's identity and one's relationship with the divine *for oneself*. Such a metaphor strategically allows for a sense of self in becoming and a social and embodied sense of self-in-relation, rather than a 'masterful' coherent subject (Haraway 1997[1991]: 39) defined as separate and in opposition to an object.

10.6 Embodiment and Space

In the same way that participants felt that the church has restricted or been ambivalent towards women within the space of the church and their relation to God, participants felt that the church restricted embodied imagery (expressed through language, embodied experience and space). Over and over, my informants told me that 'it's so difficult to even enter a discussion [in the church about alternative images of God]. There's no space. And this kind of conversation we just don't have' (Brenda). Nevertheless, women felt the need to get embodied imagery for God on the agenda and to attempt to reclaim and revalue women's embodiment, in part because, as feminist geographer Rose writes, this can enable 'imagining a space in which women might really be free' (1993: 79). Participants felt that a re-evaluation and re-theologizing of embodiment was a necessary step away from the strong church history of misogyny and body hatred. Christina was adamant that

> The history of Christianity is littered with these wonderful (in some ways) men [theologians] who helped to develop our understanding of our faith, but also helped …to develop a hatred of women, a loathing of our physical bodies, a mistrust of our physical needs, and a deep fear of sexuality and the power of sexual desire. And this has really, really skewed our understanding of what it means to be a human being on planet earth. …I mean [it's] a very tragic aspect of Christianity, and we haven't shaken that off.

Women yearn to use the liberating and explicitly embodied images of God so beautifully explored in the work of feminist theologians such as Carter Heyward (1989) (whom they often quoted during interviews), whilst at the same time they prefer the use of inclusive, universal images of God because they do not wish to be exclusive. This gives rise to what I have elsewhere called an 'inclusivity consciousness' (2007). However, like other feminists, they also struggle with a tension between wanting to revalue female embodiment with the desire not to essentialize women.

For example, Mary (Church of England) and others insisted that 'female language and images for God had a really powerful effect on me. It reached places I never knew existed in my own body! … I felt like I was coming to life in my uterus, in my sex!' However, she was not alone in saying that such imagery would 'shock' many men in the church. Indeed, embodied imagery for the divine seems to belong to the hidden or private spirituality of Christian feminist women. It may be affirming and liberating personally, it may be a strong theme in feminist theology, but it is unlikely to be used publicly in liturgy or even spoken about in church contexts. Even Megan, who has exhibited her art on the female divine, noted that a common reaction to it is that it is 'blasphemous'.

Instead, women are careful about the images they use publicly because they don't wish to exclude anyone and because they fear that using female imagery for God may be misconstrued by the male hearer. As Christina put it,

> If I'm speaking to a female-only group, I can use bodily images 'cause it won't gross anyone out! [laughter] And I can talk about the experience of giving birth and breast feeding, knowing it will not have sexual connotations for anybody. When you say the word 'breasts' in a congregation, you know some guys are just thinking of boobs!

This inclusivity consciousness tends to reinforce a public/private split in the spiritualities of Christian women. In not wanting to exclude anyone by publicly using female imagery for God, and fearing that female sexual imagery for God will be misconstrued by the male hearer, women tend to use female imagery only in the private realm. The public/private split in their spirituality is reflective of women's position on the margins of the church. Use of highly embodied imagery for God (especially female embodied imagery) in church spaces only underlines their marginality by being different to traditional imagery. At the same time, women's desire to not exclude others in the way that they themselves have been (and continue to be) excluded also highlights their marginal position.

The restriction of embodied imagery in the church (expressed through language, embodied experience and space) is linked to the restriction and ambivalence that the church has had towards women within the space of the church and their relation to God. Feminist Christian women's re-imaginings of God are bound up with the church's attitude, so that they alternately challenge it and collude with it. Participants' pleas that 'we should preach on this a lot more' (Kaatje, United Reformed) are not generally put into practice, because of the lingering culture of silence on embodiment issues in the church. Participants thus wrestle with conflicting feelings about embodiment. Megan said, 'I can remember feeling very powerful going to church. I can remember trembling with it during the service. …But I couldn't relate to the story they were telling me, you know about how bad I was'. It was the church's attitude towards 'fleshiness' that drove Megan out of the church. Those who remain must constantly 'hold the pain of it' (Mary) whilst at the same time attempting to midwife a re-imagined and embodied God.

10.7   Re-imagining Church Spaces: Recolonization

The inclusive God is one tactic that Christian women employ to ameliorate their displacement from traditional constructions of God and church. However, participants also emphasized the creation of inclusive church spaces with various methods for doing so. One major tactic is to 'recolonize' the space of the traditional church and the main way that women can do that is by their presence behind the altar. When a woman officiates at the Eucharist or leads a church liturgy, a powerful statement is made that is most obvious to those who did not grow up with this as a possibility. As Julie (Catholic) said, 'I've grown up *always* seeing men distributing the host and the wine. …And it was a revelation when I saw a woman presiding over the Mass, the service. It made it whole, made it full.' If women have been excluded from certain spaces in the church, one way to reclaim that space is to literally fill it. Kaatje spoke of the effect this has:

> In every congregation that I've stood up in front of, everybody loves it that there's a woman standing there. Because it gives them the idea that there is a still a future for this, this business [of Christianity]. And it gives them the idea of a different kind of future than if it were a man standing there—because the men have been standing there for the last two thousand years!

By her very presence, then, a woman leading the service suggests a dynamic and inclusive church space. If the male priest reflected the maleness of God and Jesus (Ruether 1990: 8), then the female celebrant reflects the possibility of other images of God and opens up the space for questioning received assumptions about God, Jesus and the church. As Crang has written, tactical spatial transgressions 'mean that things are not what they seem, …[they change] our notion of what currently is' (Crang 2000: 149). It is this, perhaps more than anything else, that makes women's presence as liturgical leader or preacher a powerful statement; it begins to *re-story* church space. In Massey's terms, a woman changes the 'power geometry' of a place by subverting the 'there and thens' in the here and now (2005). At the same time, she highlights the difference between the *now* and *then*.

In other ways, Christian women try to subvert and re-symbolize the built environment of a church (e.g. the priest/minister up front on a raised platform or pulpit). A minister informant from an email list for Christian feminist women wrote:

> You will be highly amused when I say I really, really, really wanted to strip the interior of the church ..., cut the pews in half and make them easier to move around ..., turn the interior around completely (so that people could enjoy the lovely stained glass window); tear down the pulpit; create a 'snug' in the sanctuary area where the communion table sits raised in all its glory ... until I realised that I was wasting much needed energy on that which was impossible!! ...I began to embrace the space/s and love them. I polished all the wood with lovely oils ... I gradually introduced candles as a way of acknowledging specific events ... I purchased beautiful flowing fabrics and began to combine fabric and candles to create a different visual impact. ...now we weave [the fabric] around and drape [it] over the cross, where it flows down over the communion table' (Sherri, Presbyterian, 19/01/07).

In a way typical of my Christian feminist informants, Sherri *bends* rather than *breaks* the rules of the space. She sees such rules as 'shiftable' (Sister Anne, Catholic). She does not, in the end, 'strip' the interior of the church in order to undo its material ideology, but she creates changes that have the same effect as using inclusive language 'to lead people on from where they are' (Jan, Baptist). In polishing the woodwork, Sherri nurtures the traditional space, but she also subtly demonstrates her eco-theology by revealing the 'trees' in this sacred space. Sherri softens the hard Presbyterian space with fabric and materializes a theology of the creative, flowing power of God in the fabric, which is wrapped round the cross and flows down over the communion table to bring that energy amongst the congregation.

10.8 Parallel Churches

Sherri, being in a leadership position, thus, has the privilege of beginning to materially re-conceive the built space of the church, and with that re-conception she re-theologizes the space.[7] However, most other women don't have that option and so must find other spaces or tactics. In my research, it quickly became apparent that many women were sidestepping the problems with traditional church spaces by their formation of what I term *parallel churches*. In parallel churches, women take into their own hands the responsibility for catering to their spirituality and creating the spaces in which to come together. Winter et al. (1994) call this 'defecting in place', but Lemming points out that many women

---

[7] Since the time of this communication, Sherri has moved into hospital chaplaincy, in part because the politics of remaining in the church grew too personally and professionally painful.

would take issue with that label. They do not see themselves as defecting, but rather as living their baptismal call. …They hold church to its catholicity and engage to 'do the work'
of making and preserving spaces for woman-consciousness, even when formal organizational structures seem to exclude or fail to provide these spaces (2007: 86).

This is most obvious in the formation of small ritual groups, but it may also arise
out of study groups or such organizations as the Catholic Women's Network.
Although organizations like the CWN are ostensibly lobbying on particular issues,
they have also taken over many of the roles a traditional parish would normally fulfil
(pastoral, Eucharistic, etc.). Some women's religious organizations (e.g. convents),
which are officially under the control of the larger church, may also act like parallel
churches.

Except for a convent or a small group attached to a church, a parallel church usually
exists outside of a woman's regular church. It may come into being or women may
join it as a replacement for the loss of traditional community (as Megan or Phillipa
did), or a woman may use a parallel church as a way of filling a need not being met in
her church/denomination (as was the case for many of the women in the ritual group
with which I worked). The ethos of all the parallel churches I encountered was summarized by Phillipa: 'Joining the Catholic Women's Network was something of an
eye-opener for me in that I met other women who were asking questions like myself,
and who weren't prepared to just sit there every Sunday and be told'. In other words,
going to a parallel church is a proactive response to the lack of space that women feel
in traditional churches. It is the creation of new space. But unlike the semi-permanent
space of the physical church, the theology of which is often experienced as similarly
static, parallel churches tend to be held in women's houses. Their locations move
about, reflecting not just the feminist, democratic values of participants but often also
their 'homelessness' in terms of a traditional church community.

Women who participate in parallel churches are quite conscious that the space
they use, especially when celebrating the Eucharist or sharing food together, is
highly charged symbolically. As Leming writes, women are aware that 'sacred
space is contested terrain' (2007: 85) whether that is traditional space or a new
space. This consciousness was, perhaps, most powerfully related to me by Anya
(Unitarian), who told me about a Church of England group which she attended that
met regularly together before women won the right to be ordained. The priest in
charge of the church in which they met was sympathetic to their cause, but he was
not allowed by the diocese to let them celebrate in the actual space of the church
itself. So they met in an anteroom. During meetings, they celebrated the Eucharist
at an altar they set up on the threshold of the church space—literally in the doorway.
This practice underlined their marginalization by the church, but it also expressed
the subversive and challenging way in which they used their forced positioning.
This group was a parallel church that existed physically alongside the church space,
though it was not allowed to cross the line. This example nicely illustrates the way
in which 'the performance of resistance and subversion also has spatial consequences' (Knott 2005b: 162). Some women are able to remain within the church, 'in
part because they have created spaces inside the church that are meeting their needs,
despite a sense of discontent' (Leming 2007: 86). Women may thus hold together

multiple communities, participating in the more public traditional church spaces (often quietly changing exclusive liturgical language under their breath during worship) and participating in semiprivate parallel churches wherein they receive the spiritual and spatial nourishment they need to continue to function in and negotiate with the restrictive spiritual spaces elsewhere.

10.9   Storying Place

Whilst interviewing the Catholic nuns in my study, I was struck by the sense of solidarity they had with their community even whilst acknowledging theological and personality differences inside the convent. Sister Placida's (in her eighties) sense of community included the historical members of the order. When she told me the story of the coming of her order to England, she spoke of it in the present tense, as if she herself had lived through it, despite it happening over three centuries ago: 'we had no intention whatever of coming to England [from France], but we got blown off-course in the Channel....' Though she is very much a part of the Catholic Church, the space of her order is a parallel one within that church that gives her an identity that is 'woman conscious' (Leming 2007: 86). Sister Placida also turns this foundational myth into a space of memory. Memory is a spatial tactic that allows women to 'position themselves with reference to structural religion in ways that help them negotiate' their dual Christian and female identities (Leming 2007: 87). Crang argues that this sort of tactic does not limit memory to the past but 'propels' it to the present (2000: 150). Mediated by memory, Sister Placida maintains a sense of 'woman-conscious' parallel space even within the context of the Catholic Church.

Similarly, June positions herself in solidarity with women's history of struggle in the churches through a hymn she wrote to commemorate a suffragette and the first woman ordained in the Unitarian church, though as she says, many of the images are too explicitly female to enable the use of the hymn in traditional contexts:

> We rejoice, we rejoice in our foremother's faith
> We rejoice, we rejoice in an inclusive grace
> We'll keep pressing onwards in courage and love
> And soar on the wings of God's free-flowing dove.
> God groans as she watches us struggle and fight,
> Her belly is stretching and aching for right.
> Tears flow in her travail, Her pain is revealed,
> She waits and She hopes that her wounds may be healed.
> God's wings are unfolding and circling the earth,
> She dreams of the time when She brought it to birth.
> Laments how the systems of patriarchs' power
> Have stopped her from bringing Her world into flower.
> God joys in our leaping, our dances of faith,
> She laughs as She opens her arms in embrace.
> We gather within Her as sisters in grace,
> Our strength is increasing as we find our place (Boyce-Tillman 2006, 77).

10.10   Ritualizing Place

Women who participated in parallel church groups used ritual as a tactic to explore issues surrounding their place as women within and without the churches. For example, I participated in a women-only parallel church ritual group. For a ritual during the Advent season (the time leading up to and including Christmas), we were asked to think about the theme of thresholds in our lives. This theme was significant: the threshold is a border, an edge, which represents the Christian feminist marginality in the church, and yet their desire to be part of that church. This particular evening, we began with a contemporary Advent prayer written by one of the women. We were then invited to share stories and poems on the theme of thresholds. Women spoke about where they were in their lives and the different sorts of thresholds they were experiencing. One woman spoke about coming up to retirement age, another of wanting to leave her job, and still another about the changing dynamics of her relations with her aging parents. Jane, who is a Baptist minister, said she feels she is constantly 'pushing boundaries' with her congregation in terms of challenging them as a feminist woman. She mentioned not believing anymore in a lot of what she has to say as a minister, which made me feel that she stood at a threshold in terms of her faith. She read a poem about the push and pull of change, how one minute we embrace it, and the next we pull back and are frightened by it. Jan read a poem entitled 'The Door', which went something like this:

> Open the door,
> maybe there will be sunshine
> and green fields outside.
> Open the door,
> even if it is raining outside,
> bleak and grey.
> Open the door,
> even if there is nothing outside.
> Open the door,
> at least there'd be a draft in here (from fieldnotes).

The women reacted to this poem with much knowing laughter. Afterwards, the group danced a circle dance and were then invited to physically cross the threshold of a doorway. Each woman was given a lit candle and supported by the words: *'[Name] we bless you with wisdom and courage as you take the next step into your future'*. As each woman crossed the threshold, others welcomed her and gave her something to drink and eat.

Though we worked from a preset liturgy during this ritual, space was built into it for improvisation and hearing each other. During my fieldwork, women often mentioned the lack of this kind of open space in traditional liturgies. It is important to note also that the women used the ritual space in several different ways, moving physically about it in the circle dance and in crossing the threshold. The space was clearly dynamic. It was also inclusive: the women sat and danced in a [non-hierarchical] circle and each had the chance to lead or contribute.

The spatial symbolism of the threshold seemed to echo the church position of many of the ritual participants. Some women were in an ambiguous space in terms of their beliefs and spiritual home. Some seemed poised to step into a new, as yet unnamed, spirituality, and I wondered about their future in the traditional church. It was significant that in this group, references to the divine were almost always ambiguous (in this ritual, God was referred to as 'Great Spirit') and in this ritual there was a notable absence of images of the divine in the liturgy. This I interpreted as an open space in which to insert my own ideas and images, but also as an uncertainty on the part of some of the women as to what they would insert, both a freedom *and* an emptiness, much like the metaphor of God as space discussed above.

The poem that provoked so much hilarity seemed particularly reflective of the position of Christian feminists: opening the door of feminist deconstruction may bring liberation, or it may bring a confused destruction of faith, but it will certainly bring change. In the end, it was change and the desire to move into a space different from the traditional church space that the women of the ritual group chose. Leming refers to this desire for change as an 'urgency' that 'gives rise to strategic practices' (2007: 79). Here both the urgency and a strategic practice of parallel church were ritualized and spatialized. The women of the ritual group attempted to make their marginal position positive by *celebrating* the threshold and by supporting each other in that space, but the poem revealed their ambiguous position and conflicting feelings about their marginality. The dark humour of the poem revealed both the need for a sense of humour in such a space and also the great fear that feminist women might indeed be left with nothing but 'a draft' if they deconstruct or move outside the traditional spaces of the church.

10.11   Conclusion

A Christian feminist's negotiation (and transgression) of space (and particularly religious spaces) challenges existing gender relations simply through her embodied presence and movement in spaces where men have traditionally been dominant. Here I have shown how Christian feminists are aware of the political and social ramifications of traditional received space and of their recolonization, transgression and creation of space. For Christian feminists, received spaces have certain theologies or concepts of deity embedded within them. Thus, their transgression or re-imagination involves engagement with theology.

Christian feminists who are active in traditional churches must live with 'received spaces' which treat them as 'second-class citizens' (Christine). For them, the mental, social and embodied effects of such received spaces are ongoing and pronounced. I have argued that one effect of living with such spaces is the displacement of women or marginalization, in the churches. However, most participants developed spatial tactics to cope with, sidestep, or transgress their marginal position in the churches. These tactics ranged from recolonization of positions of prominence within church space (e.g. the pulpit, or behind the altar), to the formation of 'parallel churches' and ritual spaces, to materially remaking the interiors of churches.

Woodhead (2007, 2008) and Marler (2008) have argued that 'religious change in the West—particularly the rise and decline of Christian denominations and congregations—is strongly influenced by long-term and largely unexamined changes in women's lives' (Marler 2008). Brown (2001) argues that this process of change in the way that women construct their lives and their identities is inextricably linked to the sharp decline in women's church attendance starting in the latter half of the twentieth century. Woodhead, Marler and Brown show in various ways how social change affects religion and religiosity. What is less clear in their work is how Christianity may be reshaped in any way other than simple decline.

The rise of feminism and the detraditionalism and non-traditionalism that accompany such a worldview makes the research of religious feminists particularly interesting in the context both of religious change and in terms of why and how some feminist women remain in traditional religion, but *also* how the changes in women's lives, particularly over the last 50 years, may give rise to new ways of being religious and new encounters with traditional religion. That is, the findings I have outlined here provide glimpses of how liberal Christianity is being reshaped, and they point to the 'simultaneous appearance of manifestations of decline and of growth and transformation' (Vincett et al. 2008: 15) of Christianity in the contemporary world.

References

Aune, K., S. Sharma, and G. Vincett (eds.). 2008. *Women and religion in the west: Challenging secularization*. Aldershot: Ashgate.

Boyce-Tillman, June 2006. *A rainbow to heaven*. London: Stainer and Bell.

Brierley, P. (ed.). 2006. *UKCH religious trends No.6 (2006–2007)*. London: Christian Research.

Brown, C. 2001. *The death of Christian Britain*. London: Routledge.

Butler, J. 1990. *Gender trouble and the subversion of identity*. New York: Routledge.

Crang, M. 2000. Relics, places and unwritten geographies in the work of Michel de Certeau (1925–86). In *Thinking space*, ed. M. Crang and N. Thrift, 136–153. London/New York: Routledge.

Csordas, T.J. 1994. Introduction: The body as representation and being-in-the-world. In *Embodiment and experience: The existential ground of culture and self*, ed. T.J. Csordas, 1–26. Cambridge: Cambridge University Press.

Daly, M. 1992. *Outercourse: The be-dazzling voyage*. San Francisco: Harper San Francisco.

Hampson, D. 2002[1996]. *After christianity*. London: SCM Press.

Haraway, D. 1997[1991]. Gender for a Marxist dictionary: The sexual politics of a word. In *Space, gender, knowledge: Feminist readings*, ed. L. McDowell and J.S. Sharp, 23–43. London/New York: Arnold.

Heyward, C. 1989. *Touching our strength: The erotic as power and the love of god*. San Francisco: Harper & Row.

Knott, K. 2005a. *The location of religion: A spatial analysis*. London: Equinox.

Knott, K. 2005b. Spatial theory and method for the study of religion. *Temenos* 41(2): 153–184.

Lefebvre, H. 1991. *The Production of Space* (trans: Donald Nicholson-Smith). Oxford: Blackwell.

Leming, L. 2007. Sociological explorations: What is religious agency? *The Sociological Quarterly* 48: 73–92.

Marler, P. 2008. Religious change in the west: Watch the women. In *Women and religion in the west: Challenging secularization*, ed. K. Aune, S. Sharma, and G. Vincett, 23–56. Aldershot: Ashgate.

Massey, D. 1994. *Space, place and gender*. Cambridge: Polity Press.

Massey, D. 2005. *For space*. London: Sage.

McDowell, L.1999. *Gender, identity and Place: Understanding feminist geographies*. Cambridge, UK: Polity Press.

McGuire, M. 1988. *Ritual healing in suburban America*. New Brunswick: Rutgers University Press.

McGuire, M. 1990. Religion and the body: Rematerializing the human body in the social sciences of religion. *Journal for the Scientific Study of Religion* 29(3): 283–296.

Morton, N. 1985. *The journey is home*. Boston: Beacon.

Rose, G. 1993. *Feminism and geography: The limits of geographical knowledge*. Cambridge: Polity Press.

Ruether, R.R. 1990. Women's body and blood: The sacred and the impure. In *Through the devil's gateway: Women, religion and taboo*, ed. A. Joseph, 7–21. London: SPCK.

Smith, J.Z. 2005[1987]. To take place. In *Ritual and religious belief: A reader*, ed. G. Harvey, 26–50. London: Equinox.

Thapan, M. 1997. Introduction: Gender and embodiment in everyday life. In *Embodiment: Essays on gender and identity*, ed. M. Thapan. Mumbai: Oxford University Press.

Tweed, T.A. 2006. *Crossing and dwelling: A theory of religion*. Cambridge, MA: Harvard University Press.

Vincett, G. 2007. Feminism and religion: A study of Christian feminists and goddess feminists in the UK. Unpublished PhD thesis. Lancaster: Lancaster University.

Vincett, G., S. Sharma, and K. Aune. 2008. Introduction: Women, religion and secularization: One size does not fit all. In *Women and religion in the west: Challenging secularization*, ed. K. Aune, S. Sharma, and G. Vincett, 1–22. Aldershot: Ashgate.

Winter, T., A. Lummis, and A. Stokes. 1994. *Defecting in place: Women claiming responsibility for their own spiritual lives*. New York: Crossroad.

Woodhead, L. 2007. Gender differences in religious practice and significance. In *Handbook of the sociology of religion*, ed. J. Beckford and J. Demerath III, 550–570. Los Angeles/London: Sage.

Woodhead, L. 2008. Because I'm worth it': Religion and women's changing lives in the west. In *Women and religion in the west: Challenging secularization*, ed. K. Aune, S. Sharma, and G. Vincett, 147–164. Aldershot: Ashgate.

Chapter 11
Somewhere Between Religion and Spirituality? Places of Retreat in Contemporary Britain

David Conradson

11.1 Introduction

> Scholars of religion refer to the current metamorphosis in religiousness with phrases like the 'move to horizontal transcendence' or the 'turn to the immanent'. But it would be more accurate to think of it as the rediscovery of the sacred *in* the immanent, the spiritual *within* the secular. More people seem to recognise that it is our everyday world, not some other one, that, in the words of the poet Gerard Manley Hopkins, is 'charged with the grandeur of God'. (Cox 2009: 2)

Since the nineteenth century, a number of scholars have argued that traditional forms of religious belief in western Europe are in decline. There has been a shift, they contend, from belief in metaphysical realities towards a view that this world and this life are all that there is. It is claimed that people no longer feel there is any immaterial outside to which they can refer, no other worldly dimension or higher beings from which moral guidance or existential solace may be sought (Bruce 2002; Cuppitt 1980, 1984). In Britain, some would argue that this ontological shift is evident in the falling numbers of people who declare a belief in a personal God, whilst a link might also be made to declining church attendance (Davie 1994, 2002).[1]

Although these narratives of religious decline enjoy some empirical support, they are far from the full story. It is the case that fewer people in Britain now participate in traditional Judaeo-Christian forms of worship, for instance, but the number of mosques and temples in many cities has grown. And despite the general fall in attendance at Christian churches, many Pentecostal and evangelical congregations are

---

[1] This shift in religious practice is not, of course, a global phenomenon. Whilst fewer people in western European nations now identify with Judaeo-Christian belief and practice than was previously the case, the opposite situation exists in some areas of the Global South.

D. Conradson (✉)
Department of Geography, University of Canterbury, Christchurch, New Zealand
e-mail: david.conradson@canterbury.ac.nz

P. Hopkins et al. (eds.), *Religion and Place: Landscape, Politics and Piety*,
DOI 10.1007/978-94-007-4685-5_11, © Springer Science+Business Media Dordrecht 2013

vibrant and expanding. So whilst some forms of religious association and expression are waning, others are relatively stable or even on the ascendant. Accounts of religious change in the West need to recognise this complexity rather than overlook it.

It is also important to take account of the diverse expressions of spirituality beyond religious institutions. If we understand 'the sacred' as that which affords some access to the numinous, then despite variable engagement with the formal spaces and structures of religious communities, it would seem that many people in Britain today are mindful of the sacred dimensions of this world (Partridge 2004a). For these individuals, life remains enchanted in ways that seem to defy accounts of secularisation (Bruce 2002; Heelas 2008). The sacred is no longer accessed primarily or exclusively through formal participation in religious communities, however, or by living in accordance with external forms of authority. Nor is it necessarily a matter of reaching beyond oneself to engage with a divine Being or beings, however these are understood. Instead, the sacred is more often sought within everyday life, in that which is close up and nearby, rather than far off. This kind of here-and-now, earthly spirituality can be seen at New Age and Mind Body Spirit festivals, in yoga and meditation classes, and in many alternative healing clinics.

The flourishing of spirituality outside of religious institutions has been described by some as a 'spirituality revolution' (Tacey 2004; Heelas and Woodhead 2005; Lynch 2007). In these writings, 'spirituality' typically denotes a concern for an enduring dimension of human life that relates to issues of meaning and purpose. This dimension may or may not be metaphysical in nature. The term 'revolution' is intended to signal a profound change in how contemporary humans negotiate and articulate their spirituality. Rather than living in adherence to external forms of religious authority, such as holy texts and endorsed leaders, it is claimed that many people now give greater weight to their own subjective evaluations of what makes spiritual sense (Partridge 2004a, b).

In a number of respects, the landscape of belief and spirituality in contemporary Britain is thus shifting. In this chapter, I consider one particular associational form within this landscape: the spiritual or religious retreat centre. In the barest of terms, spiritual and religious retreat centres offer people an environment in which they can (a) achieve some distance from the immediate demands of work and home and (b) engage to a greater degree than may normally be possible in personal and spiritual reflection. Many retreat centres are informed in some way by one or more religious or spiritual traditions, such as Christianity, Buddhism, Hinduism and New Age practice. Unlike most churches, synagogues, mosques and temples, however, retreat centres often lie outside or are somewhat peripheral to religious authority structures. This positioning affords them a measure of freedom from the expectations and dictates of external bodies. In principle, retreat centres thus offer significant scope for exploring spiritual and religious issues, and perhaps for spiritual innovation.

My discussion of these issues has two main parts. I begin by considering how the spirituality revolution might be playing out within particular places, and where retreat centres might fit in this process. I then examine two particular retreat centres in southern England. Each of these places enabled guests to engage in spiritual exploration and reflection, albeit within certain structures and rhythms of practice. On the basis of guests' experiences of each site, I suggest that these two retreat centres – and indeed retreat centres more generally – can be understood as places that lie somewhere between 'religion' (in the sense of obligation to external authorities and traditions) and 'spirituality' (in the sense of a subjective quest for meaning and connection).

11.2 Geographies of the Spirituality Revolution

The contemporary shift from traditional expressions of religious belief towards spirituality is visible across a number of settings. Part of the picture lies in the established churches. Although two thirds of the British population attended a weekly Christian worship service in 1950, less than 8% do so today (Brierley 2001; Lynch 2007). The congregations of many mainstream Christian denominations, such as Presbyterianism, Anglicanism and Catholicism, are consequently ageing and undergoing numerical decline. People may still identify with a Christian understanding of the Divine – perhaps as part of what Grace Davie (1994) has referred to as 'believing without belonging' – but Christian churches are now less central to popular engagement with the sacred.[2] To understand the spirituality revolution, we need to look beyond these 'official' religious sites, as Kong (2010) has described them.

Heelas and Woodhead's (2005) study of Kendal, a market town in the English Lake District, offers useful insights in these respects, for it encompasses both traditional religious institutions and a number of sites associated with new spirituality. At the outset, Heelas and Woodhead distinguish between two broad types of setting for religious and spiritual practice in Kendal. The first was the *congregational domain* of Christian churches and chapels in the town and its immediate environs. As Kendal has no numerically significant Jewish, Muslim or Hindu communities, Christian congregations were the most visible form of local religious association. The second type of setting was the more diffuse *holistic milieu* associated with New Age and alternative spiritualities. This category included the community halls, practitioner centres and private homes in which yoga, meditation, *t'ai chi* and Reiki massage were offered. By documenting the balance of these two settings in Kendal, Heelas and Woodhead sought to evaluate the extent to which a 'spiritual revolution' was occurring locally.

Heelas and Woodhead argue that the spirituality revolution is best understood as part of a broader process of cultural change. Of central importance is the idea of a culture-wide 'subjective turn', entailing 'a turn away from life lived in terms of external or "objective" roles, duties and obligations, and a turn towards life lived by

---

[2] The spiritual experiences some people report whilst visiting architecturally inspiring cathedrals and chapels are an important exception to this statement. But such visits tend to be occasional and in the capacity of an observer, rather than as a participating member of the faith community most directly associated with the sites.

reference to one's own subjective experiences (relational as much as individualistic)' (2005, p. 4). In their view, the call of the subjective life is

> not to defer to higher authority, but to have the courage to become one's own authority. Not to follow established paths, but to forge one's own inner-directed, as subjective, life. Not to become what others want one to be, but to 'become who I truly am'. (p. 4)

A subjective-life orientation involves heightened recognition of one's own values and needs in determining a way forward. It is argued that a subjective turn is occurring in many western countries across the domains of work, personal relationships and leisure, as well as with respect to religion and spirituality (Taylor 1991).

Building on this subjectivisation argument, Heelas and Woodhead develop a set of propositions around what they describe as *life-as* and *subjective-life* forms of the sacred. As they describe it, 'life-as forms of the sacred… emphasize a transcendent source of significance and authority to which individuals must conform at the expense of the cultivation of their unique subjective lives' whilst '… subjective-life forms of the sacred… emphasize inner sources of significance and authority and the cultivation or sacralisation of unique subjective-lives' (2005, p. 6). Rather than seeking guidance from an external religious authority, whether divine or human, subjective evaluation becomes a primary source of discernment.

If the spirituality revolution was occurring in Kendal, Heelas and Woodhead hypothesised that life-as forms of religion would be in decline, whilst subjective-life spirituality would be growing. They therefore sought to compare the vitality of Christian faith and practice with local holistic forms of spirituality (including t'ai *chi*, Reiki, yoga, the use of crystals and tarot-based divination). When gathering this information, Heelas and Woodhead were careful not to conflate Christianity with life-as forms of religion. They recognised that within Christian congregations and communities, there would be many different ways of relating to the sacred. Some of these would likely involve subjective-life spirituality.[3] Where expressions of subjective-life spirituality retained significant elements of life-as religion, however, such as the notion of a transcendent God, Heelas and Woodhead combined their terms to suggest these should be described as 'life-as spirituality'.

Within Kendal, Heelas and Woodhead found that church attendance had declined markedly since the 1950s, with only 8% of the local population regularly attending a service. Somewhat surprisingly, popular interest in New Age beliefs and spiritual practices had not grown to anything like a compensating extent. Although quite visible, only around 1.6% of the community were directly involved in these forms of holistic spirituality. This finding raised the possibility that there had been no spirituality revolution in Kendal.

---

[3] In the Church of England, for example, the term 'fresh expressions' describes efforts to develop new ways of doing and being church (Croft and Mosby 2009; Milbank 2008). A good number of these initiatives emphasise contemplative, immanent and sacramental forms of Christian belief which, at least at face value, bear some relation to subjective-life spirituality. Where they retain reference to an externally located transcendental God, however, they might be more accurately described as 'life-as spirituality' (Heelas and Woodhead 2005).

After some reflection, Heelas and Woodhead concluded that focusing on the *congregational domain* and *holistic milieu* had caused them to overlook other important local sites for religious and spiritual expression. To acquire a fuller picture, they argued it would be important to look beyond both traditional sites of religious expression (here churches and chapels) and the centres, homes and recreational settings associated with New Age spirituality. This would involve a '… thorough investigation of the presence or absence, growth or decline of life-as religion and subjective-life spirituality in the educational system, in health provision, in the workplace' (p. 68). As a small step in this direction, Heelas and Woodhead analysed the content of books, newspapers and magazine articles on sale locally. This work suggested that popular engagement with subjective-life spirituality significantly exceeded interest in life-as forms of religion. With respect to Kendal, they therefore concluded that '… although the spiritual revolution has not taken place with regard to weekly associational activities, it looks very much as though it has occurred, or is occurring, in significant sectors of the general culture – that is, the culture to which the majority of people have access and on which they exert influence, particularly by way of market demand' (Heelas and Woodhead 2005, pp. 72–73).

Heelas and Woodhead's call for attention to religious and spiritual expression across a range of settings resonates with recent developments in geography. As Kong (2010, p. 757) explains, geographers interested in religion and belief are now investigating '… a variety of religious practices and sites beyond churches, temples, mosques, synagogues'. She notes that

> … [s]uch studies properly recognise religion as neither spatially nor temporally confined to 'reservations', practised only in officially assigned spaces at allocated times. Instead, there are many ways in which everyday spaces can be implicated in religious meaning-making, legitimating, maintaining and enhancing, but also challenging religious life, beliefs, practices and identities.

The 'unofficially sacred' sites examined in this work include museums, schools, sacred groves, roadside shrines, mediaspaces, streetscapes and home-spaces (Kong 2010). These are places where people experience the sacred in personally meaningful ways, but which are seldom officially endorsed or recognised for such purposes.

In a number of respects, Christian retreat centres might be thought of as places that lie between the 'official' and 'unofficially' sacred. Most Christian retreat centres make some connection to historic Christian thought and practice, whether favourably or more critically. Unlike most churches, however, retreat centres are seldom incorporated into denominational structures of authority and accountability. They more typically enjoy a measure of independence from such structures. So whilst there are normally recognisable elements of Christian belief and practice at a Christian retreat centre, there is also often an implicit or explicit invitation to question and explore that tradition. In some Christian retreat centres, guests are also encouraged to engage with other religious and spiritual traditions (Whiteaker 2004).

Heelas and Woodhead (2005) suggest that some Christian retreat centres may function as extra-ecclesiastical spaces in which subjective-life spirituality is welcomed and encouraged. Many retreat centres do of course foreground the contemplative, mystical and monastic dimensions of the Christian tradition. As such, they may be places where subjective-life spirituality is supported. But it is not too difficult to imagine situations in which life-as religiosity and life-as spirituality might also be part of retreat centre life. The balance between these different styles of engagement with the sacred will of course vary between retreat centres.

11.3   Othona and Worth Abbey: Two Christian Retreat Centres

Popular engagement with retreat centres has grown across western countries in recent years (Whiteaker 2004). This growth reflects contemporary interest in spirituality as well as a demand for places that offer respite from the busyness of everyday life (Conradson 2008, 2011). Here I consider two particular retreat centres, Othona and Worth Abbey, each of which is based around a residential spiritual community in the Christian tradition. As part of a retreat programme, these communities offer members of the public the opportunity to stay in a restful and peaceful environment and to engage with contemplative, spiritual and therapeutic practices. The intention is to facilitate well-being, personal reflection and spiritual growth. Guests are asked to contribute to the costs of their stay, but the retreats are run on a not-for-profit basis.

The first of the retreat centres, Othona, is located in coastal Dorset, a rural county in southern England. Its advertising materials describe it as a 'centre for community and spirituality', 'rooted in the Christian heritage… open to the widening future'.[4] The residential community consists of six adults, assisted by two to three long-term volunteers. The overall setting is restful and scenic, with views of the nearby sea and coastline (Fig. 11.1).

The Othona community seeks to provide guests with a supportive environment for personal and spiritual growth. A range of weekend and week-long courses and retreats are offered to this end, with accommodation for nearly 40 guests at any one time. Recent retreats include 'The Future of Spirit', 'Focusing – A Tool for Transformation', 'Nature and Spirit: Exploring the Vital Connection', 'Enneagram Explorations: Freeing the Life Force', 'Singing the World' and 'The New Universe Story'. In an average year, there are approximately 700–800 residential retreatants, with day visitors in addition to this. The guests include a significant proportion of Christians, as well as people of other faiths and spiritualities, and those who do not identify themselves in any such terms. Importantly, Othona is an independent charitable organisation. Whilst it may receive support from churchgoing individuals, it is not formally accountable to any church or other religious body.

Around 150 miles east of Othona, Worth Abbey is a Benedictine monastery in East Sussex. With a residential community of 25 Roman Catholic monks and an associated secondary school, the grounds are extensive. The site includes a distinctive

---

[4] Excerpt from the Othona website (www.othona-bb.org.uk)

Fig. 11.1   The Othona chapel and grounds (Source: Author's photo)

circular church (Fig. 11.2), accommodation for residential retreatants, meeting rooms for day visitors, the monks' accommodation and a quiet garden. As a Benedictine monastery, the Abbey's core focus is work and worship, but a range of retreats is offered to members of the public as well. Illustrative examples include 'Finding Silence', 'Finding Sanctuary', 'Personal and Spiritual Growth', 'Summer Stillness: Reflective Retreats' and 'Managing Conflict in our Relationships: The Benedictine Way'.[5] These retreats are offered through the 'Open Cloister' and attract over 2,000 residential guests each year. A significant proportion of those attending self-identify as Roman Catholics, but there are others without an active connection to the church, as well as the non-religious and spiritual seeking. In contrast to the relative independence of Othona, Catholic ecclesiastical authority exerts a quiet but recognisable influence upon life at Worth Abbey. The Abbey is also affiliated to the English Benedictine Congregation, a group of 13 monasteries within the international Benedictine Confederation.[6]

As part of a broader project on the revalorisation of stillness in contemporary Britain, interviews were conducted with key members of the residential spiritual communities at Othona and Worth Abbey during 2008 and 2009. At a later date, I then attended an organised weekend retreat at each centre in a participant observer capacity. This research was undertaken with the agreement of the residential community

---

[5] For further information, see www.worthabbey.net

[6] For further information, see http://www.benedictines.org.uk and http://www.osb.org/intl/confed/confed.html

Fig. 11.2 Worth Abbey church (Source: John Barrett©. Licensed for reuse under Creative Commons Licence)

at each place, on the understanding that all guest-related information would be anonymised. At the end of each retreat, a set of questionnaires was left with a staff member for voluntary completion by future guests. The aim was to gather quantitative and more open-ended qualitative information regarding retreatants' experiences at each place. Twenty guests at Othona completed a questionnaire, whilst 32 did so at Worth Abbey.[7] Their responses provide some insight into the experience of attending a religious or spiritual retreat centre.[8]

11.4   Retreatant Characteristics

The average age of the Othona sample of retreatants was 63 years. There were more women (61%) than men (39%) and a significant proportion of retirees (65%). The retreatants at Worth Abbey were younger, with an average age of 45 years, and

---

[7] Questionnaire respondents were drawn from a number of weekend and day retreats at each site, rather than the specific retreat at which participant observation took place. All of the retreats nevertheless shared an emphasis on the cultivation of stillness through prayer, meditation and other contemplative techniques.

[8] Given the relatively small numbers and the non-random sampling strategy, these figures cannot be considered representative. Nevertheless, the religious and spiritual characteristics of the participants are broadly in line with how staff at each centre described their guests in general.

Table 11.1 Retreatant characteristics: Othona and Worth Abbey

Characteristic	Othona (%) (n = 20)	Worth Abbey (%) (n = 32)
Importance of the spiritual/religious dimension of the retreat		
Unimportant	0	0
Of little importance	0	0
Moderately important	33.3	6.3
Important	38.1	12.5
Very important	28.6	81.3
Involvement with faith or spiritual communities outside the retreat		
Regular contact/involvement	36.0	71.9
Occasional contact/involvement	16.0	15.6
Rare contact/involvement	8.0	9.4
'Spiritual but not religious'	16.0	3.1
Agnostic	4.0	3.1
Atheist	0.0	0
'Spiritually searching'	16.0	0
Other	4.0	0
Personal identification with		
Christianity	53.3	90.6
Buddhism	13.3	6.3
Judaism	6.7	3.1
Hinduism	0	0
New Age	3.3	0
None	6.7	0
Other	16.7	3.1

nearly equal numbers of men and women. They were also more likely to be undertaking paid work, whether full-time (56.7%) or part-time (20%).

In terms of religious and spiritual affiliations, almost three quarters (72%) of Worth Abbey retreatants had regular contact or involvement with a spiritual or faith community. Nearly all (91%) personally identified with the Christian faith (Table 11.1). At Othona, by contrast, a little over a third (36%) of retreatants had regular contact or involvement with a spiritual or faith community. Others described themselves as having occasional contact/involvement (16%), as 'spiritual but not religious' (16%) or as 'spiritually searching' (16%). In contrast to Worth Abbey, only half of the Othona retreatants identified with Christianity (53.3%), with others indicating a connection to Buddhism (13.3%) or New Age spirituality (3.3%). Interestingly, 6.7% described themselves as having no religious or spiritual affiliation, whilst a sizeable group selected 'other' (16.7%). Responses in this latter category included 'Quaker', 'Druid' and 'Native American', as well as two people who described themselves in universalist terms (using phrases such as 'I can see the good in all religions').

The range of religious and spiritual affiliations amongst Othona retreatants arguably reflects the community's openness to spiritual exploration. There was no expectation that a guest adhere to Christian doctrine or practice. As the web pages explain:

> You don't have to be Christian to enjoy Othona or to be welcome here. Many Othona people are Christian, but some are of other faiths. And many others are reluctant to be identified with any one religion, seeing themselves on a spiritual search.

Whether this aspiration for openness was borne out in guests' experiences is of course a matter for enquiry. But if we assume that people attend retreat centres on a largely voluntary basis, then Table 11.1 might suggest that individuals seek out retreats which are broadly consonant with their religious and spiritual positions, as well as their preferred ways of being. A larger proportion of Worth Abbey retreatants appear to have relatively traditional religious affiliations, whilst Othona retreatants include a greater proportion of the 'spiritual but not religious' and those who are spiritually searching. With these differences in mind, we can now look at the nature of each retreat in a little more detail.

11.5   Stillness and Reflection

Most residential retreats at Othona and Worth Abbey are between 3 and 7 days in length. Although each retreat has a distinctive focus, common elements include input from members of the residential community or visiting teachers, opportunities for personal reflection and contemplation, shared meals and free time. By way of illustration, Fig. 11.3 shows the programme for a 4-day retreat at Worth Abbey (attended by a number of the participants in this study). Each day included a mix of group and individual activities, structured around morning, midday and evening prayer. The retreats at Othona had similar elements, but tended to be a little less structured, with more scope for interaction between retreatants and less direct 'instruction' or teaching.

A range of thoughts and feeling states emerged at these retreats. At Worth Abbey, guests emphasised their appreciation of time away from home and work demands, as well as the opportunity for personal spiritual reflection. When asked what they most appreciated about the Abbey, they spoke of stillness, silence and the opportunity to think and connect with God. The following comments are illustrative:

'Tranquillity and time to think'

(Royal Air Force officer, male, 40–49)

'The strong presence of God in the peace and silence and the daily offices of prayer'
(Town planner, female, 50–59)

'Silence, solitude, community, monastic rhythm and prayer'
(Minister of religion, male, 40–49)

Fig. 11.3 Worth Abbey
'Open Cloister' retreat
schedule

Worth │ The Open
Abbey │ Cloister

Finding Sanctuary
6ᵗʰ – 9ᵗʰ October 2008

Monday 6ᵗʰ

16:00   Arrivals (Tea/Coffee)
17:00   *Welcome Meeting* in St. Bruno's
17:30   Community Mass in Church
18:00   Personal Reading and Prayer
18:40   Evening Prayer in Church
19:00   Supper in St. Bruno's
20:15   *Introductory Session*: in St Bruno's
21:00   Compline in Church

Tuesday 7ᵗʰ and Wednesday 8ᵗʰ

6:20   Office of Readings
        Personal Reading and Prayer
7:30   Morning Prayer
        Breakfast
        Personal Reading and Prayer
10:00   *Session*
11:00   Tea/Coffee
11.30   *Session*
13:00   Midday Prayer
13:15   Lunch
14:00   walk or rest
16:00   Tea/Coffee
16:30-17:15 Introduction to Lectio Divina *(Tuesday only)*
17:30   Community Mass
18:00   Personal Reading and Prayer
18:40   Evening Prayer
19:00   Supper
20:15   *Informal Discussion/Social*
21:00   Compline in Church

Thursday 9ᵗʰ

6:20   Office of Readings
        Personal Reading and Prayer
7:30   Morning Prayer
        Breakfast
        Personal Reading and Prayer
10.00   *Session*
11:00   Tea/Coffee
11:30   Quiet time/Prayer/Reading/Walk
13:00   Midday Prayer
13:15   Lunch
14:00   Departures.

'The divine silence... the joy of creation in a beautiful landscape, reminding me that God is here now'

(University lecturer, female, 50–59)

'Ordered periods of study and discussion interspersed with a lot of time for "nothingness" and "stillness"'

(Royal Air Force officer, male, 30–39)

The reference here to a 'monastic rhythm' of activity speaks directly to the daily rhythm of prayer and reflection at Worth Abbey. This is a rhythm which characterises

Benedictine monastic communities in general, the collective life of which builds on the teaching and practices of St. Benedict (480–547AD) (de Dreuille 2002).

Worth Abbey was clearly a place in which contemplation was valued. Retreatants were given a number of opportunities to reflect upon their personal faith and spirituality, within a relatively quiet and calming setting. Throughout the retreats, the monks mobilised particular understandings of God, the saints and the church. Prayer was offered to an external deity, and the monks made themselves available to guests for spiritual direction. The Open Cloister was thus well suited to those who wished to explore contemplative spirituality, but to do so within an environment characterised by life-as forms of religiosity. In Heelas and Woodhead's (2005) terms, the Abbey could perhaps be described as supporting life-as expressions of spirituality. To be sure, there were significant opportunities for personal reflection and contemplation, in a manner which at times represented or came close to subjective-life forms of spirituality. But these opportunities took place in a setting which tended to reinstate a transcendent rather than immanent understanding of the Divine.

Retreats at Othona were somewhat different, particularly in terms of the interaction between the residential community, guests and external teachers. The residential community and volunteers worked to provide an environment that supported reflection, contemplation and personal growth. They maintained the accommodation, prepared meals, managed advertising and reservations and generally sought to offer guests a warm and inclusive welcome. In keeping with Othona's declared ethos of 'being rooted in the Christian heritage… open to a widening future', the teaching and spiritual/creative practice elements of most Othona retreats were often provided by external practitioners and teachers. Many of these individuals were recognised for their efforts to further spiritual and theological understanding, blending psychological, scientific and religious insights in new ways (e.g. O'Murchu 2004).

Given the diversity of its guests and the use of external teachers, Othona was a place in which different spiritual ideas and traditions came together. A range of perspectives could frequently be observed in the ways guests spoke (or not) about God, faith, spirit and life and in the nature of their spiritual practices (e.g. prayer and meditation). For the most part, it seemed that these different ideas and ways of being were able to coexist harmoniously, although there was mild discomfort or awkwardness on occasion. Whatever the interpersonal dynamics, retreats at Othona were generally organised to enable interaction and dialogue amongst guests, as well as between guests and the teachers. The schedule was less structured than at Worth Abbey, and this allowed more possibility for both harmonious and less harmonious encounters to emerge.

Many Othona retreatants were seeking meaningful spirituality beyond the certainties of institutional forms of religion. Othona was very open to people engaged in this kind of quest. As the advertising for a recent 'Future of Spirit' retreat put it,

> Do you think you are – or might be – 'spiritual, not religious'? One of the features of our time is the emergence of spiritualities no longer anchored in institutional religion. Some are closer to nature mysticism, some look to an integration of science and spirit. What's going on? How does it touch us? Some people feel these emerging spiritual paths are actually the

great religions' truest offspring, their gift to the future; others see them as completely separate. Using film, online resources, group exercises and creative celebrations we'll try and discern the outlines of the spiritual future. Want to join the discussion? Share your experiences? Meet other people on parallel paths?…[9]

During the retreat I attended, it seemed to me that Othona strongly welcomed and encouraged this kind of spiritual exploration. And this was not just about solitary enquiry. There was an implicit invitation to join with others in co-creating new forms of spiritual understanding and practice.

To summarise, both Worth Abbey and Othona encouraged guests to engage in personal and spiritual contemplation. This contemplation extended beyond what would normally occur in a church meeting, both in duration and intensity. In terms of spiritual exploration and experimentation, Othona was more directly and explicitly supportive of this than Worth Abbey. The Benedictine rhythm of monastic life at the Abbey appeared to operate as a form of 'bounding' structure for retreatants, encouraging contemplative reflection within a Christian framework more than critical evaluation of it. The difference between Othona and Worth Abbey in this respect in part reflected their relationships to structures of religious authority and power. As a Benedictine monastery, Catholic belief and tradition inevitably shaped the teaching and spiritual practices of Worth Abbey. In contrast, Othona's independence of the church gave it the freedom to invite a diverse range of external teachers and practitioners, from the relatively mainstream through to the avant-garde.

11.6   Encountering Difference

At both Othona and Worth Abbey, the retreatants encountered individuals whose religious and spiritual perspectives differed from their own. Sometimes these encounters proved uncomfortable or difficult, as noted earlier. Table 11.2 summarises the main difficulties identified by guests at each place, providing a starting point for discussion.

Interestingly, over half the retreatants at each centre indicated there was 'nothing' they found problematic about their particular retreat. At Worth Abbey, the most significant difficulty was with the spiritual or religious dimensions of the overall retreat centre. Participants made it clear that they were largely referring to their struggle with its Catholicism. When asked what they felt least able to connect with, the following responses were illustrative:

The Roman Catholic perspective given during the study periods, as I am C of E (Church of England). But I accept that the retreat is rooted in a Catholic monastery!
(Royal Air Force Officer, male, 30–39)

_____

[9] Excerpt from http://www.othona-bb.org.uk/programme-of-events/event-135/

Table 11.2 Elements of retreats identified as 'difficult'

Area of difficulty	Othona (%) (n = 20)	Worth Abbey (%) (n = 32)
'Nothing'/no response[a]	45.0	59.4
Religious and/or spiritual dimensions of the retreat centre	5.0	21.9
An idea or theological issue encountered during the retreat	0	6.3
Other retreatants in general	15.0	3.1
Other retreatants' religious and/or spiritual views	30.0	6.3
Other	5.0	3.0

[a]This category combines statements along the lines that 'nothing was a problem' as well as blank responses. Whilst blank responses are not the same as a positive statement of there being no problems, they were deemed sufficiently similar to justify combination here.

Some of the more overt Catholic practices in worship.

(Company secretary, male, 60–69)

I'm not yet sure about some aspects of the Catholic church.

(Psychotherapist, female, 60–69)

The primary area of difficulty for retreatants at Worth Abbey was thus its Catholicism. A relatively small percentage of people (9.4%) indicated they experienced difficulties with other retreatants, either in general or as a result of their religious or spiritual views. Although the Worth Abbey sample is relatively homogenous in terms of Christian religious and spiritual affiliations (Table 11.1), the lack of reported tension between retreatants is unlikely to be solely a function of similar views within the group. 'Christian', after all, is a very broad category, extending from the conservative evangelical to the liberal. A more complete explanation might be derived by reviewing the nature of Worth Abbey retreats. A significant amount of time at these retreats was normally spent either in structured group sessions led by the monks or by oneself in silent reflection. This mix of activities did not enable much in the way of in-depth interaction amongst retreatants. With less opportunity for interaction and dialogue, there was also less opportunity for differences in views to become apparent. The limited nature of social interaction between guests is likely to have contributed to the low numbers who experienced difficulties with fellow retreatants.

In contrast to Worth Abbey, nearly one third (30%) of those sampled at Othona experienced some difficulty with the spirituality or religious views of other retreatants. There was some tension between evangelical and less evangelical guests, for instance, as the comments from this retired man and young women suggest:

Being a born-again Christian, while I appreciate listening to other people's experiences and beliefs, I do find a dearth of what I would describe as 'biblical truth' – indeed a rejection of same.

(Retiree, male, 60–69)

... the only thing is that some of the visitors this week are more traditional in their views,
and so I have had a little discomfort in relating to them.

(Nurse, female, 20–29)

This kind of interaction is understandable if we recall the diversity of Othona's
retreatants, which ranged from Christian and Buddhist through to New Age and
Druid (Table 11.1). In addition, as already noted, there was significant opportunity
at Othona for interaction and sharing of views, all set within an environment in
which the residential community had little vested interest in promoting any particular line of thinking. In this context, the most commonly reported difficulties concerned interactions with other retreatants. No direct comments were made about
problems with the spirituality of Othona as a retreat centre.[10]

These interactions amongst guests reflected not only their personal characteristics
and dispositions but also the retreat environment. It is clear that retreatants came to
Othona and Worth Abbey with personal qualities and needs. At the same time, each
retreat centre differed in terms of how much it expected guests to adapt their behaviours to local norms. A guest's experience of retreat emerged to a significant degree
out of this interaction between the individual and the organisational domains.

The situation at Othona and Worth Abbey was also part of a bigger picture. A
staff member at the Retreat Association – a national charitable body which handles
enquiries, marketing and public representation for several hundred Christian retreat
centres in Britain – suggested there were three main groups of retreatants in the UK.
She described these groups as:

1. The *'established faithful'*: 'The person who is in touch because they want to go
   on retreat and it's part of their pattern and rhythm, and they are established in a
   local church.'
2. The *'refugees from institutional religion'*: 'The person who's hurt and disillu-
   sioned by church, but wants to continue a journey with God, and thinks the retreat
   movement might be a place where that could happen.'
3. The *'non-religious spiritual seeker'*: 'The person who's never been to church,
   who doesn't want to go to church, isn't interested in church in any shape or form,
   but understands themselves to be a spiritual person, and is looking for a place
   where they might explore that, where they're not going to be given a direction
   which they should/ought/must go, that kind of what they would consider judging
   language. And that group of people is the group that has grown in the time that
   I've been working here.'

(Retreat Association interviewee, 2008)

With 78% of Worth Abbey retreatants in regular or occasional contact with a
religious community, we might assume that many in this group could be described

---

[10] One of the staff members at Othona nevertheless commented that, at any given retreat, there
would sometimes be guests who found it 'too Christian' for their preferences, whilst others would declare
the same retreat 'not Christian enough'. Such comments reflected the dynamic between retreatant
preferences and retreat characteristics.

as the 'established faithful'. The established faithful are likely to prefer retreats which value life-as religiosity and have clear connections to their church communities. For this group, attending a retreat is likely to be an occasional supplement to their normal religious practice. At Othona, in contrast, there was a significant proportion of 'non-religious spiritual seekers', as one third (32%) of the retreatants indicated they were either 'spiritually seeking' or 'spiritual but not religious' (Table 11.1).

It seems safe to suggest that Othona and Worth Abbey differ in the proportion of their guests which might be considered 'established faithful' or 'non-religious spiritual seekers'. This difference reflects the character of each centre and connects again to the notion of a spiritual marketplace in which retreat centres operate. As directories like the Good Retreat Guide (Whiteaker 2004) indicate, retreat centres differ in size and religious affiliation, whether or not they have a residential spiritual community, as well as the type of retreats offered (e.g. silent vs. talking, group vs. individual, structured vs. unstructured). It is unsurprising that members of the public seek retreats or retreat centres that to some degree accord with their own spirituality and beliefs.

11.7   Conclusions

In this chapter, I have considered two Christian retreat centres in southern England and the experiences of their guests. Stepping back a little, a number of points emerge about the place of retreat centres in contemporary landscapes of religion and belief. Although social life is inevitably messier than the categories we bring to it, I would argue that retreat centres can be understood as places somewhere between 'religion' (in the sense of obligation to external authorities and traditions, and life-as forms of the sacred) and 'spirituality' (in the sense of a subjective quest for meaning and connection, and subjective-life senses of the sacred). If these terms are understood in this way, Othona and Worth Abbey could be said to encompass elements of both religion and spirituality. On the one hand, each of these retreat centres has developed a collective life that is distinct from congregational Christianity. The atmosphere and spirituality of each place is consistently more contemplative than most mainstream Christian churches. At the same time, this is not a spirituality which has been fashioned *ex nihilo*, out of the nothing. It instead emerges out of the breadth and richness of the Christian tradition, foregrounding parts of that tradition – such as Christian mysticism, monasticism and the so-called Desert Fathers of the third and fourth centuries – whilst downplaying others. Whilst drawing on these theological and practical resources, the communities at Othona and Worth Abbey are also exploring their own perspectives and new ways of 'being faithful'. In doing so, they combine elements of both life-as religion and subjective-life spirituality whilst also bearing witness to the broader subjective turn of which the spirituality revolution is part (Taylor 1991; Heelas and Woodhead 2005; Heelas 2008).

Many of the participants in this study were on retreat because they recognised their spiritual needs were not being fully met in their local environment. In response, they had chosen to move to a setting which they hoped would facilitate rest, insight and perhaps spiritual growth. Irrespective of whether or not these hopes were realised, the impulse to go on retreat has much in common with subjective-life spirituality (Heelas and Woodhead 2005). For the retreatant prioritises subjectively felt needs and seeks to address them, in the hope of finding stillness, renewed perspective and open-minded spirituality. In this study, subjective-life forms of spirituality were most evident at Othona, in part because it welcomed spiritual exploration and supported open discussion between guests and teachers. In contrast, the contemplative spirituality evident at Worth Abbey was enfolded by the a broader Benedictine environment, where life-as religion was arguably to the fore. The overall outcome was perhaps akin to what Heelas and Woodhead (2005) describe as life-as forms of spirituality.

It would seem that Christian retreat centres cater to several different constituencies. Some people go on retreat as an occasional supplement to a local congregational involvement, without having any desire to move beyond this form of religious expression. Others visit these places because their spiritual journey has taken them well beyond the mainstream, and they are in real need of support and like-minded community. For these individuals, retreat centres may function as a form of spiritual refuge as well as a theological and emotional resource. In addition, the residential communities at many retreat centres are often engaged in their own processes of spiritual development and learning. This work might involve representing the contemplative and mystical strands of the Christian tradition to contemporary audiences or integrating ideas from consciousness research and psychotherapy with spirituality (Heelas 2002; Lynch 2007; Tacey 2004). To the extent that they develop genuinely new ideas and perspectives, some retreat centres may thus function as sites of spiritual innovation. For all these reasons, retreat centres are a fascinating associational form within contemporary landscapes of belief and spirituality.

Acknowledgements I am grateful to the editors for helpful comments on an earlier draft of this chapter, to the British Academy for financially supporting the research (SG44-237), and to the staff and guests at Othona and Worth Abbey who participated in the study.

References

Brierley, P. (ed.). 2001. *UK Christian handbook: Religious trends 3 (2002–2003)*. London: Christian Research.

Bruce, S. 2002. *God is dead: Secularization in the west*. Oxford: Blackwell.

Conradson, D. 2008. The place of retreat: Experiential economies of stillness in contemporary Britain. In *Therapeutic landscapes: Advances and applications*, ed. A. Williams, 31–48. Aldershot: Ashgate.

Conradson, D. 2011. The orchestration of feeling: Stillness, spirituality and places of retreat. In *Stillness in a mobile world*, ed. D. Bissell and G. Fuller, 71–86. London: Routledge.

Cox, H. 2009. *The future of faith*. New York: Harper Collins.

Croft, S., and I. Mosby (eds.). 2009. *Ancient faith future mission: Fresh expressions in the sacramental tradition*. Norwich: Canterbury Press.

Cuppitt, D. 1980. *Taking leave of god*. London: SCM Publishers.

Cuppitt, D. 1984. *The sea of faith: Christianity in change*. London: BBC.

Davie, G. 1994. *Religion in Britain since 1945: Believing without belonging*. Oxford: Blackwell.

Davie, G. 2002. *Europe, the exceptional case. Parameters of faith in the modern world*. London: Darton Longman & Todd Publishers.

de Dreuille, M. 2002. *The rule of St. Benedict: A commentary in light of world ascetic traditions*. New York: Paulist Press.

Heelas, P. 2002. The spiritual revolution: From religion to spirituality. In *Religions in the modern world*, ed. L. Woodhead, 357–377. London: Routledge.

Heelas, P. 2008. *Spiritualities of life: New age romanticism and consumptive capitalism*. Oxford: Blackwell.

Heelas, P., and L. Woodhead. 2005. *The spiritual revolution: Why religion is giving way to spirituality*. Oxford: Blackwell.

Kong, L. 2010. Global shifts, theoretical shifts: changing geographies of religion. *Progress in Human Geography* 34(6): 755–776.

Lynch, G. 2007. *The new spirituality: An introduction to progressive belief in the twenty-first century*. London: IB Tauris.

Milbank, J. 2008. Stale expressions: The management-shaped church. *Studies in Christian Ethics* 21(1): 117–128.

O'Murchu, D. 2004. *Quantum theology*. New York: Crossroad Publishing Company.

Partridge, C. 2004a. *The re-enchantment of the West. Volume 1: Alternative spiritualities, sacralization, popular culture and occulture*. London: Continuum.

Partridge, C. 2004b. Alternative spiritualities, new religions and the re-enchantment of the West. In *Oxford handbook of new religious movements*, ed. J.R. Lewis, 39–67. New York: Oxford University Press.

Tacey, D. 2004. *The spirituality revolution – The emergence of contemporary spirituality*. London: Brunner-Routledge.

Taylor, C. 1991. *The ethics of authenticity*. Cambridge, MA: Harvard University Press.

Whiteaker, S. 2004. *The good retreat guide*, 5th ed. London: Random House.

Chapter 12
The Space That Faith Makes: Towards a (Hopeful) Ethos of Engagement

Julian Holloway

12.1 Introduction

> The idea is to form an *interim vision*, one which must be *visualized* by many in order to be *felt*, and *felt* in order to energize action in interwoven institutions and individuals….
> (Connolly 2008: xi, original emphasis)

In recent times, there seems to be widespread recognition that religion is here to stay and is much more than an affair of private interest. Theories of secularisation, where matters of faith and spirituality gain less and less purchase on society and politics and find their 'legitimate' sphere only in the private spaces of the individual, have been rent asunder by a series of contemporary events and movements. Moreover, it seems that Western and European political philosophy has begun to find room for a rapprochement with religion and issues of theological concern – something that has been paralleled in the evident consolidation of the study of the geography of religion and belief (Kong 2010). Leading thinkers such as Derrida (1998), Eagleton (2009), Habermas (1998) and Žižek (2001), in admittedly divergent ways, have engaged with matters of the religious. This has led to talk of an emergent 'post-secularism' which recognises (without totally discarding) the limits of reason, rationality and secularism, the restrictions of a liberal consensus of separate public-political and private-religious spheres, and a political pluralism that, by necessity, includes constituencies of the religious and faithful (Harrington 2007; McLennan 2007; Sigurdson 2010).

Emerging from this nascent post-secularism is the recognition that religion and spirituality when scrutinised from an apparently secularised social scientific viewpoint

J. Holloway (✉)
Division of Geography and Environmental Management,
Manchester Metropolitan University, Manchester, England, UK
e-mail: j.j.holloway@mmu.ac.uk

P. Hopkins et al. (eds.), *Religion and Place: Landscape, Politics and Piety*,
DOI 10.1007/978-94-007-4685-5_12, © Springer Science+Business Media Dordrecht 2013

undergo a series of epistemological erasures. Accordingly, too often religion and belief are reduced to and made a function of the logics of society:

> From any standpoint of phenomenological adequacy to religious experience, the general problem with functionalist theories of religion is that they tend to reduce religious understandings of the absolute to functions of fulfilment of ulterior social dynamics that categorically fall outside of the horizons of the self-descriptions of the participants. (Harrington 2007: 546)

The epistemological violence inherent to such approaches has been recognised and a new spirit of engagement with religion is emerging. It seems therefore that the investigation of religion is moving beyond the point where Latour (2005: 233, original emphasis) can ask 'Why is it that when faced with religion, we tend to limit our inquiry to its 'social dimensions' and take as a scientific virtue *not* to study religion itself?' (see Roberts 2004, 2006). So in a spirit of epistemic and ontological generosity, I wish to give some space for the theological in this chapter. Hence, I want to give some room to those extraordinary forces that the faithful will *always* say move them to action (Latour 2001).

The aims of this chapter are located precisely at this increasingly fuzzy and fluid border between the religious and non-religious. It aims to elucidate an ethos of engagement with theological and faithful sensibilities and, as such, contribute to this budding movement of post-secularism. I begin by exploring the importance of affective techniques in the generation of religious and spiritual subjectivities, focussing on the intensive performance of ritual and the generation of faithful dispositions. This forms the basis for the second section of the chapter wherein I seek out points of intersection and resonance between the religious and non-religious through a discussion of the idea and affective force of hope in the impossible–virtual. As I will show in the third section, these nexus of connection, such as those which emerge through thinking about hope and being hopeful, are central to an ethos of engagement yet can only emerge with a reflexive awareness of the contingency and contestability of ultimate claims. It follows that forging an ethos of engagement that is respectful and creative in its endeavours will always require the retention of critical scrutiny: religions do result in domination and exclusion; they can pathologise and they can discriminate. Thus, religion should never be approached in way that abandons critique, but this critique is not totally reliant on a social scientific discourse 'untainted' by religion and theology (Cabezón 2006). Theology and religion present multiple 'resources for political reflection' (Sigurdson 2010: 177), and it is in exploring these resources that new modes of engagement might find their generation. How we might begin working on new dispositions to realise these modes of engagement is briefly touched upon in the conclusion.

12.1.1 On the Affective Techniques of Religion and Ritual

I wish to start by describing some guiding principles that organise my approach to religion and spirituality in order that they might be drawn upon in the development of an ethos of engagement. Principally then, religious and spiritual orderings – how space and time are realised as imbued with the sacred and the divine – require continual practice and performance. Thus, without continual re-enactment, the traditions, beliefs and sensibilities of the faithful would wither and disappear. In this section, I wish to explore the broad contours of this practice in order to set the ground for exploring a specific characteristic of faith in the next section (for more specific examples, see Holloway 2003a, b, 2006, 2011a, b). Specifically, I will begin by outlining the intensive affirmation of faithful practice before investigating the more extensive realisation of religiosity and spirituality in space and time.

Being religious, spiritual or faithful is enacted through many different registers of emotion and affect – from quiet contemplation to ecstatic expression, from serious reflection to peaceful assurance, from joy to humbleness, from anger to awe. These registers emerge in all manner of spaces and times that are too many to detail here. Yet one space and time that is central to the realisation of faith and spirituality is that of the ritual. Rituals can take a myriad of forms, consistencies and durations dependent on the religious formations under investigation. However, at the heart of many rituals I would argue is the move to re-presence, evoke or respond to, in some form or other, a sense of the divine or the sacred. In other words, rituals attempt to bring forth bodies and selves in the presence of that which is held ultimate. As such, I want to move away from analysing rituals and religious practices as solely *representing* something. To ask what a ritual or a religious practice represents is very often a misunderstanding. Instead of being a mere vehicle for symbolic meanings, and hence referring to something outside of their performative context, rituals *do things*. As Amy Hollywood (2004: 58) puts it, 'that to which they refer is constituted in [the ritual] action itself'. Indeed, the performative outcome of many ritual spaces and times is the impress of faith onto and through the bodies of the participants. What rituals do (and redo) is to produce religious bodies and modes of subjectification.

Rituals are always events of relation. By this, I mean that the presencing of the divine and sacred in the ritual space–time is the outcome of an assemblage of heterogeneous materialities and immaterialities: texts, talk, bodies, objects, architectures, atmospheres of mood, smell, touch and sound, rhythms and emotion combine and intersect to realise the ritual space–time. This relationality we can call the *patterning* of ritual space–times. The term patterning speaks to the skein of ritual but also to the intensity and consistencies of these space–times: each is generated through and generates what we might call affective atmospheres of the sacred or the divine. These intensive atmospheres occur:

> before and alongside the formation of subjectivity, across human and non-human materialities, and in-between subject/object distinctions…[They] belong to collective situations and yet can be felt as intensely personal. (Anderson 2009: 78, 80)

These atmospheres are toned, coloured and shaded differently; these consistencies might be stimulating, introspective, calming, energising, reflective, powerful, severe, and so on. There is then a *patterning of qualitative intensity* that varies in tone and atmosphere in the ritual space–time.

The intensities generated in and through these differently patterned ritual space–times have the capacity to impress on the bodies present certain affective registers whilst simultaneously being generated through these bodies and practices of embodiment. Put differently, they generate registers of affect by working to bring forth and confirm certain intensities of feeling that are corporeally sensed. These intensities, continually generated in different space–times of ritual, confirm and reconfirm religious subjectivities. Furthermore, they tone and colour what it is to have faith as a sensibility or disposition in and to the world. Emphasising that ritual produces and reproduces faithful sensibilities through techniques of affect and sensation is not to say that faith is only pre-reflective and pre-cognitive. Indeed, discursive techniques, through the creedal and doctrinal elements of belief are worked into, work upon and help inform the way faith as a sensibility frames the world. Faith, to quote and extend William Connolly (2008: 71), is 'composed of at least two elements, a creedal dimension and the lived sensibility infusing it'. Therefore, this is not to abandon the importance of the discursive trajectories of belief. Rather, we can see doctrine and belief imbricated in a series of relays with techniques that work on the affective and visceral to inform a faithful sensibility and disposition.

Rituals then are a means by which faithful dispositions are formed and reformed, amplified and affirmed. These dispositions are not however confined to the ritual space–time. Instead, we must see faith as something that informs more extensive geographies and temporalities. Faithful sensibilities are continually patterned through the myriad space–times that religious subjectivities pass, act in and practice. Faith as a way the religious shape or approach the world is an ongoing and continually formed sensibility in, and disposition to, the world. One way in which faith shapes and grasps the world is through the giving of value and the formation of judgment. In other words, faithful dispositions order the salience of different geographies and temporalities. By according relevance and significance to space and time, the faithful might ask, is this space in need of faithful action? Different geographies are sensed as full of, or lacking in, divine significance. One writer, who has attempted to understand faith as this readiness for action in space and time, is the theologian Mark Wynn. His work explores how theistic experience comes about via a felt or affective response to the world. As he puts it, the faithful must recognise

> …the possibility that God's presence may be registered directly in our *felt responses*… and the possibility that the moral considerability or 'humanity' of our fellow human beings may be recognised *directly in feeling*; and…the possibility that the goodness of the world (and its parts) may be registered in an *affectively toned appreciation* of its character (and not in some affect-independent way). (Wynn 2005: 90–91, emphasis added)

Faith as a sensibility of judgment is informed by a series of what Wynn calls somatic markers:

> …somatic markers help to frame our problems of practical decision-making, by highlighting some possible choices as worthy of further consideration and excluding others, and thereby may help to determine the course of our discursive reflections. (2005: 116).

As such, faith weighs up or sorts the geographies that the faithful move through, via both affectively felt and discursively organised responses.

Through highlighting how faith orders the salience of different spaces, places and times, *beyond* the affirmation of faithful sensibilities in ritual space–times alone, we begin to see how faithful sensibilities inform wider and more extensive geographies and temporalities. In the more extensive sense, faithful dispositions affect judgment, and the way space and time bends or acts back upon these sensibilities. Two consequences follow. First, at different times and in different places, we need to trace how faith is either, and to varying degrees, foregrounded or backgrounded. Thus, the different interactions and events that the faithful move through are not, as Latour (2005: 202) calls them, isobaric. In other words, different spaces and times will be composed through practices in which different pressures emerge. Subsequently, faith may not everywhere and at all times be something made relevant to the event. This does not mean that faith is absent, or the traces of the ritual space are completely invisible or ignorable. Rather, faith is not explicitly drawn on or brought to the fore in certain spaces and times, whereas in others it is a more apparent and organising force. Second, the more extensive realisation of faithful dispositions points to how different (and more or less) religious sites are associated or linked together. The chains of association that compose and link different spaces in which the faithful interact point towards practices and patterns of religious scaling. Thus, rather than positing on the one hand the local space–time of ritual and then, on the other, faith on a global scale, we might begin to map the traces and practices of faithful sensibilities from one site to another and how the resulting spatial assemblage composes. This way, we can think of faithful sensibilities as assemblages that compose and associate different spaces together such that faithful dispositions travel, gain consistency and potentially influence further and wider. Indeed, as we shall see, the notion that faith is an assemblage composed through multiple practices with different contingencies and connections provides a template for an ethos of engagement between the religious and the non-religious – but more of that later.

12.2   The Affect of Hope and Sensibilities of the Impossible

Thus far, I have explored and emphasised how rituals and religious practices seek to amplify and affirm religious sensibilities. Through a variety of techniques which work on both affective and discursive registers of action, religious dispositions of faith are generated and sustained. The fortification and shading of faith through different rituals and techniques are both intensive, as they work on corporeal intensities of feeling in particular religious spaces at particular times, and extensive, in that they are carried forth and scaled out into wider geographies and temporalities and affect how these space–times show up, are valued and acted in by the faithful.

In this section, I want to draw attention to a particular trajectory in these sensibilities, one which colours how the faithful respond to and give meaning to space and time. The particular relation to the world I want to explore is that of hope. It strikes me that faith and hope are inextricably entwined in the performance of religious dispositions. For what is a faithful sensibility if it is not one woven through hope in something better, something more just and benevolent, sourced in the past, emerging in the present or in the future? Hope is a force of organisation and judgment that surges through many religious orderings such that the faithful hope to transcend the juncture where 'even the fresh leaves of spring are tinged with brown'

(Taylor 1984: 72). Hope then is realised in faith through the hope for a better life beyond this one, a hope in forgiveness, a hope for grace, a hope for providence, a hope for intervention through prayer, a hope in revelation, a hope in the realisation of prophecy, a hope in the Second Coming, a hope in a shift in global spiritual consciousness, a hope for revenge, a hope for transcendence and love, a hope that the ancestors are listening and appeased, a hope for oneness and peace, and many more hopes beside. Different faiths hold out different hopes and practices by which they are sustained: in this chapter, I will focus on broadly Christian dispositions of hope.

The notion of hope and its attendant spaces has come back onto the human geographical agenda in recent years (in tandem with work on anticipation, prediction and the future – see Evans 2010). Arguably it was Harvey's (2000) reengagement with utopianism that ushered in this focus, but it is Anderson's work (2006a, b; Anderson and Fenton 2008) that has profitably extended and developed the examination of hope. Key to what Anderson seeks (via a reappraisal of Bloch's work on the topic) is an exploration of 'what the event of hope, and the act of hoping, *does*' (Anderson and Fenton 2008: 78, emphasis added). In other words, hope affects those who practise it or are formed through its event. Hope is a particular relation to space and time wherein those moved *by* hope or moved *to* hope cultivate or are obliged by 'an ethos of engagement with the world' (Anderson 2006a: 692). This ethos, or what we might call (in line with the terms of this chapter) a sensibility or disposition, affects and is affected by the hope in something better. The possibilities and potentialities of the world act to forge a way of relating to and acting in space and time such that 'hopefulness, therefore, exemplifies a disposition that provides a dynamic imperative *to action* in that it enables bodies to *go on*. As a positive change in the passage of affect, it opens the space–time that it emerges from to a renewed *feeling* of possibility' (Anderson 2006b: 744, original emphasis).

The performative force of hope is one which enacts a relation to the world that is made full of its possibilities and potentialities. Faith can be taken as imbued and formed through hope such that faithful sensibilities tone and shade space and time through hope. Moreover, the techniques described in the previous section can be seen as modes of practice through which hopeful–faithful dispositions are forged or renewed. A sermon or prayer, for example, works through and realise affective charges that instil or revivify hopeful dispositions of faith. These affective charges are (partly) made of 'flows of hope that take place as transindividual affectivities which move between bodies' (Anderson 2006b: 741). Hope as an affective capacity of these techniques is always relational: it is a transversal (and sometimes precarious) emergent outcome of the ritual assemblage through which it is generated and in which it takes place. Religious talk, texts, objects, atmospheres and bodies coalesce to instil and distil faithful registers of hope: 'Hope is a relational phenomenon precisely because processes of hoping are always already scored across a range of human and nonhuman materialities' (Anderson and Fenton 2008: 78). Furthermore, the intensiveness of the techniques which express and impress hopeful bodies are made more extensive as these hopeful–faithful dispositions (so generated) grasp or anticipate a series of space–times as hopeful or in need of hope. Hope, then, is one charge of faith that realises a disposition that colours judgment and salience in and through space–time such that the 'Good News' (a story of hope that we will return to) is carried further afield.

Relational, intensive and extensive dispositions of hope are part of the production of faithful subjectivities: they generate certain sensibilities that characterise what it is to have faith or be one of the faithful. These sensibilities, as we have seen, are worked on and through the body. Therefore, there is something viscerally felt by these faithful bodies as they are organised and affirmed by religious techniques: hopefulness thus emerges 'as a constellation of specific bodily background feelings emergent from the expression of affect' (Anderson 2006b: 741). The propositional stance of faithful bodies emerges in and through a felt relation of hope in and towards the world. Hope is engineered by faithful bodies whilst generating and making its mark on those bodies in particular ways. Put differently, bodies have the capacity to affect and be affected by hopeful–faithful dispositions, with hope often being 'felt in a renewed animation of the proprioceptive and visceral senses' (Anderson 2006b: 743). Yet when interrogating hope as it animates and stirs different bodies, one must look to how the faithful body per se is particular in its constellations of hope and affect. Thus, the faithful body that hopes is often organised and intensified in particular ways.

In Christian faith, the source of this hope is one of centuries of contest which makes its determination difficult; space here does not allow the detailed exploration of this long history of struggle. Yet we can at least trace the broad contours of this source in order to give the peculiarity of the faithful–hopeful body some shape. As such, the faithful Christian body is made hopeful through another body – the 'Good News' of the body of Christ, its crucifixion and its resurrection. However this body is made sense of, however it is presenced again, however it is used politically (conservatively or progressively), it seems relatively uncontroversial to state that events of *this* body are of central content to how the Christian faithful body hopes. The force of hope, as it works on and through faithful bodies in the here and now, congeals out of the story of a particular body in the past (crucified and crossed) and the particular transformation of this body and other bodies in the past, present and future (the resurrected body). As the philosopher-cum-theologian John Caputo (2007: 75, 76) puts it,

> [Jesus'] body is the site of hope, providing the setting for the events that will transform the flesh of those laid low by suffering...[Christ's is] the first body in a chain of bodies to undergo such transformation that is set in motion by the body of Jesus.

The event of the crucified and resurrected body therefore is told (in sermons, in texts, in hymns, in prayers, and so on), performed (in communion, in baptisms, and so on) and presenced again and again (in the continual performative casting of these techniques) in the Christian faith such that the event of this body is impressed and expressed in the hopeful dispositions of faithful bodies. Through a variety of techniques, both discursive and corporeally felt, this event is sedimented into the sensibilities of the faithful Christian body that hopes.

The particularities of the faithful Christian body are therefore played out through a defeated and transformed body, and the hope impressed through the salvation seemingly insured by its resurrection: 'This is to say that there is a contradiction in the subjectivity of the Christian between the promise that solicits a calling forth from the self to a fulfilled eschatological space-time and the experiential reality of current space-time' (Sanderson 2008: 97). In this way, hope both more broadly and within the particular affective registers of the faithful Christian body, works with and through its converse – that of tragedy, defeat and despair. Thus, the annihilations of the past and the simultaneous possibilities for prevailing over that destruction form the spark of hope that surges through and energises the faithful body in the present: 'The risen body is freedom from this body of flesh and death' (Caputo 2007: 81). Once instilled into the sensibilities of the Christian faithful, this embodiment of hope arises from the ongoing defeats in the present into the (hopeful) becoming transformed of the future. Hope here is composed of dispositions that find assurances in the destructive *and* resurrected transformations of bodies in the past-in-the-present, in the what-has-become and in the future. Such faithful dispositions of hope usher forth spaces of hope: for example, Sanderson (in her work with faith-based community groups in Fiji and Tanzania) found that conceptualisations of community development are embodied by place-based dispositions of eschatological and messianic hope:

> Hoped for development, as expressed from within these communities, is a becoming of the Body of Christ – a body offensively malformed…and yet resurrected and therefore bringing and challenging hope as a protest against that malformation. (Sanderson 2008: 103)

The body of Christ is impressed on bodies in and through space such that different geographies are infused with a hope as a 'transindividual beginning again that reanimates the present in response to the transmission of despair and grief' (Anderson 2006b: 745).

The faithful Christian body and its hopeful dispositions are renewed through a particular event and its hopeful present and future realisation. Herein, sensibilities of hope emerge 'through processes of qualification and are distinguished by possessing a determinate object' (Anderson 2006b: 741). Yet (and eluded to above), the determinate object of this qualification and, the event out of which hopeful bodies emerge are and have been a source of contest. Moreover, the event and object of hope in Christianity has been a source for violence on others. Certainly and in recent events, when this determinate object of hope is aligned with readings of Revelations and the 'End Times' such that a section of humanity (the evangelical Right) see themselves as somehow 'chosen', a series of resent-filled acts are performed on those who fail or cannot be born again (see Dittmer 2008). And, as Connolly (2008: 4) so expertly reveals, when this evangelical resentment resonates with 'cowboy' capitalism in various ways, the outcome is an ethos of revenge which

> finds its expression in punitive orientations towards others outside the fold: in a bellicose orientation to other faiths, states, and civilizations, in patterns of scandal and gossip, in an extreme sense of entitlement of your constituency, and in a tendency to devalue the claims and needs of other constituencies.

The determinate object of hope for the evangelical Right is translated into a source of hope for the salvation of the special few and revenge over everyone else. And this poses a problem if (and for some this 'if' is still a step too far) we wish to approach religion with some form of respect and an ethos of creative and critical engagement.

Put differently, if dispositions of faith and hope have as their source and object something that can be assembled to serve out discrimination and subordination, then how are we (those geographers of religion who wish to critically and respectfully engage with religion) to approach the force of hope in (Christian) faith? One way to tackle this question is to explore modes of faith that refuse to posit a determinate and obdurate object of hope that can lend itself to these sensibilities of revenge and resentment. Thus, we must seek out other faithful dispositions where the question 'Faith in?' (or equally 'Faith in What?') is answered with a reflexive sense of contestability as to the object of hope. Thus, Right wing evangelism as a form of

> Fundamentalism is an attempt to shrink the love of God down to a determinate set of beliefs and practices, to make an idol of something woven from the cloth of contingency, to treat with ahistorical validity something made in time…It represents a failure of religious nerve, a failure to see that the love of God is uncontainable and can assume uncountable and unaccountably different forms. (Caputo 2001: 107)

To seek out these other trajectories in the sensibilities of faith is important for at least two reasons: first, in order that we fall short of equating the evangelical Right with the totality of contemporary Christian thinking; and second, in order that the groundwork is done for the critical and creative ethos of engagement that I wish to detail in the next section.

For Anderson and Fenton (2008: 77), a secular ethos of hope is distinguished from that of the religious or sacred sensibility in that non-religious formations lack a determinate source or object of or for hope. Thus,

> In the absence of a telos or ultimate ground that would guarantee hope, a secular practice or ethos of hope becomes a way of embodying the conviction that the future may be different from the present.

This is a crucial first step if a critique of the revengeful evangelical Right is to be forged and a different ethos of hope developed. Yet, religious and sacred trajectories of hope are too easily represented here as the opposite of secular concerns and hence *only* built on fixed teleologies and ultimate grounds. In doing so, contemporary theological attempts to work with post-structuralist thinking in order to disrupt the secure foundations of more traditional theology are ignored (see Griffin et al. 1989; Hart 1989; Tilley 1995; Ward 2001; Vanhoozer 2003; Robbins 2004). Elsewhere I have explored the work of Mark C. Taylor (1984) who works at the border zone between post-structuralism and the Western theological tradition (see Holloway, 2011a, b). Here I wish to, albeit very briefly, furnish insight from Caputo's (2001) treatise *'On Religion'* which is part of his wider project of what has been called 'weak theology' (see Caputo 1997, 1999, 2003, 2006; Caputo and Scanlon 1999).

Whilst not specifically about hope per se, Caputo's *'On Religion'* resonates with ideas of faith and its object in the past, present and future. Caputo is keen to distinguish and wrest himself from those who insist on an absolutist interpretation of the

Scriptures as 'God's own Word', and thus he emphasises contingency over totalising readings and perspectives:

> The faithful need to concede that they do not cognitively *know* what they *believe* by faith in any epistemologically rigorous way. While faith gives the faithful a way to view things, they are not lifted by the hook of faith above the fray of conflicting points of view…There is indeed something deeply true about religion, but it is, I claim, *a truth without knowledge*, by which I mean without absolute or capitalized Knowledge, without laying claim to enjoying privileged cognitive, epistemic, propositional information that has been withheld from others. (Caputo 2001: 111, original emphasis)

This sense of complexity and contingency in interpretation allies with his take on how and what the faithful hope for and what they hope in. Caputo (2001: 7) makes a key distinction between the 'future present' of faith and attendant hopefulness by which he means 'the future of the present, the future to which the present is tending, the momentum of the present into the future that we can more or less see coming', and the 'absolute future' in which

> …we [sic] move, or we are moved, past the circle of the present and of the foreseeable future, past the manageable prospects of the present, beyond the sphere in which we have some mastery, beyond the domain of sensible possibilities that we can get our hands on, into a darker and more uncertain and unforeseeable region, into the domain of 'God knows what' (literally!). (2001: 9)

Caputo argues that it is this future, inconceivable and unknowable (i.e. without the totality of capitalised Knowledge), where hope and faith should find their nourishment. Caputo (2001: 10), drawing on Derrida (see Derrida and Marion 1999; Sherwood and Hart 2005), calls this uncertain and unforeseeable future the impossible, and advises the faithful to "revisit the idea of the impossible and to see our way clear to thinking the possibility of the impossible, of the impossible, of the possible as the "im-possible," and to think of God as the "becoming possible of the impossible," as Derrida also says". As such the possibility of the impossible, a non-knowing in answer to what the faithful hope in, is a faith in becoming 'continually exposed to discontinuity' (2001: 34). Without the assurances of an ultimate ground, faith and hope are constantly renewed in their source and object, and their determinate contours cannot be traced because of the impossibility of fully and forever knowing the source and object of hope; 'For after all, to believe what seems highly credible or even likely requires a minimum of faith, whereas to believe what seems unbelievable, what it seems impossible to believe, that is really faith' (2001:12). For the hopeful disposition of faith the 'only recourse is to hang on by our [sic] teeth, that is, to have faith and hope, and to love this possibility of an impossibility and unmasterable future which is not in our hands. Love and hope and faith are the virtues on the impossible' (2001: 14).

The impossible, or more precisely the possibility of the impossible, is without ground and determinate form. Therefore, the object or source of hope in this formulation becomes more of a horizon always present and always possible, but escaping, becoming impossible, as soon as one seeks to reach it. Significantly, this non-teleological formation of faith and hope resounds with Anderson and Fenton's

(2008, 78–79) argument that hope is always composed through the excess or the virtuality of the 'not-yet':

> The topos of the 'not-yet' is not only a question of the temporal extension of the present into the future. It also involves thinking of space as animated by (im)possibilities, potentialities and virtualities – some of which we find in the past life of spaces, some of which can be predicted to occur in the future, and some of which are impossibilities 'to come'.

Consequently, the horizon of the impossible in which Caputo finds hope and faith can be made to resonate with more secular understandings that find a hopeful ethos in a 'qualitative "more" outside something that has "become"' (Anderson 2006a, b: 696). Both share a sense of the impossibilities that are immanent and incipient forces of and for hope. Indeed, through a mutual appreciation of excess, becoming and the impossible, we see the potential for religious and non-religious sensibilities to come together and connect. How such moments of connection, between seemingly intractable and opposed positions, can be forged and cultivated is something I turn to now.

12.3   An Ethos of the Ineffable and the Impossible?

There are then potential moments of intersection between an ostensibly secular ethos of hope without 'telos or ultimate ground', and one composed through a faithful disposition of hope without 'absolute or capitalised knowledge'. If seemingly divergent understandings of hope can be brought into relation, then this, in turn, provides hope that other secular and religious dispositions can also be made to resonate. Feelings of despair that the secular and sacred are intractably separated might be assuaged if we seek out such lines of compatibility – a renewed sense of possibility is animated by this nexus of imbrication. Endeavouring to discover these mutual resonances between religious and non-religious sensibilities will no doubt be resisted by some. Some will argue that the public sphere should seek consensus through rational dialogue requiring a concomitant relegation of religion to the private realm. Conversely, some will raise the moral deficiencies of this 'neutral' secular vision and argue for a necessary return to an absolutist reading of Scripture and a telos that promotes the rights of the chosen. It becomes difficult to hold out any hope for these naysayers. Only hopelessness ensues when these two sides meet and look upon each other from afar. Such a divided congregation can only lend 'a saddened, nay, melancholy, tone to time' (Taylor 1984: 72).

Yet moments of respectful and post-secular coincidence can be pursued. The first step in this, potentially arduous, journey is to reveal moments of resonance such as those outlined above. The second is to detail what is going on and what needs to be done in order that further moments can be engendered. Key to this detailing is the recognition of contestability. For Connolly (1999: 44), the awareness of contingency and the knowledge that an identity 'contains an element of difference within itself from itself that tends to be blurred or obscured by the representations it makes of itself to others' must be made central to an emergent ethos of engagement:

> The key is to acknowledge the comparative *contestability* of the fundamental perspectives you bring into public engagements while working hard not to convert that acknowledgement into a stolid or angry stance of existential resentment...For a positive ethos of public life requires more constituencies to respond graciously and generously to elements of comparative contestability in their own religions, secular, and asecular faiths. (Connolly 1999: 8, 15, original emphasis)

The contest intrinsic to issues of central concern, and the indeterminacy inherent to any claims at absolute determinacy, is one point of connection where a more charitable response may form. This recognition of hesitancy and contingency is both a self and mutual awareness such that each constituency is aware of its own and others' attempts to fix and make unambiguous; 'It is when the relations 'between' resonate with reciprocal appreciation of elements of contestability in the fundamentals of each party that positive possibilities begin to glow' (Connolly 1999: 154).

However, this is not a matter of jettisoning everything that energises the sensibilities through which one values and makes sense of the world. Instead, the drive to place determinate and fixed assumptions at the centre of engagement and ultimate saliency (at the expense of and violence to others) is necessarily abridged and subject to a generous reserve. Modes of creative and benevolent engagement with and between the religious and non-religious therefore involve the appropriate and '*selective desanctification of elements in your own identity*' (Connolly 1999: 146, original emphasis), but without a total abandonment of what moves you to action. A reflexive awareness of contestability, which falls short of deserting animating assumptions and passions, involves an appreciation of the politics of becoming:

> The politics of becoming is purposive without being teleological...Here many constituencies appreciate a little more actively the uncertain element of historical contingency in their own constitution, and this discernment informs their responses to movements by alter-identities to reconstitute the terms of their institutional identification and regulation...They convert the cultural disturbance of what they are into energy to respond reflectively to new lines of flight. (Connolly 1999: 58)

Engaging in the appreciation of becoming involves gratitude towards change, the emergent and surprise that has the potential to destabilises obdurate dispositions. The politics of becoming allows new sensibilities to crystallise which take shape across and with difference, but without self-defeat or nihilism. The creative yet critical resonances that ensue have the potential to animate new assemblages of engagement. These assemblages, or what Connolly has called 'resonance machines', are 'composed through relations of imbrications, infusion, and intercalation between heterogeneous elements that simultaneously enter *into* one another to some degree, *affect* each other from the outside, and generate residual or torrential *flows* exceeding the first two modes of connection' (2008: 11). These 'machines' therefore have points of contact and mutual imbrication, whilst maintaining trajectories of identification or disposition that take flight without necessarily become fused or folded together. As such, these assemblages are connected rhizomatically 'in which a plurality of constituencies divided along several dimensions enter into a complex network of differences and connections informed by a general ethos unmarked by a single cultural constituency at the center' (Connolly 1999: 89).

There are then multiple points and moments of connection in resonance machines. Many issues have the potential to become a nexus of resonance, but the one that concerns us here is that between the religious and the non-religious. Thus, I have highlighted above one point where these two constituencies might associate and emulsify: the moment of resonance between Caputo's possibility of the impossible and Anderson's (Deleuzian inspired) notion of the virtual, as the reservoir of potentialities that accompany the 'not-yet' of any event or space. In both, we see an appreciation of excess and incipient potentialities of becoming. Enhancing and amplifying this further (without too much translation), we can see here a nexus of resonance that takes as its point of inception the ineffable and the quasi-mysterious. In other words, a protean movement between the religious and non-religious might begin to take shape around the impossibilities and indeterminacy of the geographies and temporalities we move through. So whilst Caputo finds (theistic) faith and hope in the possibility of the impossible, other formations of hope find a renewed engagement with the potentialities and impossibilities of the virtual and its movement through space and time. In both, we find a register of something overwhelming, beyond actualisation and hence infused with (differing degrees of) mystery. Both find faith and hope in something that cannot be fully grasped and made determinant. Both resonate together and find their point of juncture in articulations of excess: that which remains elusive but nonetheless presses on space and time, and gives hope and faith. Consequently, we could direct Connolly's following statement to and with Caputo's faith in the impossible:

> …when you encounter unfathomable mystery in your faith in the right spirit, you may become inspired to appreciate corollary elements of paradox, mystery, or uncertainty at different points in other faiths; this very appreciation can encourage a positive connection with them across differences. (2008: 128)

Yet and at the same time – for this is a nexus of resonance – this statement could also speak to those Deleuzian-inspired thinkers (like Anderson) for whom the virtual presents an ineffable excess of potentialities incipient to space and time. Therefore, at the point of resonance between the non-religious and religious we see potential for an ethos of creative and critical engagement cultivated around the ineffability of the impossible–virtual (Bennett 2001). The resonance machine generated around such intersections need not mean a loss of a secularised critical impulse or the dampening of the energising force of what the faithful will call God or the story of the 'Good News'. Yet simultaneously both refuse to reduce their relation with the other to either a secularised determination of faith and religion, such that it has 'little or no purchase on the nature of things' (Caputo 2001: 56), or to a series of (often revengeful) theistic determinate presuppositions. Instead, both resonate so as to make a new ethos for the secular and sacred, the non-religious and the religious to emerge.

12.4 Conclusions

An appreciation of renewal and reinvention, namely, the politics of becoming, and mutual resonance through the possibility of the impossible and the virtual potentialities of time and space, provides for a nexus where the religious and non-religious might engage. Such a point of imbrication and connection has no time and space for that which lives through a determinate and fixed set of presumptions, that finds no hope in the moment by moment revitalisation of time and space, that moves forth through a resentful faith founded on ultimate and unshakeable grounds, or finds its ultimate means of engagement in a world purified of the passions of religious faith.

There are no doubt other points of connection that might allow a resonance machine of the religious and the non-religious to emerge and take shape. The geography of religion, belief and spirituality needs to seek out such sites of engagement and work with them. This work involves cultivating a respectful and creative ethos of engagement, yet one that can remain critical to the violence (symbolic, material, spatial, and so on) that some modes of the religious and secular are ordered through. Indeed, it might be that we need to work on ourselves (and I identify myself here with the secularity that animates the geography of religion) in similar ways to how the religious sediment the sensibilities of ritual. In other words, we must engineer and affect a different disposition that colours and animates the interaction, interpretation and engagement we perform with religious and spiritual orderings when we come to study them. Such a sensibility of engagement will be realised in and worked upon via 'the visceral register of being as well as the more refined intellectual register to which the visceral is linked by multiple circuits', in order that this disposition 'infiltrates habits of desire, conscience, and perception as well as the presumptions of reflective judgments' (Connolly 2008: 70). It seems that the politics and poetics of a nascent post-secular age demand this protean disposition be animated and amplified.

References

Anderson, B. 2006a. Transcending without transcendence: Utopianism and an ethos of hope. *Antipode* 38(4): 691–710.

Anderson, B. 2006b. Becoming and being hopeful: Towards a theory of affect. *Environment and Planning D: Society and Space* 24(5): 733–752.

Anderson, B. 2009. Affective atmospheres. *Emotion, Space and Society* 2(2): 77–81.

Anderson, B., and J. Fenton. 2008. Spaces of hope. *Space and Culture* 11(2): 76–80.

Bennett, J. 2001. *The enchantment of modern life: Attachments, crossings and ethics*. Princeton: Princeton University Press.

Cabezón, J.I. 2006. The discipline and its other: The dialectic of alterity in the study of religion. *Journal of the American Academy of Religion* 74(1): 21–38.

Caputo, J.D. 1997. *The prayers and tears of Jacques Derrida: Religion without religion*. Bloomington: Indiana University Press.

Caputo, J.D. 1999. Apostles of the impossible: On God and the gift in Derrida and Marion. In *God, the gift and postmodernism*, ed. J.D. Caputo and M.J. Scanlon, 185–223. Bloomington: Indiana University Press.

Caputo, J.D. 2001. *On religion*. London: Routledge.

Caputo, J.D. 2003. Without sovereignty, without being: Unconditionality, the coming God and Derrida's democracy to come. *Journal for Cultural and Religious Theory* 4(3): 9–26.

Caputo, J.D. 2006. *The weakness of God: A theology of the event*. Bloomington: Indiana University Press.

Caputo, J.D. 2007. Bodies still unrisen, events still unsaid. *Angelaki* 12(1): 73–86.

Caputo, J.D., and M.J. Scanlon. 1999. Introduction: Apology for the impossible: Religion and postmodernism. In *God, the gift and postmodernism*, ed. J.D. Caputo and M.J. Scanlon, 1–20. Bloomington: Indiana University Press.

Connolly, W. 1999. *Why I am not a secularist*. Minneapolis: University of Minnesota Press.

Connolly, W. 2008. *Capitalism and Christianity, American style*. Durham: Duke University Press.

Derrida, J. 1998. Faith and knowledge: The two sources of 'religion' at the limits of reason alone. In *Religion*, ed. J. Derrida and G. Vattimo, 1–78. Cambridge: Polity.

Derrida, J., and J.-L. Marion. 1999. On the gift: A discussion between Jacques Derrida and Jean-Luc Marion (moderated by Richard Kearney). In *God, the gift and postmodernism*, ed. J.D. Caputo and M.J. Scanlon, 54–79. Bloomington: Indiana University Press.

Dittmer, J. 2008. The geographical pivot of (the end of) history: Evangelical geopolitical imaginations and audience interpretation of left behind. *Political Geography* 27(3): 280–300.

Eagleton, T. 2009. *Reason, faith, and revolution: Reflections on the God debate*. New Haven: Yale University Press.

Evans, B. 2010. Anticipating fatness: Childhood, affect and the pre-emptive 'war on obesity'. *Transactions of the Institute of British Geographers* 35(1): 21–38.

Griffin, D.R., W.A. Beardslee, and J. Holland. 1989. *Varieties of postmodern theology*. Albany/New York: State University of New York Press.

Habermas, J. 1998. Notes on post-secular society. *New Perspectives Quarterly* 25(4): 17–29.

Harrington, A. 2007. Habermas and the 'post-secular society'. *European Journal of Social Theory* 10(4): 543–560.

Hart, K. 1989. *The trespass of the sign: Deconstruction, theology and philosophy*. Cambridge: Cambridge University Press.

Harvey, D. 2000. *Space of hope*. Edinburgh: Edinburgh University Press.

Holloway, J. 2003a. Make-believe: Spiritual practice, embodiment and sacred space. *Environment and Planning A* 35(11): 1961–1974.

Holloway, J. 2003b. Spiritual embodiment and sacred rural landscapes. In *Country visions*, ed. P. Cloke, 158–175. Harlow: Prentice Hall.

Holloway, J. 2006. Enchanted spaces: The séance, affect and geographies of religion. *Annals of the Association of American Geographers* 96(1): 182–187.

Holloway, J. 2011a. The spiritual life. In *A companion to social geography*, ed. P. Cloke, V. Del Casino, R. Panelli, and M. Thomas. Oxford: Blackwell.

Holloway, J. 2011b. Tracing the emergent in the geographies of religion and belief. In *Emerging geographies of belief*, ed. A.C. Bailey, C. Brace, S. Carter, D. Harvey, J. Hill, and N. Thomas. Newcastle: Cambridge Scholars Publishing.

Hollywood, A. 2004. Practice, belief, and feminist philosophy of religion. In *Thinking through rituals: Philosophical perspectives*, ed. K. Schilbrack, 52–71. London: Routledge.

Kong, L. 2010. Global shifts, theoretical shifts: Changing geographies of religion. *Progress in Human Geography* 34(6): 755–776.

Latour, B. 2001. 'Thou shalt not take the Lord's name in vain' – Being a short sermon on the hesitations of religious speech. *Res: Journal of Anthropology and Aesthetics* 39: 215–234.

Latour, B. 2005. *Reassembling the social*. Oxford: Oxford University Press.

McLennan, G. 2007. Towards a postsecular sociology. *Sociology* 41(5): 857–870.

Robbins, J.W. 2004. Weak theology. *Journal for Cultural and Religious Theory* 5(2): 1–4.

Roberts, T. 2004. Exposure and explanation: On the new protectionism in the study of religion. *Journal of the American Academy of Religion* 72(1): 143–172.

Roberts, T. 2006. Between the lines: Exceeding historicism in the study of religion. *Journal of the American Academy of Religion* 74(3): 697–719.

Sanderson, E. 2008. Eschatology and development: Embodying messianic spaces of hope. *Space and Culture* 11(2): 93–108.

Sherwood, Y., and K. Hart. 2005. Other testaments. In *Derrida and religion: Other testaments*, ed. Y. Sherwood and K. Hart, 3–26. London: Routledge.

Sigurdson, O. 2010. Beyond secularism? Towards a post-secular political theology. *Modern Theology* 26(2): 177–196.

Taylor, M.C. 1984. *Erring: A postmodern a/theology*. Chicago: University of Chicago Press.

Tilley, T.W. 1995. *Postmodern theologies: The challenge of religious diversity*. Maryknoll: Orbis.

Vanhoozer, K.J. (ed.). 2003. *The Cambridge companion to postmodern theology*. Cambridge: Cambridge University Press.

Ward, G. (ed.). 2001. *The Blackwell companion to postmodern theology*. Oxford: Blackwell.

Wynn, M. 2005. *Emotional experience and religious understanding*. Cambridge: Cambridge University Press.

Žižek, S. 2001. *Did somebody say totalitarianism? Five interventions in the mis(use) of a notion*. London: Verso.

Index

P. Hopkins et al. (eds.), *Religion and Place: Landscape, Politics and Piety*,
DOI 10.1007/978-94-007-4685-5, © Springer Science+Business Media Dordrecht 2013